Free DVD  Free DVD

Essential Test Tips Video from Trivium Test Prep

Dear Customer,

Thank you for purchasing from Trivium Test Prep! Whether you're looking to join the military, get into college, or advance your career, we're honored to be a part of your journey.

To show our appreciation (and to help you relieve a little of that test-prep stress), we're offering a **FREE *CDL Essential Test Tips* Video** by Trivium Test Prep. Our video includes 35 test preparation strategies that will help keep you calm and collected before and during your big exam. All we ask is that you email us your feedback and describe your experience with our product. Amazing, awful, or just so-so: we want to hear what you have to say!

To receive your **FREE *CDL Essential Test Tips* Video**, please email us at 5star@triviumtestprep.com. Include "Free 5 Star" in the subject line and the following information in your email:

1. The title of the product you purchased.
2. Your rating from 1 – 5 (with 5 being the best).
3. Your feedback about the product, including how our materials helped you meet your goals and ways in which we can improve our products.
4. Your full name and shipping address so we can send your **FREE *CDL Essential Test Tips* Video**.

If you have any questions or concerns please feel free to contact us directly at 5star@triviumtestprep.com.

Thank you, and good luck with your studies!

CDL Study Guide 2025-2026
6 Practice Tests and CDL Permit Prep Book
[2nd Edition]

B. Hettinger

Copyright ©2025 Trivium Test Prep

ISBN-13: 9781637988237

ALL RIGHTS RESERVED. By purchase of this book, you have been licensed on copy for personal use only. No part of this work may be reproduced, redistributed, or used in any form or by any means without prior written permission of the publisher and copyright owner. Trivium Test Prep; Accepted, Inc.; Cirrus Test Prep; and Ascencia Test Prep are all imprints of Trivium Test Prep, LLC.

Federal Motor Carrier Safety Administration (FMCSA) and Department of Transportation (DOT) were not involved in the creation or production of this product, is not in any way affiliated with Trivium Test Prep, and does not sponsor or endorse this product.

Image(s) used under license from Shutterstock.com

Table of Contents

INTRODUCTION ... 2
- How is the CDL exam scored? ... 5
- How is the CDL exam administered? ... 6

1. CONTROLLING THE VEHICLE ... 9
- Accelerating, Stopping, and Steering ... 9
- Backing Safely ... 10
- Shifting Gears ... 11
- Retarders/Auxiliary Brakes ... 13
- Answer Key ... 15

2. DRIVING SAFELY ... 16
- Seeing ... 16
- Communicating ... 18
- Speed and Braking ... 21
- Managing Space ... 24
- Distracted Driving ... 29
- Aggressive Drivers and Road Rage ... 32
- Railroad Crossings ... 34
- Alcohol and Drugs ... 38
- Hazardous Materials Rules for All Commercial Drivers ... 40
- Answer Key ... 44

3. DRIVING IN HAZARDOUS CONDITIONS ... 47
- Driving at Night ... 47
- Driving in Fog ... 51
- Driving in Winter ... 52
- Driving in Hot Weather ... 55
- Mountain Driving ... 57
- Answer Key ... 61

4. DRIVING HAZARDS AND EMERGENCIES ... 63
- Seeing Hazards ... 63
- Hazardous Roads ... 63
- Hazardous Drivers, Vehicles, and Nondrivers ... 64
- Antilock Braking Systems (ABSs) ... 66
- Skid Control and Recovery ... 69
- Answer Key ... 72

5. TRANSPORTING CARGO ... 73
- Basics of Transporting Cargo ... 73
- Inspecting Cargo ... 74
- Cargo Weight and Balance ... 74
- Securing Cargo ... 77
- Cargo Needing Special Attention ... 86
- Answer Key ... 89

6. THE AIR BRAKE SYSTEM ... 90
- Overview of Air Brakes ... 90
- Parts of the Air Brake System ... 90
- Dual Air Brake Systems ... 98
- Answer Key ... 99

7. INSPECTING AND USING AIR BRAKES ... 100
- Inspecting Air Brakes ... 100
- Normal Stops with Air Brakes ... 104
- Emergency Stops with Air Brakes ... 105
- Brake Lag ... 105
- Braking on a Downgrade ... 106
- Parking Brakes ... 106
- Low Air Pressure ... 108
- Answer Key ... 109

8. COMBINATION VEHICLES ... 110
- Controlling a Combination Vehicle ... 110
- Combination Vehicle Hazards ... 114
- Combination Vehicle Air Brakes ... 116
- Antilock Braking Systems (ABSs) in Combination Vehicles ... 119
- Coupling Tractor Semitrailers ... 120
- Uncoupling Tractor Semitrailers ... 123
- Coupling a Pintle Hook ... 125
- Uncoupling a Pintle Hook ... 125
- Coupling a Drawbar ... 126
- Uncoupling a Drawbar ... 127
- Coupling a Gooseneck Hitch ... 128
- Uncoupling a Gooseneck Hitch ... 128
- Inspecting a Combination Vehicle ... 129

Answer Key	132

9. DOUBLE AND TRIPLE TRAILERS — 134

Safely Pulling Double and Triple Trailers	134
Coupling Twin Trailers	135
Uncoupling Twin Trailers	138
Coupling and Uncoupling Triple Trailers	139
Inspecting Double and Triple Trailers	139
Double and Triple Trailer Air Brakes	140
Answer Key	142

10. PASSENGERS — 143

Vehicle Inspection	143
Loading and Starting the Trip	145
On the Road	147
After-Trip Vehicle Inspection	149
Prohibited Practices	149
Brake-Door Interlocks	150
Answer Key	151

11. TANK VEHICLE — 152

Requirements for Tank Vehicle Endorsement	152
Inspecting Tank Vehicles	152
Tank Vehicle Loads	153
Safely Driving Tank Vehicles	155
Answer Key	157

12. HAZARDOUS MATERIALS — 158

Introduction to Hazardous Materials	158
Purpose of Hazmat Regulations	160
Hazmat Transportation Roles	160
Classifying Hazardous Materials	161
Hazmat Placards	163
Identifying Hazardous Materials	167
Hazmat Shipping Papers	170
Hazmat Package Labels	172
Loading and Unloading	174
Loading Precautions for Specific Materials	174
Bulk Packaging	178
Parking	179
Driving	181
Emergencies Involving Hazardous Materials	183
Emergency Responses to Specific Materials	186
Answer Key	189

13. SCHOOL BUS — 192

Danger Zones	192
Mirrors	193
Loading Students	195
Unloading Students	197
Emergency Exit and Evacuation	199
Railroad Crossings	201
Managing Students	202
Special Safety Considerations	203
Answer Key	205

14. METAL COILS — 206

The Securement and Application of Metal Coils	206
Securement Requirements and Orientation	207
Roll Prevention	212
Answer Key	214

15. VEHICLE SAFETY INSPECTION — 215

Specific Issues to Look For	215
The 7-Step Inspection Method	218
During-Trip Inspections and the After-Trip Inspection Report	226
The Vehicle Inspection Test	227
Answer Key	241

16. BASIC VEHICLE CONTROL SKILLS TEST — 242

Scoring	242
Exercises	243
Answer Key	247

17. ROAD TEST — 248

How You Will Be Tested	249
Answer Key	256

PRACTICE TEST #1 — 257

General Knowledge	257
Combination Vehicles	263
Double and Triple Trailers	266
Passengers	269
Tank Vehicles	273
Hazardous Materials	276
School Bus	279
Metal Coil	282

PRACTICE TEST #1 ANSWER KEY — 286

General Knowledge	286
Combination Vehicles	288
Double and Triple Trailers	289
Passengers	290
Tank Vehicles	291

Table of Contents

HAZARDOUS MATERIALS...................................292
SCHOOL BUS..294
METAL COIL 295

Online Resources

Trivium includes online resources with the purchase of this study guide to help you fully prepare for the exam.

Practice Tests

In addition to the practice test included in this book, we also offer five online tests. Since many exams today are computer based, practicing your test-taking skills on the computer is a great way to prepare.

From Stress to Success

Watch "From Stress to Success," a brief but insightful YouTube video that offers the tips, tricks, and secrets experts use to score higher on the exam.

Feedback

Let us know what you think!

Access these materials at: triviumtestprep.com/cdl-online-resources

Introduction

Congratulations on choosing to take the Commercial Driver's License (CDL) exam! By purchasing this book, you've taken the first step toward becoming a licensed commercial driver.

This guide will provide you with a detailed overview of the CDL exam, so you will know exactly what to expect on test day. We'll take you through all of the concepts covered on the exam and give you the opportunity to test your knowledge with practice questions. Even if it's been a while since you last took a major test, don't worry; we'll make sure you're more than ready!

What is the CDL exam?

The CDL exam consists of two parts: the knowledge exam and the skills test. Together, these tests evaluate an applicant's understanding of safe driving and how to properly operate a commercial motor vehicle (CMV). Applicants must pass all portions of each of the required knowledge and skills tests.

The knowledge and skills tests are described in detail in the next section. Briefly, knowledge tests are written exams that evaluate an applicant's general understanding of how to operate a CMV. Applicants must pass all required knowledge tests before they are allowed to take the skills test.

The skills test is a hands-on exam divided into three parts, each of which is described in the next section. Each portion must be taken—and passed—in the following order: vehicle inspection, basic vehicle control, and on-road test.

What is on the CDL exam?

Knowledge Tests

All CDL applicants must first pass a general knowledge test, regardless of the CDL Class (see CDL Classes and Descriptions Table) for which they are seeking licensure. Depending on the types of endorsements needed, applicants may be required to take additional knowledge tests (see "Types of Knowledge Tests" table).

The knowledge tests are written exams with questions based on federal guidelines. Questions are multiple-choice, matching, and/or fill-in-the-blank. In most states, the question breakdown for the basic general knowledge test is as follows:

- Class A license:
    - 50 questions (written general knowledge test)
    - 20 questions (written combination vehicles test)
- Class B license: 50 questions (written general knowledge test)
- Class C license: 50 questions (written general knowledge test)

Introduction

CDL Classes and Descriptions

Class A

any combination of vehicles with a gross combination weight rating of 26,001 pounds or more, provided the gross vehicle weight rating (GVWR) of the vehicle or vehicles towed exceeds 10,000 pounds

Class B

any single vehicle with a gross vehicle weight rating of 26,001 pounds or more, any one of those vehicles towing a vehicle that does not exceed a 10,000 pounds GVWR, and any vehicle designed to transport 24 passengers or more, including the driver; restricted to operating buses under 26,001 pounds GVWR if the skills test is taken in a bus with a GVWR of less than 26,001 pounds

Class C

any single vehicle or combination of vehicles that is not a Class A or Class B if the vehicle is: 1) designed to transport 16 to 23 passengers including the driver; or 2) used in the transportation of hazardous materials that require the vehicle to be placarded under 49 CFR, Part 172, Subpart F

Regulations vary from state to state, as do the required knowledge and endorsement exams that an applicant must pass. It is imperative to understand the requirements needed for the state in which you will take your CDL exam and the cargo you plan to transport with a CDL.

Types of Knowledge Tests

Type of Knowledge Test	Description	Applicants Who Must Take Test
General knowledge	assesses basic knowledge needed to operate a CMV	all CDL applicants
Air brakes	assesses knowledge of air brakes and their features	required for all applicants who will drive a CMV with air brakes and/or air-over-hydraulic brakes
Combination vehicles	assesses the special knowledge needed to safely operate combination vehicles	all applicants planning to drive combination vehicles; applicants for Class A licenses
Passenger transport (endorsement-specific knowledge test)	assesses the special knowledge needed to drive a passenger CMV	all applicants for bus driving
Hazardous materials (endorsement-specific knowledge test)	assesses knowledge of how to safely transport hazardous materials (as defined in 49 CFR 383.5)	applicants who plan to transport hazardous materials and who have already passed a TSA background check
Tank vehicles	assesses special knowledge needed to safely operate tank	required for applicants who plan to transport liquids or

3

Types of Knowledge Tests

(endorsement-specific knowledge test)	vehicles with individual rated capacities of at least 119 gallons and aggregated rated capacities of at least 1,000 gallons	gases in the described tanks, which can be either temporarily or permanently attached to the vehicle or chassis
Doubles/triples *(endorsement-specific knowledge test)*	assesses knowledge of how to safely pull double or triple trailers	required for all drivers planning to pull double or triple trailers
School bus *(endorsement-specific knowledge test)*	assesses the special knowledge needed to operate a school bus	required for all applicants planning to drive a school bus

Skills Tests

The skills test can only be taken once the applicant passes the required knowledge tests. There are three separate portions of the skills test (see "Skills Test Portions" table below). Each must be taken—and passed—in the following order before the applicant can move on to the next skills test portion:

1. vehicle inspection
2. basic vehicle control
3. on-road test

The skills test MUST be taken in the type of vehicle for which the applicant is seeking a CDL. The vehicle used CANNOT have any marked or labeled components.

Skills Test Portions

Type of Skills Test	Description
Vehicle inspection	<ul><li>evaluates the applicant's ability to determine if the vehicle is safe to drive</li><li>requires pointing/touching items as requested by the examiner and explaining the purpose of inspecting those items</li></ul>
Basic vehicle control	<ul><li>evaluates the applicant's skills on how to control a CMV</li><li>involves performing basic maneuvers in a defined area as instructed by the examiner; includes a mandatory engine start, in-cab inspection, and coupling inspection</li></ul>

On-road test	<ul><li>evaluates the applicant's ability to safely operate a CMV in a variety of traffic conditions</li><li>includes performing various maneuvers as instructed by the examiner</li></ul>

Chapters 15, 16, and 17 of this study guide provide more in-depth information about the three skills tests portions. The following website also contains state-specific information concerning both the knowledge and skills tests: https://online-cdl-test.com.

How is the CDL exam scored?

General Knowledge Test

A total minimum score of 80% (at least 40 correct answers out of 50 questions) is required to pass the written general knowledge test. Class A CDL applicants must also earn a total minimum score of at least 80% (16 correct answers out of 20 questions) on the written test on combination vehicles.

Skills Test

Each component of the skills test is scored separately; please note that the following information may vary by state:

- Vehicle inspection: The examiner will keep track of how many items are properly inspected. Of the list of items included in the vehicle inspection, the CDL applicant must properly inspect at least 80% of them:
    - If the CDL applicant fails this portion, the examiner will review the missed items with the applicant before officially concluding the exam.
    - If the applicant successfully completes the inspection but finds that it is not properly equipped or unsafe, the examiner will require the applicant to reschedule the rest of the skills test portions until the vehicle is safe to drive.
- Basic vehicle control: CDL applicants are allowed NO MORE THAN 12 points on the basic vehicle control portion of the exam; however, certain maneuvers carry separate penalties and may still result in failure—even if the 12-point threshold has not been met. If you score more than 12 points, you will have failed the exam and will need to reschedule it. The basic vehicle controls skills test is scored based on your performance of the following:
    - **Encroachments:** You will be scored on the number of times you cross over or touch a boundary; each time you encroach, it will be counted as an error. **More than 3 encroachments results in failure.**
    - **Pull-ups:** Two pull-ups are allowed for each exercise EXCEPT the straight-line backing maneuver, where only 1 pull-up is allowed. **Using more pull-ups than allowed for a particular exercise will result in failure of the test.**
    - **Outside vehicle observations ("looks"):** Two outside vehicle observations are allowed for each exercise EXCEPT straight-line backing, where only 1 look is allowed; **too many looks will result in failure of the test.** Not safely securing and/or exiting the vehicle can result in an automatic failure of this skills test. The following are all scored as looks:

opening the door, moving from a seated position (when in control of the vehicle), and/or walking to the rear of a bus to check the view.
- **Inside parallel/final position:** The applicant must maneuver the vehicle into its final position EXACTLY as described by the examiner; penalties or automatic failure of the test can result otherwise.
- On-road test: The on-road test is led by the examiner, who determines whether a required maneuver is performed correctly. Errors result in deductions; the number of deductions that will result in failure of the test varies by state, but typically applicants must have 30 deductions or less to pass. Other causes of failing the road test are
  - having or causing an accident/crash,
  - driving in a dangerous manner,
  - being uncooperative with the examiner, and/or
  - any violations of the law.

How is the CDL exam administered?

Knowledge Tests

The written knowledge and skills tests are administered at a DMV CDL in the state in which the applicant is trying to earn the license. It is important for applicants to check with their local DMV to ensure the tests are administered there, learn about any required fees, and confirm the documentation requirements to be eligible to take the tests. Typically, applicants must provide

- proof of age,
- proof of citizenship or permanent residency,
- a report of their driving history over the past 10 years from any and all states which issued them a license, and
- a current Department of Transportation medical card.

Applicants will have 60 minutes to complete the general knowledge test (50 questions). Class A CDL applicants will have 20 minutes to complete the written exam on combination vehicles (20 questions).

Skills Test

Applicants must hold a valid commercial learners permit (CLP) for at least 14 days, pay all fees, and successfully complete entry-level driver training in order to take the skills test. The skills test portions are administered by a tester affiliated with the licensing state or a third-party tester that has been approved by that state.

You must check the requirements in your licensing state to determine whether you need to bring your own vehicle or if one will be provided for you. If bringing your own vehicle, you must ensure that it matches the type of vehicle for which you are seeking a CDL. Remember: if any parts of the vehicle do not pass the inspection portion of the skills test, you will be asked to address those issues and reschedule the exam.

The vehicle inspection portion of the exam typically takes around 40 minutes. The basic vehicle control portion requires performing maneuvers within a time limit specified by the examiner for each maneuver. While the on-road test can take up to one hour, applicants are reminded that this portion of the exam is not a "speed test." Applicants must obey all traffic laws and drive safely at all times during the exam (and after they earn their CDL).

About Trivium Test Prep

Trivium Test Prep uses industry professionals with decades' worth of knowledge in their fields—proven with degrees and honors in law, medicine, business, education, the military, and more—to produce high-quality test prep books for students.

Our study guides are specifically designed to increase any student's score. Since our books are shorter and more concise than typical study guides, you can increase your score while significantly decreasing your study time. We're pleased you've chosen Trivium to be a part of your professional journey.

1 Controlling the Vehicle

Accelerating, Stopping, and Steering

- **Do not roll back** when starting to accelerate.
  - Rolling back can damage property or injure people who are close behind the vehicle.
  - For a manual transmission: partly engage the clutch and then take your right foot off the brake.
  - **Use the parking brake to prevent rolling back:** release the parking brake when enough engine power has been applied to prevent rolling back.
  - A trailer brake hand valve will keep the truck from rolling back.
- Accelerate slowly and smoothly without jerking the vehicle; rough acceleration can damage the vehicle or coupling.
- **When traction is bad, speed up slowly.**
  - The wheels will spin if too much power is applied.
  - **Take your foot off the accelerator if the drive wheels are spinning.**
- Push the brake pedal down gradually to stop.
  - The amount of brake pressure needed is determined by the speed of the vehicle and how quickly it needs to stop.
  - **Control the brake pressure** to ensure that the vehicle stops safely and smoothly.

> **Helpful Hint**
>
> Manual transmission vehicles require the clutch to be pushed in as the engine reaches the idle stage.

1. Controlling the Vehicle

- The steering wheel should be **held firmly with 2 hands at all times**.
  - Your hands should be placed on opposite sides of the wheel ("10 and 2").
  - You can lose control of the wheel if you do not keep a firm, two-handed grip.

Figure 1.1. Proper Steering Wheel Grip

Quick Review Question

1. Where should your hands be placed on the steering wheel?

Backing Safely

- **Backing is ALWAYS dangerous and should be avoided**.
- Park in a way that allows you to pull the vehicle forward upon departure.
- Basic safety rules must be followed if backing is necessary:
  - Position the vehicle based on the type of backing needed.
  - Inspect the line of travel: walk around the vehicle; check clearance on all sides, including above the vehicle.
  - Check mirrors on both sides often; exit the vehicle if needed to verify that the path is clear.
  - **Back slowly using the lowest reverse gear**; this helps you correct steering errors and/or come to a sudden stop if needed.
  - **Back and turn toward the driver's side**; this may include repositioning the vehicle to prevent backing toward the right/passenger side.
  - Backing and turning toward the driver's side allows the rear of the vehicle to be viewed from the side window.
  - Ask helpers to stand behind the vehicle to help navigate blind spots; agreeing on hand signals, especially for "stop," is extremely important.

1. Controlling the Vehicle

Quick Review Question

2. Toward which direction should you turn when backing up?

Shifting Gears

Shifting Up

Learn the vehicle's operating rpm range (found in the driver's manual).

- Shift up when the engine hits the top of the tachometer's range. (See Figure 1.2.)
- Learn which speeds are appropriate for which gears so that the speedometer can be used to determine when it is time to shift.
- **Become familiar with the various engine sounds, which indicate when it is time to shift.**

Shift up at the top of the tachometer range.

Figure 1.2. Engine Reaching Top Range of a Tachometer

- The basic method for shifting up with a manual transmission is as follows:
    - Release the accelerator and push in the clutch while simultaneously shifting to neutral.
    - Release the clutch.
    - Allow the gears and engine to slow down to the rpm needed for the next gear.
    - Shift to the higher gear while depressing the clutch; these should be simultaneous movements.

- Depress the accelerator while releasing the clutch.
- Use double clutching to change gears in vehicles with unsynchronized manual transmissions.
- Staying in neutral too long while using a double clutch can prevent shifting to the next gear; return to neutral and match engine speed with road speed before trying again.

Quick Review Question

3. What are the two ways to determine when to shift?

Shifting Down

Knowing when to downshift is equally as important as knowing when to upshift.

- **Use the speedometer or tachometer to downshift at the correct rpm or road speed.**
- The basic method for shifting down with a manual transmission is as follows:
  - Simultaneously release the accelerator, push in the clutch, and shift to neutral.
  - Release the clutch.
  - Depress the accelerator and increase the engine and gear speeds to the rpm that is required in the lower gear.
  - Push the clutch in while simultaneously shifting to the lower gear.
  - Press the accelerator and release the clutch at the same time.
- The following steps explain how to shift down when going down a hill:
  - **Downshift and slow down to a manageable speed BEFORE starting down a hill.**
  - Be in a gear that is low enough, which is often lower than the gear needed to climb the hill.
  - **Avoid braking hard** by slowing down and downshifting; otherwise, the brakes could overheat and malfunction.
- The following steps explain how to shift down before a curve:
  - **Slow down, ensure a safe speed, and downshift to the correct gear BEFORE entering a curve.**
  - Slowing and downshifting ahead of a curve allow more power to be used through the curve.
  - Using more power through a curve promotes vehicle stability while turning and makes it easier to increase speed after the curve.
- **Auxiliary transmissions and multispeed rear axles provide extra gears.**
  - These contain numerous shift patterns.
  - It is critical to understand the correct way to shift gears in each vehicle that will be driven.
  - The extra gears are usually controlled by a switch on the gearshift lever of the main transmission or by a selector knob.

1. Controlling the Vehicle

- Automatic transmissions allow a low range to be selected for greater engine braking when driving down a grade.
- Lower ranges prevent the transmission from shifting up past the selected gear (except if the governor rpm is exceeded).
- **It is important to select a low range when going down grades.**

Quick Review Questions

4. What is the purpose of multispeed rear axles and auxiliary transmissions?

5. What do lower ranges aim to prevent?

Retarders/Auxiliary Brakes

- **Retarders offer an alternative way to slow down and reduce the wear on primary brakes.**
- All retarders have the option of being turned on or off.
- Some vehicles allow for retarders to be adjusted.
- When in the "on" position, retarders activate their braking power whenever the driver fully lets up on the accelerator.
- **Retarders apply to drive wheels only.**
- There are 4 types of retarders:
    1. exhaust
    2. engine
    3. hydraulic
    4. electric

> ### Helpful Hint
> *Jake Brake* is short for the *Jacobs Engine Brake*, a diesel engine retarder. Certain regions use the term in signage to indicate that retarders are not allowed.

- Keep the following in mind when using retarders:
    - Retarders are known to be noisy; **some areas restrict their use**.
    - Since retarders apply only to drive wheels, drive wheels with poor traction can skid when retarders are applied.

- Retarders should be turned off in inclement conditions (e.g., when roads are wet, snowy, or icy).

Figure 1.3. Jake Brake Sign

Quick Review Question

6. What kind of road conditions require retarders to be turned off?

Answer Key

1. Your hands should be placed on opposite sides of the wheel ("10 and 2").

2. Back and turn toward the driver's side so that you can see better.

3. Two ways to determine when to shift are 1) using your engine's speed (rpm) by monitoring the tachometer; and 2) learning the appropriate road speed for each gear, which allows you to use the speedometer to decide when to shift.

4. Multispeed rear axles and auxiliary transmissions provide extra gears.

5. Lower ranges prevent the transmission from shifting up past the selected gear.

6. Retarders should be turned off in wet, icy, snowy, or other inclement conditions.

2 Driving Safely

Seeing

- **Failure to look properly and far enough ahead is a leading cause of accidents.**
- Drivers must look far enough ahead to:
    - know what is happening all around the vehicle, and
    - stop and change lanes.
- **Look 12 – 15 seconds ahead**, which shows how far you will travel in that same amount of time.
    - This equals approximately 1 block at lower speeds.
    - At higher speeds, this distance is roughly a quarter of a mile.
- Safe driving requires looking far enough ahead AND being aware of things that are closer.
- Look for vehicles on all sides: entering highways, switching lanes, or turning.
- Watch for others' brake lights; adjust speed and change lanes in time to avoid problems.
- Look ahead at a green traffic light.
    - Pay attention to how long it has been on.
    - Noticing this will help you know when to slow down and anticipate stopping.
- Check mirrors often to see what is happening behind and on all sides of the vehicle.
    - Regular checks let you be aware of traffic and monitor your own vehicle.
    - Check mirrors regularly to see if other vehicles have moved into blind spots.
    - Mirrors help drivers spot overtaking vehicles.
- **Mirrors must be adjusted before a trip, while the trailer is straight.**

- Each mirror must show a portion of the vehicle—a reference point for gauging the position of other things outside of the vehicle.

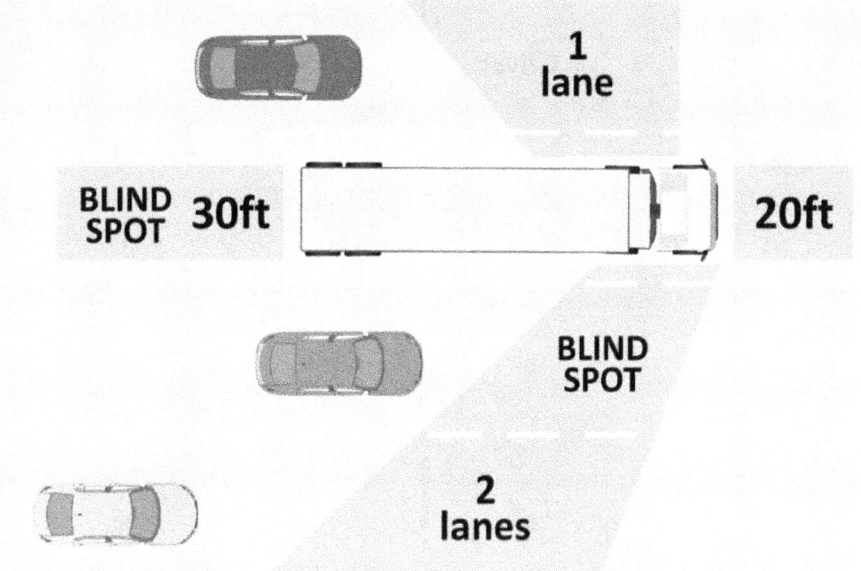

Figure 2.1. Blind Spots

- **Use mirrors to inspect your own vehicle.**
    - Mirrors let you check the tires and spot tire fires or potential blowouts.
    - Use mirrors to check open cargo and spot loose straps, flapping tarps, etc.
- Check mirrors more frequently when changing lanes, turning, merging, or performing tight maneuvers.
- **Changing lanes:** check mirrors before changing lanes to ensure there is enough room.
    - Check to make sure vehicles are not in blind spots AFTER signaling.
    - Check that the path is clear IMMEDIATELY AFTER starting to change lanes.
    - Check the mirrors again AFTER the lane change is finished.
- **Turning:** use mirrors to be sure the rear of the vehicle will not collide with anything.
- **Merging:** use mirrors to gauge whether a traffic gap is large enough for you to enter safely.
- **Maneuvering tight spaces:** use mirrors to ensure clearance.
- Using mirrors correctly involves checking them quickly and understanding what is seen.
    - Don't spend too long checking mirrors; this prevents seeing what lies ahead.
    - **Alternate between checking mirrors quickly and looking at the road ahead.**

> **Helpful Hint**
>
> Convex mirrors, also known as "fisheye," "bug-eye," or "spot" mirrors, offer a wider range of view but make objects appear smaller than they are in reality. Flat mirrors are also known as "plane mirrors" and create an image that is the same size as the object being reflected.

- Know the type of mirror: objects appear smaller in some mirrors than in others.

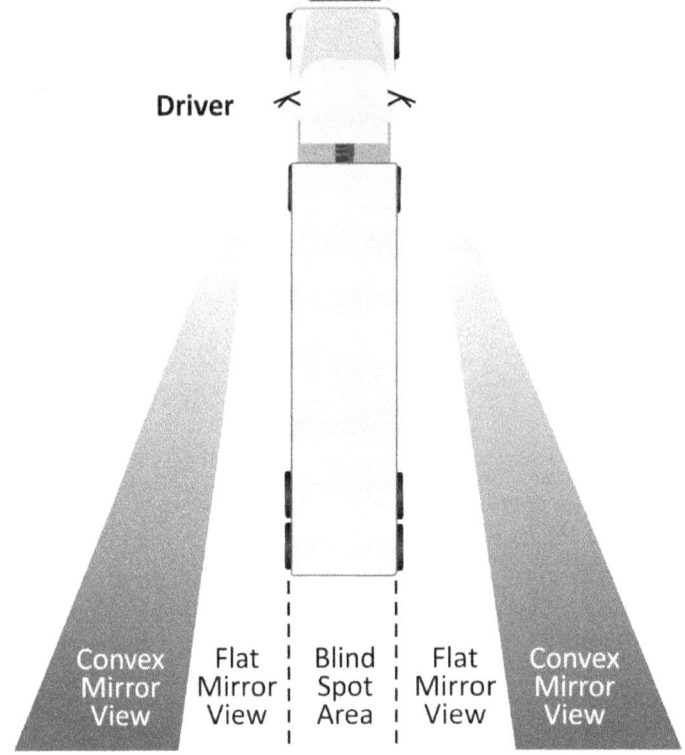

Figure 2.2. Convex vs. Flat Mirror

Quick Review Questions

1. How far ahead should a driver look?

2. What is the BEST way to see the rear and sides of your vehicle?

Communicating

Use of Signals, Lights, and Horn

Signaling is critical to safe driving and lets others know your intentions.

- Follow these signaling rules when turning:
  - Signal early with plenty of time before turning to prevent others from trying to pass.
  - Keep the signal on continuously so that both hands can remain on the wheel.
  - Do not cancel the signal until you are finished turning.
  - If your signals do not self-cancel, remember to turn them off after completing the turn.
- Turn the signal on before changing lanes to allow others to honk or avoid your vehicle.
- Flash your brake lights (tap the brake pedal) to alert others that you will be slowing down.

- Activate the emergency lights if you are driving especially slowly or are stopped.
- Use signaling to alert drivers to certain situations:
  - Flash your brake lights if you see hazards ahead so that drivers behind you are aware.
  - Let others know you need to go slowly to negotiate a tight turn: brake early, slow down gradually.
  - If you must stop on the road, flash your brake lights; do not stop suddenly.
  - Use your emergency lights to alert drivers that you are driving slowly.
- Always be aware of local laws that restrict the use of emergency lights.
- Communicate your presence—always assume others cannot see or hear you.
  - If you cannot see other drivers, they probably cannot see you.
  - Always drive carefully—even after you have communicated your presence.
- When you are passing vehicles, bicyclists, and/or pedestrians
  - honk (if legally alloweD), or
  - flash your high beams (at night).
- Turn your headlights (not ID or clearance lights) to low beam, especially when visibility is poor.
- If needed, use your horn to avoid a crash. (Never use the horn unnecessarily.)

Quick Review Question

3. What does the term *communication* mean in driving, and why is it important for safety?

Stopping Near the Road

Use 4-way emergency flashers (not taillights) when stopped at the side of the road.

- Put out **emergency warning devices/triangles** no more than 10 minutes after stopping on the side/shoulder of a road.
  - **1-way or divided highway:** put warning devices toward approaching traffic at intervals of 10, 100, and 200 ft.
  - **2-lane road or undivided highway:** put warning devices within 10 ft. of the front or rear corners of your vehicle and 100 ft. behind AND ahead of your vehicle, in the lane in which you are stopped, or on the shoulder.

- For your own safety, hold warning triangles between yourself and oncoming traffic.

Figure 2.3. Placing Warning Devices

- **When stopped on the side of a road, make sure your vehicle is visible within 500 ft.**
    - This may involve backing past curves, hills, and obstructions.
    - If a curve or hill prevents a clear line of sight: place the rearmost emergency triangle to a point farther back down the road.
- **Never direct traffic.**
    - Doing so poses a serious liability.
    - Directing traffic can cause accidents.
    - If an accident happens when you are directing traffic, it may cost you money.

Quick Review Questions

4. At what distance should your vehicle be visible to others if you are stopped on the side of a road?

5. Where should reflectors or other emergency warning devices be placed if you are stopped on a divided highway?

2. Driving Safely

Speed and Braking

Stopping Distance

Perception distance is the distance traveled.
- It starts from the moment you visually notice a hazard until your brain recognizes it.
- Physical and mental conditions, including visibility and the nature of the hazard, affect perception distance.
- The average perception time of alert drivers is $1\frac{3}{4}$ seconds (roughly 142 ft. of travel distance if driving at 55 mph).

- **Reaction distance is the length traveled BEFORE actually hitting the brakes.**
  - Alert drivers have an average reaction time of $\frac{3}{4}$ of a second to 1 full second.
  - Average reaction times at 55 mph result in roughly 61 ft. of travel distance.

- **Braking distance is the distance traveled *in ideal conditions* while the brakes are being applied.**
  - Braking distance varies depending on road conditions, especially when they are wet.
  - Driving 55 mph on dry pavement with reliable brakes equals a braking distance of around 216 ft.

- **Total stopping distance = perception distance + reaction distance + braking distance *in ideal conditions*.**
  - It represents the total minimum distance traveled until the vehicle stops completely.
  - At 55 mph, perception distance (142 ft.), reaction distance (61 ft.), and braking distance (216 ft.) equal a total stopping distance of at least 419 ft.

MPH	Total stopping distance	Perception Distance	Reaction Distance	Braking Distance
15	72'	39'	16'	17'
25	140'	65'	28'	47'
35	222'	91'	39'	92'
45	319'	117'	50'	152'
55	419'	142'	61'	216'

Figure 2.4. Stopping Distance

- **Speed directly affects a vehicle's total stopping distance and strike (impact) power.**
    - Doubling speed from 20 mph to 40 mph quadruples impact and braking distance.
    - Braking distance and impact are 9 times higher if speed is tripled from 20 mph to 60 mph.
    - Driving at 60 mph results in a stopping distance that is greater than the length of a football field.

Quick Review Questions

6. How is total stopping distance calculated?

7. How much does total stopping distance increase if you are driving twice as fast?

Factors Affecting Braking Distance

Braking distance can be reduced by slowing down.
- **Brakes must work harder and absorb more heat to stop heavy vehicles.**
    - Heavy vehicles have brakes, shock absorbers, tires, and springs that are **designed to function best when the vehicle is fully loaded**.
    - Empty vehicles have less traction, which may require greater stopping distances.
- Traction (friction between the road and the tires) is needed to both steer and brake vehicles.
- **Wet road conditions affect traction and require using lower speeds.**
    - Stopping distance is doubled on wet roads.
    - Speeds should be reduced by a third (55 mph to 35 mph) on wet roads.
    - Speeds should be reduced by at least half in packed snow.
    - Avoid driving on icy surfaces; if you must, your speed should be at a crawl.
- It is important to be aware of signs that a road could be slippery:
    - Shaded parts of a road stay slippery even when the open road around them has melted.
    - Bridges freeze before roads; temperatures around 32°F indicate that freezing is likely.
    - Ice that is partially melted is slipperier than solid ice.
    - **Black ice is often mistaken for a wet road because the asphalt is visible.**
    - Wet roads are prone to becoming black ice if temperatures drop to freezing.
    - Feel your vehicle's mirrors or antenna for signs of icing, which indicate that the road is likely icy too.
    - Oil on the road mixes with early rainfall, causing slippery conditions; the longer it rains, the more the oil is washed away.
- **Collections of water or slush on roadways can result in hydroplaning.**
    - Hydroplaning is when a vehicle's tires lose contact with a wet road.
    - Hydroplaning makes the vehicle feel like it is water-skiing.

2. Driving Safely

- o Tire splashes, clear reflections, and visible raindrops falling on the road indicate the potential for hydroplaning.
- o **Do not use brakes to slow down if your vehicle hydroplanes.**
- o Release the accelerator and push in the clutch to regain control and slow the vehicle.
- o If the drive wheels skid, push in the clutch so they can freely turn.

> **Helpful Hint**
> Only a small amount of water is needed to hydroplane, even at slower speeds (e.g., 30 mph). Worn tires or those with low pressure increase the possibility of hydroplaning.

Quick Review Questions

8. Why do empty vehicles sometimes require greater stopping distances?
9. What is hydroplaning and how is it corrected?
10. What does the term *black ice* describe?

Controlling Speed

Excessive speed directly contributes to fatal crashes.

- Adjust speed based on driving conditions and terrain.
- Manage your speed so that you can always stop within the distance ahead that is visible to you.
- **Slow to a safe speed BEFORE entering a curve.**
    - o Taking curves too fast causes tires to lose traction; the vehicle will go off the road.
    - o Even if traction is not lost, vehicles that take curves too fast can roll over.
    - o Taking curves at the posted speed can cause trucks with a high center of gravity to roll over.
    - o **Do not brake while taking a curve; it can lock the wheels and cause skidding.**
    - o Maintain control by using a gear that lets you accelerate slightly while taking a curve.
- Be sure to slow down when using low beams; they do not allow you to see as far as high beams.
- **In heavy traffic, the safest speed is the speed of the other vehicles going the same direction.**
    - o Speed limits in many states are lower for commercial vehicles than for private vehicles; be extra cautious when passing or switching lanes in these circumstances.
    - o Keep a safe following distance (see next section) and drive at the speed of the traffic if you can do so safely and legally.
    - o Going faster than other vehicles results in more passing, increasing the risk of crashing.
- Gravity causes a vehicle's speed to increase on downgrades.

- Choose and maintain speeds that are appropriate for:
    - the total weight of the vehicle and cargo,
    - the steepness and length of the grade, and
    - the weather and road conditions.
- Obey posted speed and warning signs on downgrades.
- Use the engine's braking effect as the primary way to control speed on downgrades.
    - The braking effect is best when it is near the governed rpm and lower gears are used.
    - Saving your brakes lets you slow down or stop as needed.
- **Speeding traffic is the leading cause of injury and death in roadway work zones.**
    - Always obey speed limits that are posted in a work zone.
    - Decrease your speed in poor weather and/or if workers are nearby.

Quick Review Question

11. Why should you not brake when taking a curve?

Managing Space

Following Distance

You must maintain space around your vehicle.
- Available space gives drivers time to think and take action if things go wrong.
- The space you are driving into—the area ahead—is the most important.
    - The following distance (the space between your vehicle and the one in front of you) must be long enough in order to stop in time.
    - Smaller cars ahead can stop faster; **do not follow too closely behind**, which can cause a crash.
    - Calculate how much space you need in front of you; adjust accordingly.
- **The ideal space ahead is at least 1 second for every 10 ft. of your vehicle's length.**
- Looking at the vehicle ahead of you, begin counting when that vehicle passes a landmark.
    - Count slowly: "one thousand and one, one thousand and two," and so forth until you pass that same landmark.
    - Compare your count: does it follow the rule of 1 second for every 10 ft. of your vehicle's length?
- See Figure 2.5. for following distances using the **timed interval heavy vehicle formula** for various vehicle lengths:
    - Below 40 mph: aim for at least 1 second for each 10 ft. of vehicle length.

- Above 40 mph: follow the formula used for under 40 mph and add another second.

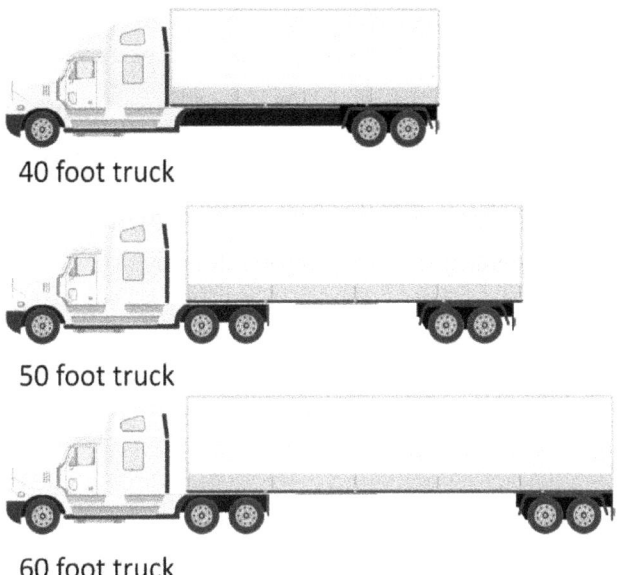

< 40 mph: 1 second for every 10 feet of vehicle
> 40 mph: 1 second for every 10 feet of vehicle + 1 second

Figure 2.5. Space in Front of the Vehicle

Quick Review Questions

12. How do you determine your vehicle's following distance?
13. When driving a 30-ft. vehicle at 55 mph, how many seconds should the following distance be?

Lane Usage

Stay to the right if others are following you too closely.

- Do not pass other slow vehicles unless passing can be done quickly and safely.
- It is common for heavy vehicles to be tailgated when they can't keep up with traffic and when going uphill.
    - If tailgated, do not make any quick changes: signal early when turning; gradually reduce speed when slowing.
    - Increase your following distance: open up room ahead of you to prevent sudden speed or direction changes and allow others to more easily pass you.
    - Maintain a low speed if being tailgated.
    - Do not trick the tailgater by using taillights for flashing your brakes.
- Commercial vehicles take up most of the lane; drivers must properly manage the small lane space available to them.
- Make sure your vehicle remains centered in its lane; this helps keep a safe clearance on either side.

- **Do not drive alongside others.**
    - Other drivers could suddenly change lanes and turn into you.
    - You could need to change lanes but find yourself trapped by other drivers.
- Ideally, you should find an open spot away from other traffic.
    - If an open spot is unavailable, try your best to keep space around you on all sides.
    - Drop back (or pull forwarD) to ensure other drivers can see you.
- Strong winds also prevent drivers from staying in their lane.
    - This is especially true for lighter vehicles and when exiting tunnels.
    - Make every effort to avoid driving alongside others in windy conditions.

Quick Review Questions

14. What should you do if you are being tailgated?

15. Why should you increase your following distance if someone is driving too closely behind?

Clearance Above and Below the Truck

Be sure to ALWAYS have overhead clearance.

- **Never assume that posted heights are correct**: bridges or overpasses could have been repaved or have packed snow, which alters the posted height (see Figure 2.6.).

Figure 2.6. Low Clearance Warning Sign

2. Driving Safely

- Cargo vans are higher after the cargo is unloaded: you may not be able to get through the same bridge or tunnel as when the van was freighted.
- Always travel slowly when passing beneath objects.
- **If there is ANY doubt whether you can safely pass under an object, find an alternate route.**
- Remember: warnings are not always posted on low bridges or underpasses.
- If the road has a tilt, try to drive slightly closer to the center line to avoid hitting trees or other objects on the road's edge.
- Always check for overhanging objects and other hazards before backing into an area.
- **Be aware of the space beneath your vehicle**; it can be limited when the vehicle is freighted.
  - This is particularly true on dirt roads or in unpaved yards.
  - Prevent getting hung up in these situations by avoiding such roads when heavily loaded.
- Cross depressions (e.g., drainage channels across roads) carefully; they can cause the end of your vehicle to drag.
- Avoid crossing railroad tracks when pulling trailers with low clearance underneath; you could get hung up halfway across.

Quick Review Questions

16. Why should you not rely on a bridge or overpass's posted height?

17. Why should dirt roads and unpaved yards be avoided when driving a heavily loaded vehicle?

Turning

Commercial vehicles can strike objects when turning and therefore need adequate space.

- **Turn right slowly**; this gives you and other drivers extra time to avoid potential issues.
- Turning right could cause you to cross into another lane (see Figure 2.7.).
  - Be sure to turn wide when completing right turns.
  - Keep your vehicle's rear near the curb to prevent others from passing you on the right.
- **Never turn wide to the left when you start a right turn:**
  - It could cause other drivers to incorrectly think that you are turning left.
  - If drivers think you are turning left, they may try to pass you on the right.
  - If they try to pass you on the right, you could hit them as you complete the turn.
- Use a buttonhook turn when making a right turn:
  - Keep close to the right-side curb and swing wide when making the turn.
  - **Never back up for oncoming vehicles**; you can hit drivers behind you.

- Give oncoming traffic in the other lane time to move or stop.

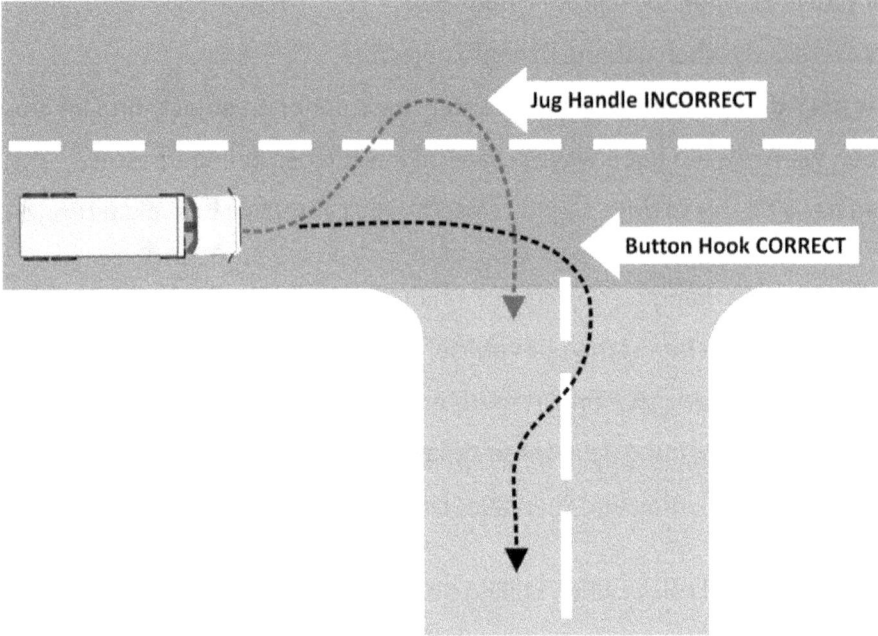

Figure 2.7. Right Turn

- **Reach the center of the intersection before making a left turn.**
- Turning left before you reach the center of the intersection can result in a crash due to off tracking.
- Always take the right turn lane if you have an option.
    - You may need to swing right if you choose the inside lane.
    - Choosing the right lane allows you to more easily see drivers on your left (see Figure 2.8.).

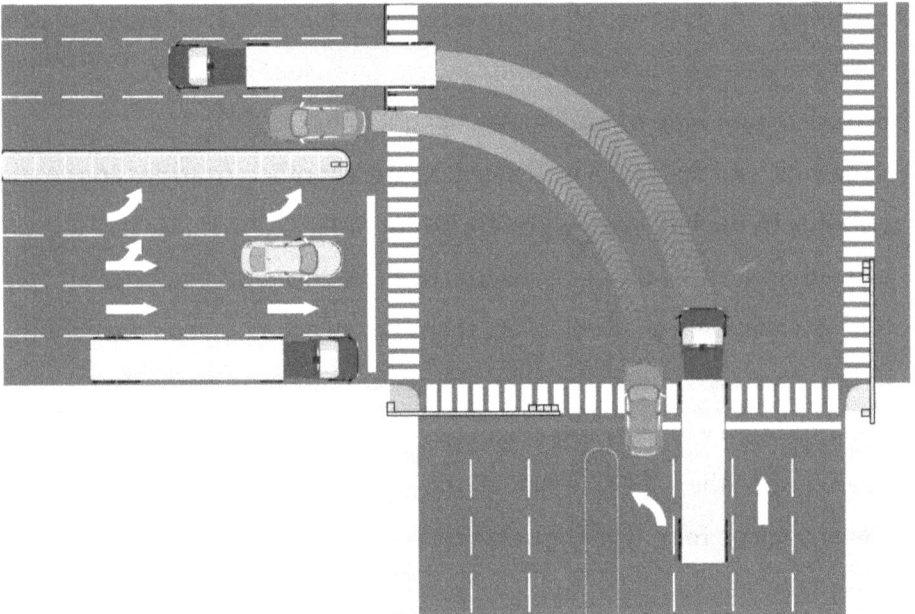

Figure 2.8. Left Turns

- **Before crossing or entering traffic, be familiar with your vehicle's size and weight.**
- Commercial vehicles often require space and have slower acceleration.
    - Plan to need a much larger gap when entering traffic.
    - If your vehicle is heavily loaded, you will need more room.
    - BEFORE crossing a road, make sure you can do so successfully before traffic reaches you.

Quick Review Questions

18. Should you swing wide to the left before negotiating a right turn? Why or why not?

19. Why is it important to be aware of your vehicle's size and weight before crossing or entering traffic?

Distracted Driving

- **Distracted driving diverts your attention and can cause injury, death, or property damage.**
- There are several causes of distraction, all of which decrease road safety:
    - physical distractions (e.g., reaching for something)
    - mental distractions (e.g., chatting with passengers or daydreaming)
    - a combination of physical and mental distractions (e.g., texting or talking on a mobile communication device)
- Distracted driving causes
    - a delay (or total failure) to perceive traffic events,
    - slow decision-making, and
    - undesirable decisions (e.g., incorrect inputs to the brakes, steering, or acceleration).
- Distracted driving occurs both inside and outside of a vehicle.
- Inside distractions include the following:
    - adjusting entertainment or climate controls
    - smoking, eating, drinking, or reading (e.g., text messages or maps)
    - using navigational tools or other electronic devices (e.g., a mobile communication device)
    - talking on the CB radio
    - various mental distractions (e.g., daydreaming)
- Outside distractions include the following:
    - traffic
    - vehicles, pedestrians, or other objects
    - crash scenes and other similar events
    - sunlight, including sunrise and sunset

- roadway objects and construction
- billboards and other advertisements

Quick Review Question

20. What are some examples of inside distractions?

Mobile Communication Devices and Texting

Federal regulations prohibit the use of handheld mobile communication devices by commercial drivers.

- Failure to comply with federal regulations results in disqualification sanctions.
- Being convicted of multiple state or local traffic regulations concerning the use of mobile communication devices is also grounds for disqualification sanctions.
- **CDL drivers are disqualified after at least 2 convictions for violations of state laws on handheld mobile communication devices.**
    - Each violation subjects drivers to civil penalties of up to $2,750.
    - Disqualification is 60 days for the second offense within 3 years.
    - Disqualification is 120 days for more than 3 offenses within 3 years.
- Employers cannot require or allow commercial drivers to use handheld mobile communication devices; employers requiring drivers to use such devices are liable to civil penalties up to $11,000.

Did You Know?

The use of any mobile communication device (including hands-free) drains brain power by 39%—energy that would otherwise be used to drive safely.

- Only hands-free mobile communication devices that are located close to the driver and are compliant with voice communication rules may be used, albeit cautiously.
- Even if you are using a hands-free device, reaching for one unsafely is a violation.
- Exceptions to these rules apply to emergency use only to call law enforcement and/or other emergency services.
- **The likelihood of a safety-critical event increases sixfold when dialing a mobile communication device while driving.**
    - Dialing while driving takes your eyes off the road for 3.8 seconds on average.
    - At 55 mph, this results in a football field's length of driving with your eyes off the road.
- Hands-free or not, the use of mobile communication devices is always a distraction.
- **Texting is the most dangerous driving distraction.**
    - Texting is not limited to mobile communication devices (e.g., phones): it includes ANY device used to write, receive, send, or read text.
    - **Federal Motor Carrier Safety Regulations prohibit texting in a commercial vehicle.**
- Driver disqualification sanctions are in place should texting regulations be violated.
    - Any state texting law that is violated is grounds for CDL disqualification.

2. Driving Safely

- A CDL will be disqualified if the driver is convicted of 2 or more texting violations.
- The disqualification timelines and violation fees for state laws on handheld mobile communication devices also apply to texting.
- Safety-critical events are over 23 times more likely to happen to drivers who are texting.
    - Sending/receiving texts diverts your eyes from the road for an average of 4.6 seconds.
    - At 55 mph, this equals driving 371 ft.—more than the length of a football field—without looking at the road.

Quick Review Questions

21. Are there any ways to use communications equipment safely while driving?
22. What is the most dangerous driving distraction?

Eliminating Distractions

Eliminate all in-vehicle distractions before driving:

- Make an assessment of any potential distractions in your vehicle.
- Anticipate distractions and create a plan to prevent or eliminate them.
- Consider possible scenarios and discuss these (if accompanied by a partner) before driving.
- **Crash chances double if your reaction time is only a half second slower.**
- Use these tips to help prevent distractions:
    - Turn off all communication devices (e.g., mobile communication devices).
    - If you must use a hands-free communication device, do so cautiously and make sure you can use it while restrained—do not reach for it.
    - **Never type or read a message while driving.**
    - Be familiar with the equipment and features in your vehicle.
    - Adjust all mirrors and controls BEFORE driving.
    - Program your preferred entertainment stations in advance.
    - Ensure cargo is secured; remove unnecessary objects from your vehicle.
    - Study maps, program the GPS, and determine your route BEFORE driving.
    - Plan ahead for eating and smoke breaks; avoid doing these while driving.
    - Avoid emotionally charged/intense conversations while driving.
    - Require occupants to abide by a commitment form.
- Noticing distracted drivers gives you more perception and longer reaction times.
- **Keep your eyes out for the following signs that other drivers are distracted:**
    - drifting vehicles—either within the lane or over the divider lines

2. Driving Safely

- inconsistent speed
- preoccupation with a mobile communication device, eating, drinking, smoking, or other distractions
- drivers having conversations
- **If you encounter distracted drivers, take preventive actions:**
  - Keep a safe following distance; let the distracted driver have a lot of room.
  - Pass distracted drivers with extreme caution; they could drift over.

Figure 2.9. Distracted Drivers

Quick Review Questions

23. How can you proactively reduce distractions in your vehicle?

24. What are some of the warning signs that a driver could be distracted?

25. What should you do if you notice a distracted driver?

Aggressive Drivers and Road Rage

- **Aggressive driving means driving selfishly, but without intent to harm**; it includes
  - operating a motor vehicle selfishly,
  - being bold and/or pushy when driving, and/or
  - showing disregard for the safety and rights of other drivers.
- **Road rage is driving with intent to harm others**, including physically assaulting other drivers and/or their vehicles.

- Avoid being an aggressive driver:
  - Your mood affects your driving: de-stress before driving and while at the wheel (e.g., listen to relaxing music).
  - Focus on driving only and avoid distractions (e.g., eating, mobile communication device use).
  - Plan ahead: anticipate delays/traffic and know the weather on the day you will drive.
  - If you are running late, accept it—do not drive aggressively to compensate.
  - Show empathy toward other drivers and give them the benefit of the doubt.
  - Slow down if you find yourself going too fast.
  - Maintain a reasonable following distance.
  - Avoid driving slowly if you are in the left lane of traffic.
  - Avoid making any gestures toward other drivers; this includes shaking your head and other seemingly harmless motions.
  - Let eager drivers pass you.
  - Get in the habit of being both cautious and courteous to other drivers.
- Avoid confrontations with aggressive drivers:
  - Get out of their way as much as possible.
  - Swallow your pride: do not challenge aggressive drivers or try to hold your own.
  - Do not make eye contact.
  - Do not react to any gestures directed toward you—ignore them.
- **Report aggressive drivers to the appropriate authorities:**
  - Call police if you can do so safely.
  - If possible, provide license plate information, a vehicle description, a location, and the direction of travel.
  - If the aggressive driver is involved in an accident, stop safely, wait for the authorities, and describe the driving behaviors you witnessed.

Quick Review Questions

26. How does road rage differ from aggressive driving?

27. An aggressive driver begins to tail you; when you let him pass, he makes an obscene gesture toward you. What should you do?

28. Why is it important to de-stress before you drive?

Railroad Crossings

- **Railroad crossings are always dangerous.**
- **Assume that a train is coming each time you approach a railroad crossing.**
- There are 2 types of railroad crossings: passive and active.
    - **Passive crossings** have no traffic control devices; you must recognize these and check for yourself if a train is coming.
    - **Active crossings** have traffic control devices with flashing red lights with or without bells and gates.
- Round black and yellow advance warning signs (Figure 2.10.) appear before railroad crossings.
    - When you see these signs, you must slow down, look, listen, and anticipate stopping.
    - Hazmat and passenger vehicles are required to stop if a train is approaching, regardless of whether there is time enough to pass.

Figure 2.10. Advance Warning Railroad Crossing Sign

- Pavement markings (Figure 2.11.) also warn you that a railroad crossing is approaching.
    - These markings have the letter *X* and the letters *RR*.
    - On two-lane roads, there are also markings to indicate that passing is not allowed.
    - If you are driving a school bus, the vehicle's front must stay behind the white stop line.

Figure 2.11. Railroad Crossing Pavement Markings

- Crossbuck signs (Figure 2.12.) mark the grade crossing; you must yield to the train.
    - If no white stop line appears, stop no less than 15 ft. and no more than 50 ft. from the nearest rail of the nearest track.
    - If the road will cross more than one track, a sign beneath the crossbuck will indicate how many tracks you will have to drive over.

Figure 2.12. Railroad Crossbuck with Elevated Gates

- Flashing red light signals are on crossbuck signs at many highway-rail grade crossings.
    - **STOP if the lights are flashing—a train is approaching.**
    - Always yield the right-of-way to the train.
    - Be certain that all tracks are clear before proceeding.
- Gates with bells and flashing red lights appear at many railroad crossings.
    - Stop before the lights flash and the gate lowers.
    - Do not proceed until the lights have stopped flashing and the gates have gone up.
- **NEVER try to beat a train to a railroad crossing.**
- Always slow down when you notice advance warning signs.
- Maintain a speed that will allow you to both see an approaching train and be able to stop if necessary.
- Table 2.1. describes other best practices when approaching railroad crossings.

2. Driving Safely

Table 2.1. Railroad Crossing Best Practices

Situation	Considerations	Best Practices
Hearing an oncoming train	<ul><li>Train horns are not allowed at some crossings—these should be identified by signs.</li><li>In-vehicle noise may prevent you from hearing a train.</li><li>By the time you do hear a train, it may be dangerously too close.</li></ul>	<ul><li>Never rely solely on hearing a train to know whether it is safe or not to cross.</li><li>Be aware of signs indicating that train horns are not allowed.</li></ul>
Relying on signals	<ul><li>They may not be at all crossings.</li><li>They may not always work properly.</li></ul>	<ul><li>Never rely on signals.</li><li>Use heightened awareness when passing crossings with no signals or gates.</li></ul>
Multiple tracks at a crossing	<ul><li>Multiple tracks mean the potential for multiple trains.</li><li>A train passing on one track could prevent you from seeing trains passing on the other tracks.</li></ul>	<ul><li>Always double-check all tracks, making sure you have a clear line of sight before passing.</li></ul>
Stopping safely	<ul><li>Traffic behind you and the type of cargo you are carrying influence what constitutes a safe stop.</li></ul>	<ul><li>Stop gradually; check for traffic behind you.</li><li>If available, use a pullout lane.</li><li>Switch on the 4-way emergency flashers.</li><li>Make a full stop when your cargo (e.g., passengers) dictates that you do so.</li></ul>
Clearing the tracks	<ul><li>**Typical tractor trailers can usually clear single tracks in 14 or more seconds and**</li></ul>	<ul><li>Never get in a situation where you have to stop on railroad tracks.</li></ul>

2. Driving Safely

Table 2.1. Railroad Crossing Best Practices

Situation	Considerations	Best Practices
	double tracks in more than 15 seconds.	<ul><li>Always be sure you can clear all tracks BEFORE attempting to cross.</li><li>Be aware of steep approaches that can cause your rig to hang up on the tracks.</li></ul>

- Other best practices for handling railroad crossings are to
    - approach yard area and city/town grade crossings with as much caution as all other crossings, and
    - not shift gears when you are crossing tracks.
- **Certain types of trailers can get stuck on raised railroad crossings:**
    - units that are low-slung (e.g., lowboys, car carriers, and possum-belly livestock trailers)
    - a tractor with a single axle pulling a long trailer that has landing gear set for a tandem-axle tractor
- If you get stuck on the tracks,
    - exit your vehicle and move away from the tracks,
    - check for signposts or signal housing to identify emergency notification information,
    - call 911 (or other emergency number),
    - provide your location and describe nearby landmarks, and
    - provide the DOT number if it is posted.

Quick Review Questions

29. Is this true or false? Railroad crossings are only dangerous when a train is approaching.

30. How many types of railroad crossings are there?

31. How long does it usually take a tractor trailer to clear railroad tracks?

32. Which types of vehicles are most at risk of getting stuck on a raised railroad crossing?

33. What should you do if you find yourself and your vehicle stuck on train tracks?

Alcohol and Drugs

Alcohol

Crashes are more likely for people who have been drinking than for those who have not.

- Alcohol impairs numerous body functions:
    - muscle coordination
    - reaction time
    - depth perception
    - night vision
    - portions of the brain responsible for controlling judgment and inhibition
- **One drink can cause impaired judgment, which also affects your ability to realize you are drunk.**

- Blood alcohol concentration (BAC) is the common measurement to determine the amount of alcohol in someone's body.
- BAC is affected by
    - the amount of alcohol consumed,
    - the rate at which the alcohol is consumed, and
    - the weight of the person consuming alcohol.
- Some alcohol exits the bloodstream through urine, sweat, and breathing. The remaining alcohol is processed by the liver, which can process $\frac{1}{3}$ oz. of alcohol an hour.

Did You Know?

Drinking alcohol and driving is extremely dangerous: alcohol-related crashes account for over 20,000 deaths per year.

- **The body processes alcohol at a fixed rate**; drinking faster than your body can process the alcohol means
    - there is more alcohol in your body, and
    - your risk of impaired driving increases.
- As BAC increases, alcohol has more of an effect on the brain; muscle control, vision, and coordination also decrease.
- All of these **signs of impaired driving** increase the chance of crashing and/or losing your license:
    - straddling lanes
    - jerky, quick starts
    - failure to signal and/or use lights
    - missing stop signs and red lights
    - improper passing
    - longer reaction time to hazards
    - erratic speed (too fast or too slow)

2. Driving Safely

- - - driving in the wrong lane
    - weaving
    - hitting or running over curbs
  - **Time is the only remedy for sobering up: coffee, fresh air, and cold showers do not work.**
  - All of the drinks below have the same alcohol content:
    - a 12-oz. glass of 5% beer
    - a 5-oz. glass of 12% wine
    - a $1\frac{1}{2}$ oz. shot of 80 proof (40%) liquor
  - **The only safe BAC while driving is 0.00.**

Number of Drinks		BLOOD ALCOHOL CONTENT (BAC) Table for Male (M) / Female (F)								Driving Condition
		Body Weight in Pounds								
		100	120	140	160	180	200	220	240	
0	M	.00	.00	.00	.00	.00	.00	.00	.00	Only Safe Driving Limit
	F	.00	.00	.00	.00	.00	.00	.00	.00	
1	M	.06	.05	.04	.04	.03	.03	.03	.02	Driving Skills Impaired
	F	.07	.06	.05	.04	.04	.03	.03	.03	
2	M	.12	.10	.09	.07	.07	.06	.05	.05	
	F	.13	.11	.09	.08	.07	.07	.06	.06	
3	M	.18	.15	.13	.11	.10	.09	.08	.07	
	F	.20	.17	.14	.12	.11	.10	.09	.08	Legally Intoxicated
4	M	.24	.20	.17	.15	.13	.12	.11	.10	
	F	.26	.22	.19	.17	.15	.13	.12	.11	
5	M	.30	.25	.21	.19	.17	.15	.14	.12	
	F	.33	.28	.24	.21	.18	.17	.15	.14	

Subtract 0.01% from BAC for each block of 40 minutes since drinking started. There is a threshold for "legally intoxicated" that carries criminal penalties. This threshold may vary by state.

Figure 2.13. Effect of Weight and Number of Drinks on BAC

Quick Review Question

34. What is the quickest way to sober up after a few drinks?

2. Driving Safely

Other Drugs

It is illegal to possess or be under the influence of drugs while driving.

- It is illegal to be under the influence of the following:
    - amphetamines: pep pills, uppers, Benzedrine ("bennies")
    - narcotics
    - **certain prescription and over-the-counter drugs that cause drowsiness (e.g., cold medicines)**
- Legally prescribed drugs are exempted if a doctor confirms they do not pose a risk to driving.
- Do not use any drugs meant to combat fatigue; rest is the only solution.
- Do not use illegal drugs.
- Be aware of side effects and warnings on both legal (e.g., over-the-counter) and legally prescribed drugs.
- Never mix alcohol and drugs.
- It is not safe to drive if you are ill.
- If you become ill while driving, go to the nearest area where you can safely stop driving.

Quick Review Question

35. Why is it illegal to be under the influence of certain prescribed and over-the-counter drugs?

Hazardous Materials Rules for All Commercial Drivers

- Be able to recognize when cargo is hazardous.
- Understand whether you can legally transport such materials (i.e., without a hazardous materials endorsement on your CDL).
- **Hazardous materials present health, safety, and property risks during transport.**
- Rules exist to contain the product, communicate risk, and ensure that drivers and their equipment are safe.
    - Containment rules tell shippers how to safely package, load, transport, and unload bulk tanks.
    - Rules about communicating risk involve shippers using shipper paper and diamond-shaped hazard labels.
- Hazardous material shipping papers must be easily located, especially in an accident.
- **Lives may depend on how quickly you can locate the shipping papers in an accident.**
- Emergency personnel can help reduce or prevent damage/injury if they know the types of hazardous materials being transported.
- Keep shipping papers on top of each other in one of the following locations:
    - in a pouch on the driver's door

- in clear view and within clear reach while driving
- on the driver's seat if you have exited the vehicle
- Hazards are divided into class numbers; each class number has a name (see Table 2.2.).

Table 2.2. Definitions of Hazard Classes

Class	Class Name	Examples
1	Explosives	- ammunition - dynamite - fireworks
2	Gases	- propane - helium - oxygen
3	Flammable	- gasoline - acetone
4	Flammable Solids	- matches - fuses
5	Oxidizers	- ammonium nitrate - hydrogen peroxide
6	Poisons	- pesticides - arsenic
7	Radioactive	- uranium - plutonium
8	Corrosives	- hydrochloric acid - battery fluid
9	Miscellaneous Hazardous Materials	- formaldehyde - asbestos
None	ORM-D (Other Regulated Material-Domestic)	- hair spray - charcoal
None	Combustible Liquids	- fuel oils - lighter fluid

- **Placards are signs that identify the hazard class of cargo.**
    - They are put on the outside of the vehicle.
    - They warn others that hazardous materials are being transported.

- They let emergency personnel know what you are transporting, which is critical if an accident happens.
- **Placarded vehicles must have 4 or more identical placards.**
- Placards are placed at the front, rear, and both sides of the vehicle.
- **Placards must be visible and readable from all 4 positions (front, rear, sides).**
- Placards must be positioned in a diamond shape and be 9.8 in. (250 mm) or larger.
- Cargo tanks (or other bulk containers) display the ID number of the contents on placards (or orange panels).

- **Not using placards when needed jeopardizes your life and the lives of those around you.**
- Placard ID numbers are 4-digit codes used by emergency personnel to identify hazardous materials.
- The same ID number may be used for more than one chemical on shipping papers.
- ID numbers have the letters *NA* or *UN* appearing before them.
- Chemicals and their assigned ID numbers are listed in the US DOT *Emergency Response Guidebook (ERG)*.
- Some vehicles that carry hazardous materials may be driven without placards.
- **If your vehicle requires placards, your CDL must have a hazardous materials endorsement.**
- Drivers with a hazardous materials endorsement must know how to load and transport hazardous products safely.
- You can only get this endorsement if you pass a written exam (see Chapter 12).
- Tank endorsements are needed for vehicles that will transport liquid or gases.
  - This applies to tank(s) with individual rated capacities of more than 119 gal. and aggregate capacities of at least 1,000 gal.
  - The tank(s) must be permanently or temporarily attached to the chassis or vehicle.
  - The liquid or gas being transported does not have to be considered hazardous.
- You must understand placard rules if you need a hazardous materials endorsement.
- **It is a crime to drive with hazardous materials if you do not have the CDL endorsement.**
  - If you do not have the endorsement and are stopped, you will receive a citation.
  - If you receive a citation after being stopped, you will not be allowed to drive your truck.
- **Not all hazardous materials can be loaded together.**
  - You must know which materials can and cannot be loaded with one another.
  - Refer to your employer and consult regulations if you are unsure which materials can be transported simultaneously.

Quick Review Questions

36. Why is it important to know where your vehicle's hazardous material shipping papers are located?

37. What are placards for hazardous materials, and why are they important?

38. Can anyone with a CDL transport hazardous materials?

2. Driving Safely

Answer Key

1. A driver should look 12 – 15 seconds ahead, which shows how far you will travel in that same amount of time.

2. Checking the mirrors regularly—and even more frequently in certain situations—is the best way to see the rear and sides of your vehicle.

3. The term *communication* means signaling your intentions to other drivers and is therefore a critical component of safe driving.

4. Your vehicle should be visible within 500 ft.

5. On a 1-way or divided highway, emergency warning devices should be placed toward approaching traffic at intervals of 10, 100, and 200 ft.

6. Total stopping distance is calculated by adding the perception distance, reaction distance, and braking distance in ideal conditions.

7. Driving twice as fast quadruples your total stopping distance (and your impact power).

8. Since empty vehicles have less traction, they may require greater stopping distances.

9. Hydroplaning occurs when a vehicle's tires lose contact with the road when roads have accumulated amounts of water or slush. Do not brake to slow down; instead, release the accelerator and push in the clutch to regain control. Or, if the drive wheels skid, push in the clutch to allow them to freely turn.

10. The term *black ice* describes when roadways look wet because the asphalt is visible. If the temperatures drop to freezing, wet roads are prone to becoming black ice.

11. Braking can lock the wheels and cause skidding.

12. Calculate following distance using the timed interval heavy vehicle formula, which is at least 1 second for every 10 ft. of vehicle length when driving under 40 mph, adding 1 second to that number if driving over 40 mph. Identify an approaching landmark and count slowly to see how long it takes the vehicle in front of you to pass that landmark. If it is less than the number you have calculated, slow down until your count follows the timed interval rule.

13. A 30-ft. vehicle driven at 55 mph should have a following distance of at least 4 seconds: 1 second for every 10 ft. of the vehicle's length (30 ÷ 10 = 3), and driving over 40 mph tacks on an extra second.

14. If tailgated, you should maintain a low speed, increase your following distance, and not make any quick changes.

15. By increasing your following distance, you are opening up room ahead of you, which prevents sudden speed or direction changes and allows other drivers to pass you more easily.

16. Posted heights on bridges and overpasses can be inaccurate, especially if there has been repaving or if there is packed snow on the road.

17. Heavily loaded vehicles have lower clearance underneath; certain terrain (e.g., dirt roads and unpaved yards) can cause such vehicles to get hung up.

18. You should never swing wide to the left before negotiating a right turn because it could mislead other drivers into thinking that you are turning left. These drivers may then think it is safe to pass you on the right, which could cause you to strike their vehicles when completing the right turn.

19. The weight of your vehicle affects acceleration: the heavier the load, the slower the acceleration. Commercial vehicles also take up more space than cars. It is therefore important to keep these factors in mind when crossing or entering traffic.

20. Examples of inside distractions include adjusting entertainment or climate controls, smoking, eating, drinking, reading, using navigational tools or other electronic devices, talking on the CB radio, and mental distractions (e.g., daydreaming).

21. Hands-free mobile communication devices located close to the driver and compliant with voice communication rules may be safely used while driving; however, they must be used with caution since they still pose a distraction.

22. Evidence has proven texting to be the most dangerous driving distraction, making a safety-critical event 23.2 times more likely for drivers who are texting than for those who are not.

23. Before driving, make it a goal to eliminate any potential distractions in your vehicle. This includes assessing for distractions, anticipating distractions and creating a plan to eliminate them, and considering possible scenarios that should be discussed before hitting the road.

24. Drifting vehicles, speed inconsistencies, using a mobile communication device, eating, drinking, smoking, and having conversations are all warning signs that a driver could be distracted.

25. If you notice signs of distracted driving, take preventive measures: maintain a safe following distance and take extreme caution when passing such drivers.

26. Road rage involves an intention to cause harm to others (e.g., physically assaulting other drivers and their vehicles). Aggressive driving is selfish driving, but it does not involve an intent to harm others.

27. When confronted with an aggressive driver, you should avoid making eye contact, swallow your pride, and not react—let it go. If the situation seems unsafe or like it could escalate, make a plan to safely call the appropriate authorities.

28. Since your mood can affect how you drive, it is important to recognize any stress and deal with it beforehand. Listening to relaxing music is one way to de-stress before—or even during—a trip.

29. This is false. Railroad crossings are always dangerous; assume that a train is coming each time you approach a railroad crossing.

30. There are 2 types of railroad crossings: passive crossings have no traffic control devices; active crossings do.

31. It typically takes standard-sized tractor trailers at least 14 seconds to clear a single track and more than 15 seconds to clear double tracks.

32. Low-slung units, such as car carriers and single-axle tractors pulling long trailers with landing gear set for tandem-axle tractors, are both at risk of getting stuck on a raised railroad crossing.

33. If you get stuck on the tracks, exit the vehicle and move away from the tracks. Check for signposts or signal housing to identify emergency notification information; provide your location and the posted DOT number if possible, and describe any nearby landmarks.

34. Allowing enough time to pass for your BAC to drop to 0 is the only proven way to sober up. Taking a cold shower, getting fresh air, and/or drinking coffee do not work.

35. Certain prescribed or over-the-counter drugs can cause drowsiness, which affects the ability to drive safely.

36. Hazardous material shipping papers must be easily located, especially in the event of an accident, since lives may be at stake. Keeping shipping papers on top of each other and accessible can help emergency personnel reduce or prevent damage/injury if they know what kinds of hazardous materials are being transported.

37. Placards are signs that identify the hazard class of cargo. They are put on the outside of the vehicle to warn others that your vehicle is transporting hazardous materials.

38. No. If your vehicle requires placards, you must have a hazardous materials endorsement on your CDL in order to legally transport certain hazardous materials.

3 Driving in Hazardous Conditions

Driving at Night

- **It is always more dangerous to drive at night.**
    - Hazards are harder to spot at nighttime.
    - Difficulty seeing hazards results in less response time.
    - Crashes are more likely when drivers are caught by surprise, which is often the case at night.
- The driver, roadway, and vehicle all contribute to the difficulties of night driving.

Vision

You must have good vision to drive safely.

- Your vision dictates your control of the brake, accelerator, and steering wheel.
- Limited vision prevents you from noticing and responding to traffic/road conditions and potential issues in time.
- Have your eyes checked regularly by a professional eye specialist.
- If you must wear glasses or contacts, do so and remember the following:
    - Always wear corrective lenses when driving, regardless of the distance being driven.
    - It is illegal to operate a vehicle without corrective lenses if your license indicates they are needed.
    - Have an extra set of corrective lenses in your vehicle.
    - Do not use corrective lenses that are dark or tinted while driving at night—they cut down the light you need for nighttime driving conditions.
- Glare from bright lights can give drivers short-term blindness.
    - At 55 mph, 2 seconds of glare blindness equates to driving more than half the length of a football field—without seeing.
    - It can take several seconds for your eyes to recover from glare.

Quick Review Question

1. How are good vision and safe driving related?

Fatigue

Driving while fatigued or drowsy is a leading cause of crashes.

- Fatigue means being physically and/or mentally tired; it impairs judgment and vision.
- Falling asleep behind the wheel can be fatal; ANY sleep behind the wheel can lead to a serious crash.
- **Nighttime drivers have a greater chance of falling asleep at the wheel.**
- **Stop driving and take a 15 – 20 minute nap (or overnight) if you experience any of these signs of fatigue:**
    - trouble focusing
    - blinking frequently or having heavy eyelids
    - rubbing your eyes and/or yawning over and over again
    - a wandering mind, daydreaming, or having disconnected thoughts
    - difficulty remembering the last few miles you drove
    - missing exits and/or traffic signs
    - difficulty keeping your head up
    - lane drifting, following closely, or hitting shoulders or rumble strips
    - restlessness and irritability
- Pushing on in the face of these warning signs can cause a fatal crash.

Risks for fatigue include having 6 or fewer hours of sleep; driving a long distance without adequate breaks; taking sedatives; and working more than 60 hours per week.

Figure 3.1. The Risks of Driving While Fatigued

- **Prevent fatigue BEFORE a trip:**
    - **Get the 8 – 9 hours of sleep per night that adults need for alertness.**
    - Plan your route carefully: identify total distance, stopping points, and other considerations.

- Plan your driving for when you would normally be awake.
- Have a passenger.
- Stay away from any medications that can cause drowsiness.
- See a physician if you have trouble sleeping, experience daytime sleepiness, or nap frequently.

- **Stay alert** while driving:
    - Use sunglasses to protect yourself from eyestrain and glare.
    - Use the air conditioner or open the window to keep your body cool.
    - Make healthy meal choices; do not eat foods that are rich or heavy.
    - Pay attention to any downtime during your day and use it to rest.
    - Take breaks every 100 mi. or 2 hours during long trips.
    - Stop driving to rest or nap whenever possible.
    - Do not rely on caffeine: it only increases your awareness for a few hours.
    - Do not take drugs: stimulants may keep you awake, but they will not make you alert.
    - **Leave the road and find a place to rest as soon as you realize you are drowsy.**

Quick Review Questions

2. What are 3 indications that you could be experiencing fatigue while driving?

3. If you are drowsy, what should you do before driving?

Roadway-Related Factors

Most roadways have poor lighting at night.

- You will need to depend on your headlights when driving at night.
- You cannot see hazards as well at night as you can during the day.
- Nondrivers (e.g., joggers, pedestrians, animals, bicyclists) often do not use lights.
- Roads can be more confusing at night, especially when there are other lights around (e.g., signs, shop windows).
- Always drive slower than usual in poor or disorienting lighting.
- Be sure that you are driving slowly enough to stop within the visible distance ahead.
- Be aware of drivers on the road who are impaired:
    - Pay special attention during closing time for bars/taverns.
    - Watch for drivers who are weaving, have difficulty maintaining speed, stop unnecessarily, or show any other signs of impairment.

3. Driving in Hazardous Conditions

Quick Review Question

4. Why is it advisable to drive slower at night?

Vehicle-Related Factors

You cannot see as much with your headlights as you can during the daytime.

- o Headlights are often your main source of light when driving at night.
- o In addition to providing light to drive, they allow other drivers to see you.
- o Low beams usually light a distance of about 250 ft.
- o High beams usually light a distance of about 350 – 500 ft.

- **Adjust your speed to keep your stopping distance within your sight distance.**
- If stopping distance is not within sight distance, there will not be enough time to stop.
- Be certain your headlights are in proper working order at all times:
  - o Keep them clean: dirty headlights can cut down your visibility and the ability of others to see you by half.
  - o Headlights must be professionally adjusted if they are not pointed in the right direction.
  - o Headlights not positioned correctly can blind others and limit your sight distance.
- Other lights on your vehicle must be maintained in order for others to easily see you:
  - o reflectors
  - o clearance lights
  - o taillights
  - o marker lights
  - o identification lights
- Always be certain your signal and brake lights are clean and functional.
- Clean windshields and mirrors are especially important at night:
  - o Oncoming bright lights create a glare against dirt on windshields and mirrors.
  - o A rising or setting sun can create near-zero visibility through a dirty windshield.
  - o Windshields should be cleaned on both the inside and outside.
- Following safety procedures for night driving increases your safety and the safety of others:
  - o Always be rested and alert; sleep if you are not.
  - o Make sure any corrective lenses are clean and unscratched.
  - o Never wear sunglasses at night.
  - o Do a thorough inspection of your vehicle, including all lights and reflectors.
  - o Clean any lights or reflectors that are within reach.
  - o **Dim your lights within 500 ft. of oncoming vehicles.**

- - **Dim your lights when you are following a vehicle.**
  - Remember: glare from your headlights shines in the rearview mirror of the vehicle in front of you.
  - Look slightly to the right of oncoming vehicles using the right lane or edge marking to avoid glare from oncoming traffic.
  - Do not retaliate with high beams if oncoming vehicles do not lower theirs.
  - **Use high beams whenever it is legal and safe to do so.**
  - Keep interior lights off and instrument lights dim; when they are on, it is harder to see outside.
  - **Always stop as soon as possible to rest as soon as you realize you are tired.**

Quick Review Question

5. Is it better to use high beams or low beams while driving at night?

Driving in Fog

- **Fog is unpredictable and extremely dangerous.**
- Be on the lookout for foggy conditions and plan to reduce your speed.
- Never assume that the fog will thin out, especially after you enter it.
- **Never drive in fog if you can avoid it**; pull over and wait for it to lift.
- If you must navigate through fog, keep the following in mind:
  - Look for and obey any warning signs about fog.
  - Slow down before entering foggy conditions.
  - Use fog lights and low beams—even in the daytime.
  - Be aware that other vehicles may not have their headlights on.
  - Use your 4-way flashers/hazard lights so you are visible to vehicles behind you.
  - **Never rely on the taillights in front of you as a guide to where the road is; the vehicle could be pulled over and not on the actual road.**
  - Look for roadside reflectors to help you gauge curves ahead.
  - **LISTEN for traffic**; do not rely on seeing it.
  - Do not pass vehicles.
  - Do not stop on the side of the road unless it is unavoidable.

Quick Review Question

6. Why is it dangerous to follow the taillights in front of you in foggy conditions?

Driving in Winter

Coolant, Heating Equipment, Wipers

Use a coolant tester to check that the cooling system is full and has enough antifreeze, which helps maintain the engine's operating temperature.

- Understand how your vehicle's heaters work before driving; this includes mirror, battery box, and fuel tank heaters.

- Be sure all defrosters are in working order.
- Check that your windshield wiper blades work and make a hard enough contact with the windshield to remove snow.
- Make sure the windshield washer works and that its reservoir has enough fluid.
- Use windshield washer antifreeze.

> **Helpful Hint**
> Coolant testers can have ball floats or disc floats, both of which let you know what the freeze protection level is in your coolant system. Disc floats offer increased visibility because they tend to be larger than ball floats.

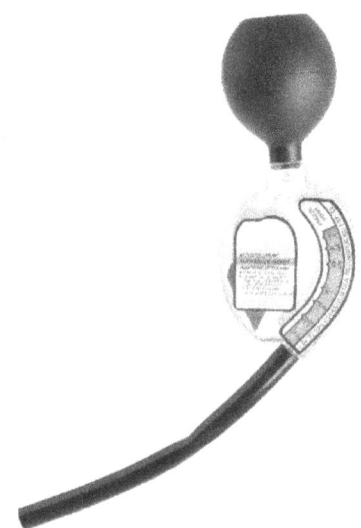

Figure 3.2. Coolant Testers

Quick Review Question

7. Why should you use a coolant tester?

Tires and Tire Chains

Use a gauge to make sure you have enough tread:

- Drive tires need traction to push the vehicle through snow and go over wet pavement.
- Steering tires need enough traction to steer your vehicle.
- **You need at least $\frac{4}{32}$ in. tread depth in each major groove on the front tires.**

3. Driving in Hazardous Conditions

- o **Tread depth for all other tires should be at least $\frac{2}{32}$ in.; more is better.**

Figure 3.3. Tire Tread

- Always have the correct number of chains and extra cross-links on hand.
    - o **Be sure they fit your drive tires.**
    - o Inspect chains beforehand: make sure there are no broken hooks, worn or broken cross-links, or bent/broken side chains.
    - o Understand how to put chains on BEFORE you have to do so in winter conditions.

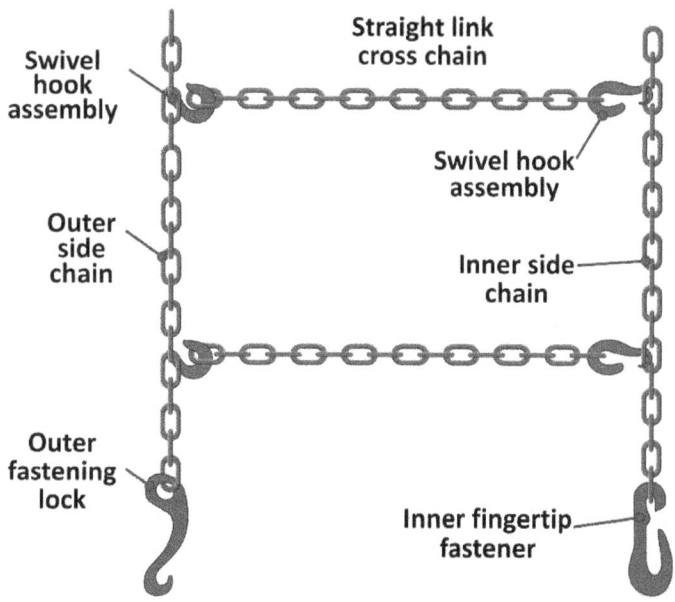

Figure 3.4. Tire Chains

3. Driving in Hazardous Conditions

> **Helpful Hint**
> Before driving, do a standard inspection and ensure your vehicle is ready for winter travel conditions.

Quick Review Questions

8. What are the correct tread depths for winter driving?

9. Which tires do you put chains on for winter driving?

Other Vehicle Checks

Check regularly to make sure that all lights and reflectors are clean and in working order.

- BEFORE driving, remove snow, ice, and debris from the windshield, mirrors, and windows.
- Clean ice and snow from any handholds, steps, or deck plates to prevent slipping.
- Clear ice from radiator shutters.
- **Check that the winterfront is not closed too tightly,** which can cause the vehicle to overheat.
- Check for loose parts and signs/sounds of leaks in the exhaust system.
    - Loose connections can cause carbon monoxide to leak into the vehicle, which can be fatal.
    - Sleepiness could be a sign of carbon monoxide poisoning.

> **Helpful Hint**
> Winterfronts cover the grill to protect the radiator from ice and snow. They help keep the engine operating at the correct temperature in extreme cold weather.

Quick Review Question

10. Why is it important to make sure that the winterfront is not closed too tightly?

Driving Strategies

Get a feel for the road conditions as soon as you start driving.

- Practice safe driving techniques on slippery roads:
    - Go slowly; make smooth movements.
    - Turn and brake gently; never brake on curves.
    - Do not pass unless absolutely necessary.
    - Look far enough ahead; increase your following distance.
    - Never use engine brakes or speed retarders, which can cause drive wheels to skid.
    - Avoid driving alongside other vehicles.
    - Anticipate stops as much as possible in order to slow down gradually.
    - Give snowplows and salt/sand trucks ample room on the roadway.

3. Driving in Hazardous Conditions

- On very icy roads, stop at the first safe place and wait for conditions to improve.
- Know the signs for ice-covered roadways:
  - **If other vehicles are not producing spray, the road is iced over.**
  - Bridges and overpasses will get icy first.
  - If your mirrors and/or wipers have ice, chances are the road will too.
- **Moisture causes brakes to weaken, apply unevenly, or grab.**
- Some **effects of wet brakes** include
  - a **loss of braking power,**
  - **jackknifing,**
  - **pulling to one side,** and
  - **wheel lockups.**
- Avoid wet brakes by not driving through deep puddles or flowing water.
- **Follow these guidelines if you must drive through deep or flowing water:**
  - Slow down and go into low gear.
  - Brake gently so that the linings press against drums or discs to prevent debris from entering.
  - Increase your engine's rpm.
  - Cross the water while maintaining light brake pressure.
  - Keep the light pressure on your brakes after exiting the water so that they can heat up and dry out.
  - When no one is behind you and it is safe to do so, test the brakes by stopping; dry them out more if needed.
  - Never apply excess brake pressure and the accelerator simultaneously—it can cause brake drums and linings to overheat.

Quick Review Questions

11. How can you determine if roadways are icy?

12. What problems can wet brakes cause, and how can you avoid getting them?

Driving in Hot Weather

- Perform a standard inspection of your vehicle.
- Pay special attention to tires:
  - Remember that air pressure increases as temperatures rise.
  - Check air pressure and tire mounting.
  - Monitor your tires every 2 hours or 100 mi.

- - Remain stopped and wait for tires to cool off if they are too hot to the touch.
  - **Never let air out of hot tires; once they cool off, the pressure will be too low.**
  - Overly hot tires can catch fire or blow out.
- Be sure there is enough engine oil.
  - Oil both lubricates the engine and keeps it cool.
  - Monitor the oil temperature gauge; be sure it is within the appropriate range.
- Heed the engine manufacturer's guidance on the amounts of water and antifreeze needed.
- Monitor the water or coolant temperature gauge periodically to make sure it is within normal range.
  - Gauges beyond the normal range indicate problems that could cause engine failure or a fire.
  - If the gauge goes beyond normal range, stop driving as soon as you can do so safely; try to diagnose the issue.
- Take precautions when inspecting an engine that is overheating:
  - Sight glasses, see-through coolant overflow containers, or coolant recovery containers allow you to safely check the coolant level while the engine is hot.
  - If the coolant container is NOT pressurized, you can safely remove the cap and add coolant while the engine is at running temperature.
  - **NEVER remove any part of a pressurized system—including the radiator cap—unless the system has cooled down.**
  - Steam and boiling water from pressurized systems can spray if still under pressure and cause severe injuries.
  - Test the radiator cap: if you can touch it comfortably with your bare hand, it is likely safe to open.

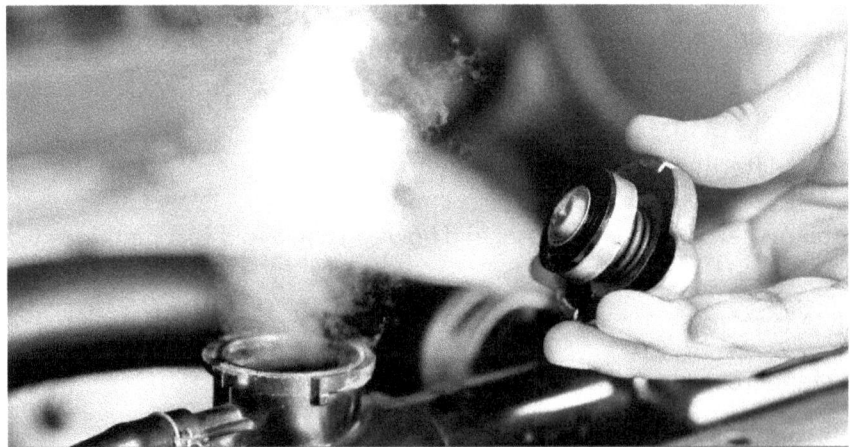

Never remove the radiator cap if the system is still hot.

Figure 3.5. Radiator Cap

3. Driving in Hazardous Conditions

- Follow special steps when adding coolant to systems without recovery or overflow tanks:
    - Be sure to shut the engine off and wait for it to cool down.
    - Use gloves or a sturdy cloth to protect your hands.
    - Release the pressure seal: turn the radiator cap slowly until it reaches the first stop.
    - Take a few steps back to let the pressure release from the cooling system.
    - When you are certain all pressure has been released, press the cap down and turn to remove it.
    - Inspect the coolant level; add more if necessary.
    - Replace the cap and return it to the closed position.
- Make sure your engine belts have no signs of wear (e.g., cracking).
- Check the tightness of all *v*-belts:
    - Press on the belts.
    - The water pump and/or fan will not turn properly if belts are loose.
    - Loose belts cause vehicles to overheat.
- Check coolant hoses:
    - Broken coolant hoses cause engine failure and fire.
    - Make sure they are in decent condition and working properly.
- Be on the lookout for "bleeding tar":
    - Bleeding tar rises to the surface.
    - It is very slippery in hot weather.
- Drive slowly in very hot weather, especially desert conditions.
- Always remember that extreme heat could cause tire failure, fire, and/or engine failure.

Quick Review Questions

13. While driving in dangerously warm weather, you notice your tires are very hot and have excess air pressure. What should you do?

14. If your vehicle's coolant container is part of a pressurized system, when can you safely remove the radiator cap to add more coolant?

Mountain Driving

- Understand the route you will be taking and any long, steep grades involved.
- If possible, connect with drivers who are familiar with the steep grades you will be traveling; ask them which speeds are safe.
- **Gravity slows you down on upgrades and speeds you up on downgrades.**
- The gears you will need to use are determined by

3. Driving in Hazardous Conditions

- o the steepness of the grade,
- o the length of the grade, and
- o the weight of the load you are carrying.
- Use lower gears
	- o with heavier loads,
	- o to climb steeper or longer grades, and
	- o when going down grades.
- When going down grades,
	- o use proper braking techniques,
	- o be sure you are in a lower gear,
	- o choose an appropriate and safe speed, and
	- o go slowly enough to prevent your brakes from getting overheated.
- Brakes that are too hot will "fade" and require more pressure to get stopping power.
- Repeatedly using brakes that are fading can prevent you from slowing down or stopping.
- Choosing a safe speed is the most critical thing to consider when mountain driving.
- **When selecting a safe speed, take into consideration**
	- o your **vehicle's total weight** (including cargo),
	- o the **length and steepness of the grade**, and
	- o the **weather and road conditions**.
- Be on the lookout for warning signs concerning a grade's length and steepness.
- Never exceed the maximum safe speed indicated by a sign.
- Control your speed using the braking effect of the engine:
	- o Engine braking works best when the engine is near the governed rpm and the transmission is in lower gears.
	- o Engine braking saves your brakes so you can use them to slow or stop when needed.
- Always shift the transmission to low gear BEFORE starting down a grade.
	- o **You will not be able to shift to a lower gear after your speed has built up.**
	- o There is a chance you will not be able to switch to ANY gears after your speed builds.
	- o The engine braking effect could also be lost if your speed has built up.
- In older trucks, choose the same gear to go downgrade as you would to go up a hill.
- Modern trucks let you use a lower gear going downgrade than you would need to go up a hill.
- Understand the type of vehicle you are driving and which gear is appropriate for the grade.
- Overusing brakes can result in too much heat and cause them to fail.

3. Driving in Hazardous Conditions

- It is important to rely on the engine braking effect to lessen wear on primary brakes.
- Brake adjustment affects brake function; out-of-adjustment brakes are prone to fading.
    - Other brakes overcompensate for a fading brake, which can cause them to overheat.
    - If the brakes overheat and fade, you will not be able to control your vehicle.
    - **Always check brake adjustment regularly**.
- Using brakes on a long/steep grade is a supplement to the engine braking effect.
- **After shifting to the appropriate low gear, use the following braking techniques:**
    - Wait until your vehicle reaches its "safe" speed.
    - Depress brakes just until you feel the vehicle slow down.
    - Release the brakes after your speed is about 5 mph below your "safe" speed.
    - When your vehicle returns to "safe" speed, depress and release the brakes again until you are 5 mph below the "safe" speed.
    - Keep repeating this process until you reach the bottom of the hill.
- For example: if your "safe" speed is 40 mph,
    - wait until you reach 40 mph before applying the brakes;
    - keep the brakes applied until you reach 35 mph, then release the brakes; and
    - repeat as needed until you reach the end of the hill.

Figure 3.6. Escape Ramp

- Look for signs and be aware of the location of escape ramps on your route.
    - **Escape ramps** save lives, cargo, and equipment.
    - They can often be **found within miles from the top of a downgrade**.
    - They **help stop runaway vehicles safely**.

- They often use a long bed of soft material.
- Some escape ramps have an upgrade.

Quick Review Questions

15. How do you determine a safe speed for a long, steep downgrade?

16. Why is it important to choose the appropriate gear before going down a hill?

17. What is the correct braking technique for a long, steep downgrade?

18. What is an escape ramp?

Answer Key

1. Since vision dictates a driver's control of the accelerator, brake, and steering wheel, it is important that a driver have good vision.

2. Missing exits or traffic signs, rubbing your eyes, and having trouble remembering the last few miles you drove are all indications that you are fatigued and must stop driving.

3. If you realize you are drowsy before driving, you should plan to get adequate rest before hitting the road. If you become drowsy while you are driving, you should pull over as soon as possible to take a nap of 15 – 20 minutes or, if possible, get a full night's rest.

4. Most roadways have poor lighting at night, making hazards difficult to see. Nighttime driving also increases the likelihood of sharing the road with drivers who are impaired.

5. If it is legal and safe to do so, you should use high beams whenever you can. High beams allow you to see up to 350 – 500 ft., which is at least 100 ft. more than the sight distance of low beams.

6. In foggy conditions, relying on the taillights in front of you to help you navigate the road is dangerous because the vehicle in front may not be on the road at all—it could be pulled over to the side.

7. A coolant tester allows you to check that the cooling system in your vehicle is full and has enough antifreeze, which helps maintain the engine's operating temperature.

8. Front tires should have at least $\frac{4}{32}$ in. tread depth in every major groove; all other tires should have a tread depth of at least $\frac{2}{32}$ in.

9. Chains should go on the drive tires. Be sure to inspect the chains and understand how to put them on BEFORE driving.

10. If the winterfront is closed too tightly it can cause the vehicle to overheat.

11. Looking for spray from other vehicles and checking for ice on your mirrors or windshield can indicate ice-covered roads. Always remember that overpasses and bridges get icy first.

12. Wet brakes weaken the braking system; cause the brakes to apply unevenly and grab; and result in jackknifing, a loss of braking power, pulling to one side, and wheel lockups. You can avoid getting wet brakes by not driving through deep or flowing water.

13. Since air pressure increases with heat, do not let any air out of the tires—the pressure will be too low once the tires cool down. Remain stopped and wait for the tires to cool down naturally to avoid having them catch fire or have a blowout.

14. Always wait for components of a pressurized system to cool down before removing them; this includes radiator caps. Be sure the system has cooled enough for you to safely remove the radiator cap without causing it to spray steam or boiling water. A good rule of thumb is to feel the radiator cap with your bare hand—if you can touch it comfortably, it is probably safe to remove.

15. To determine a safe speed for a long, steep downgrade, you must consider your vehicle's total weight (including cargo), the downgrade's steepness and length, and the road and weather conditions.

16. Failure to choose the appropriate gear before going down a hill will prevent you from shifting to a lower gear after your speed has built up. It could also cause you to lose your engine braking effect and prevent you from switching any gears.

17. For a long, steep downgrade, the correct braking technique is to apply the brakes after reaching your "safe" speed. Apply the brakes until you are 5 mph under the "safe" speed. Release the brakes, and continue this process until you have reached the bottom of the hill.

18. Escape ramps are designed to stop a vehicle whose brakes have failed on a downgrade. They help safely stop vehicles, often use a long bed of soft material, and sometimes have an upgrade. Escape ramps save lives, cargo, and equipment.

4 Driving Hazards and Emergencies

Seeing Hazards

- **Hazards are anything that could pose a danger to you while driving.**
- Hazards include road conditions and road users (e.g., pedestrians, other drivers, bicyclists).
- Reduce your risk of crashing by identifying hazards BEFORE they become emergencies.
- Familiarize yourself with hazards so that you can spot them and prepare to act.
- **Being prepared gives you time to create an action plan, which lessens danger.**

Quick Review Question

1. In driving, what is meant by the term *hazard*?

Hazardous Roads

- Look for signs concerning "move-over laws."
    - These laws require drivers to change lanes if they encounter a roadside incident.
    - Always slow down and, if possible, yield the right-of-way if you encounter emergency vehicles.

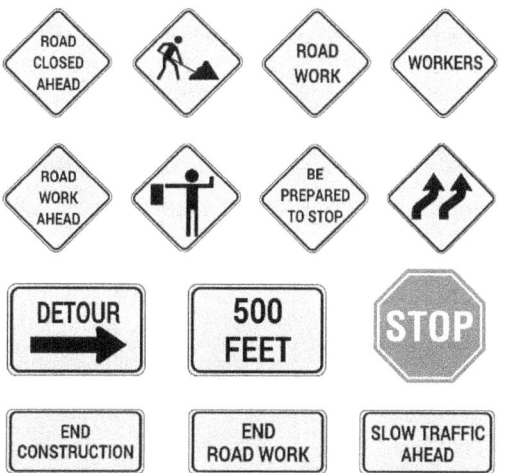

Figure 4.1. Road Work Signs

- Proceed with extra caution and always reduce speed in response to the following hazards:

- Work zones: use 4-way flashers or brake lights to alert other drivers.
- Drop-offs: stay away from the edge of the road to avoid hitting signs, tree limbs, and other roadside objects.
- Foreign objects: pay attention to items that have fallen in the road; just because they look harmless does not mean they will not cause damage to your vehicle.
- On/off ramps: keep in mind that posted speeds on ramps are meant for automobiles and adjust accordingly; never brake while turning.

"Slow moving vehicle" signs—red triangles with orange centers—alert other drivers to slow down ahead of time when approaching these types of vehicles.

Figure 4.2. Slow-Moving Vehicle Sign

Quick Review Question

2. What do move-over laws require drivers to do?

Hazardous Drivers, Vehicles, and Nondrivers

- **Hazards can turn into emergencies: spotting them means an emergency situation is possible.**
    - Recognizing hazards helps you plan and prevent emergencies; always be on the lookout.
    - Consider the emergencies that could result from various hazards.
    - Decide how you would react to hazards, create a plan, and be ready to use it if needed.
    - **Planning ahead makes you a defensive, prepared, and safe driver.**
- Hazards are not limited to the roadway itself; see Table 4.1.

Table 4.1. Hazardous Drivers, Nondrivers, and Vehicle Types

Drivers

- of vans, loaded automobiles, and cars with blocked windows
- of rental trucks (whose drivers are often not aware that the vehicles offer limited vision)
- **whom you cannot see, which means that they cannot see you**
- of delivery trucks, which offer a limited line of sight
- who are engaged in conversation
- whose attention is diverted due to a roadway accident or roadway workers
- who are tourists or other confused drivers trying to get their bearings
- who are driving slowly
- with turn signals on but who are somehow prevented from turning
- who are hurried and may feel your rig is slowing them down
- who are impaired (see Chapter 3), drowsy, and/or driving at night
- who need to adjust speed/direction to avoid a collision

Nondrivers

- who may have their back to you (e.g., pedestrians, bicyclists)
- who may be distracted by portable listening devices or engaged in conversation
- who could act spontaneously and not notice traffic (e.g., children)
- who may be unable to see you (e.g., roadway workers)

Vehicle Types

- those which are snow- or ice-covered
- those with out-of-state licenses
- those hidden by blind intersections or alleys, which may require you to stop suddenly
- those that are parked with interior movement (i.e., the driver may move the vehicle)
- stopped buses with passengers in front of or behind it who are unable to see you
- ice cream trucks, which could signal that children and other pedestrians are nearby
- those with wheels that are jacked up and/or have open hoods

Quick Review Question

3. What is the purpose of having a plan when you recognize a hazard?

Antilock Braking Systems (ABSs)

This section describes how ABSs are beneficial in hazardous or emergency situations. Please see Chapters 6 and 7 for more detailed information on these types of braking systems.

ABS Basics

ABSs prevent wheels from locking up and help you keep control of the vehicle.
- Locked up wheels cause skidding, jackknifing, and vehicle spinning.
- ABSs do not necessarily allow you to stop faster.
- ABSs help you navigate around things while braking without skidding.

- Antilock braking systems
  - are an added feature to your normal brakes,
  - do not affect how you normally brake,
  - only activate when wheels are close to locking up,
  - do not shorten stopping distance,
  - help keep your vehicle under control,
  - use computerized sensors that detect when a wheel might lock up, and
  - are faster than a driver's response in the event of wheel lockup.
- **An electronic control unit (ECU) prevents wheel lockup by decreasing brake pressure.**
- Brake pressure adjusts to offer maximum braking without causing wheel lockup.

Quick Review Questions

4. How are ABSs helpful?

5. How does an ABS prevent wheel lockup?

Which Vehicles Have ABSs?

The Department of Transportation (DOT) requires ABSs on certain vehicles (see Table 4.2.).

Table 4.2. Vehicles Required to Have ABSs by Order of the Department of Transportation (DOT)	
Vehicles with Air Brakes	**Vehicles with Hydraulic Brakes**
<ul><li>truck tractors manufactured on or after March 1, 1997</li><li>any other air brake vehicles manufactured on or after March 1, 1998:</li></ul>	<ul><li>trucks and buses:<ul><li>with a gross vehicle weight of at least 10,000 lb.</li></ul></li></ul>

4. Driving Hazards and Emergencies

Table 4.2. Vehicles Required to Have ABSs by Order of the Department of Transportation (DOT)

Vehicles with Air Brakes	Vehicles with Hydraulic Brakes
o trucks o buses o trailers o converter dollies	o manufactured on or after March 1, 1999 • Other commercial vehicles manufactured before this date have often been modified to include ABS.

Quick Review Question

6. Which types of vehicles with hydraulic brakes are required to have ABS?

How Do I Know My Vehicle Has ABS?

Indications that a vehicle is equipped with ABS vary; see Table 4.3.

- If the **yellow malfunction lamp** stays lit after the initial bulb check (in newer vehicles) or after you have been driving (in older vehicles), it may signal a loss of ABS control.

Table 4.3. Determining Whether a Vehicle is Equipped with ABS

Type of Vehicle	ABS Indication
Tractors, trucks, and buses	Yellow ABS malfunction lamps are on the instrument panel.
Trailers	Yellow ABS malfunction lamps are on the left side, either on the rear or front corner.
Dollies built on or after March 1, 1998	A yellow ABS lamp is required on the left side.
Towed units	If built before DOT mandates for ABS, an ECU and wheel speed sensor wires at the back of the brakes can indicate if the unit has ABS.
Newer vehicles	The malfunction lamp turns on for a bulb check when the vehicle is started, and then it goes out quickly.
Older vehicles	The malfunction lamp illuminates at start-up and may stay on until you begin driving more than 5 mph.

Quick Review Question

7. How can you determine if your vehicle has ABS?

Braking with ABSs

Drive and brake per usual on vehicles with ABSs.

- o Only use the braking force needed to stop safely and maintain control.
- o Keep an eye on the tractor and trailer while slowing down.
- o Safely ease up on brakes to maintain control.
- o EXCEPTION: fully apply brakes in an emergency when driving straight trucks or combinations with a working ABS on all axles.

- An ABS on only the trailer, tractor, or one axle still offers more vehicle control during braking.
  - o **ABS on tractor only:** steering control should still be possible with fewer chances to jackknife; drivers should watch the trailer closely and ease up on the brakes if the trailer begins to swing out.
  - o **ABS on trailer only:** swinging out on the trailer is not likely; if steering control is lost or the tractor begins to jackknife, ease up on the brakes to regain control.
- If the ABS malfunctions, drive and brake as you normally would.
  - o Be on the lookout for yellow malfunction lamps that indicate if the ABS is malfunctioning.
  - o Get your vehicle serviced as soon as possible after noticing an ABS malfunction light
- ABSs are helpful safety devices but do not give a free pass to ignore other safety measures:
  - o Having an ABS does not mean you can drive faster.
  - o ABSs will NOT prevent skids and jackknives caused by spinning drive wheels or turning too fast.
  - o Do not rely on ABS to shorten the stopping distance.
  - o ABSs are an accessory to normal brakes, not a replacement—stopping power is neither increased nor decreased.
  - o ABSs are not a replacement for malfunctioning or poorly maintained brakes.
  - o **Safe driving behaviors are the greatest safety feature in any vehicle.**
- ABSs can prevent serious crashes, but
  - o you should still pay attention to road conditions, and
  - o you should drive in a way that prevents you from needing them in the first place.

4. Driving Hazards and Emergencies

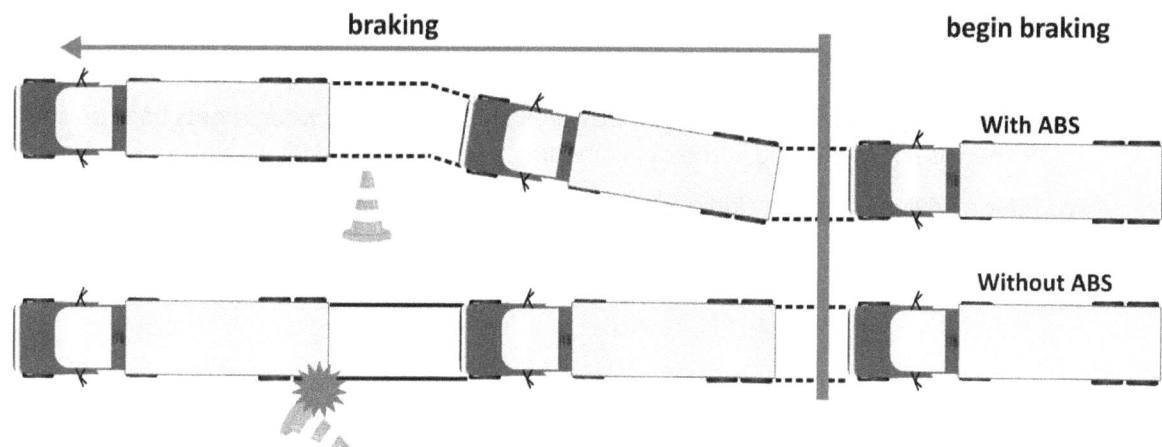

ABS will allow you to steer while braking but will not shorten stopping distance

Figure 4.3. Braking With and Without ABS

Quick Review Question

8. What is the correct braking technique in a vehicle that has ABS?

Skid Control and Recovery

- **Skidding happens when tires cannot grip the road; there are 4 causes:**
    1. braking too hard, causing wheel lockup, or using speed retarders on slippery roads
    2. oversteering by turning the wheel more than the vehicle itself can turn
    3. accelerating too hard, which gives drive wheels too much power
    4. driving too fast for the road conditions
- **Drive-wheel skids are the most common.**
    - They are caused by excessive braking or acceleration.
    - The rear wheels lose traction.
    - These types of skids typically happen on ice- or snow-covered roads.
    - Releasing the accelerator can stop the skidding.
    - In extremely slippery conditions, depress the clutch to keep wheels rolling freely and help them regain traction.
- When the rear drive wheels lock, rear-wheel braking skids happen.
    - Locked wheels have less traction than rolling ones.
    - Locked wheels cause the rear wheels to slide sideways (spin out).
    - Rear wheels spin out to try to catch up with the front wheels.
    - Buses and straight trucks go sideways in a skid.
- **Drive-wheel skids can happen in vehicles with trailers and cause a jackknife.**

- Do the following to correct a drive-wheel braking skid:
    - Stop braking in order to get the rear wheels rolling again and prevent them from sliding.
    - Turn the opposite direction of the way the vehicle is turning when it gets back on course; otherwise, it might skid in the opposite direction of its first skid.
    - Use a driving range or "skid pad" to practice these techniques.

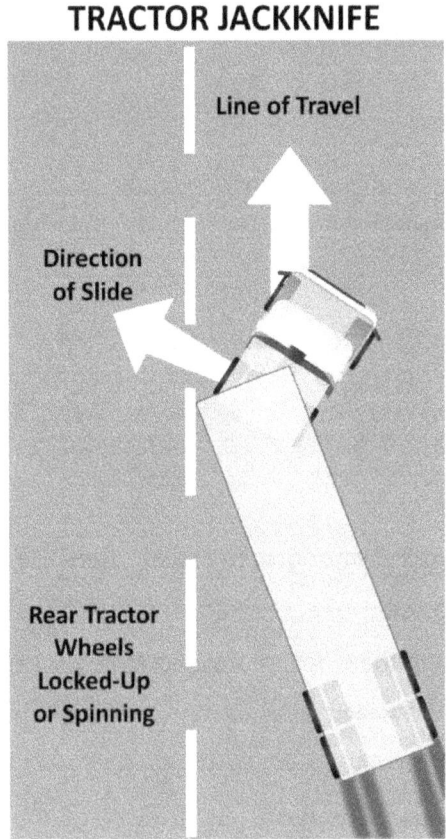

Figure 4.4. Correcting a Jackknife Skid

- Most front-wheel skids are the result of driving too fast for the conditions.
- Insufficient tread on the front tires and/or cargo loads without enough weight on the front axle can also cause front-wheel skids.
- Front-wheel skids can prevent steering and cause the vehicle to only move in a straight line.
- The only way to stop a front-wheel skid is to allow the vehicle to slow down:
    - Stop turning.
    - Stop braking hard.
    - Slow down as quickly and safely as possible without skidding.

4. Driving Hazards and Emergencies

Quick Review Questions

9. What does the term *skidding* mean, and how does skidding happen?

10. Which type of skid is the most common?

Answer Key

1. Hazards are anything that could pose a risk to you while you are driving; they include other drivers, pedestrians, and bicyclists.

2. Move-over laws require drivers to change lanes if they encounter a roadside incident, slow down if they encounter emergency vehicles, and yield the right-of-way to emergency vehicles.

3. Recognizing hazards, considering the possible emergencies that could result from them, and making a plan ahead of time in the event of an emergency can prevent a crash and make you a defensive, prepared, and safe driver.

4. Antilock braking systems (ABSs) are designed to help you keep control of the vehicle and prevent the wheels from locking up.

5. An antilock braking system (ABS) prevents wheel lockup by decreasing brake pressure through the use of an electronic control unit (ECU).

6. Trucks and buses with a gross vehicle weight of at least 10,000 lb. that were manufactured on or after March 1, 1999, must have antilock braking systems (ABSs) by order of the Department of Transportation (DOT).

7. Yellow antilock braking system (ABS) malfunction lamps indicate whether a vehicle is equipped with ABS. In buses, tractors, and trucks, the lamp is on the instrument panel. On trailers, the lamp is on the left side, either on the rear corner or front. Any dollies built on or after March 1, 1998, have the lamp on the left side. Towed units need to be checked near the back of the brakes for an electronic control unit (ECU) and wheel speed sensors.

8. Braking with an antilock braking system (ABS) is no different than regular braking—only use the force needed to come to a safe stop and maintain control. Always watch your tractor and trailer and ease up on brakes if necessary (and safe to do so). Straight trucks or combinations with ABSs on all axles can have brakes fully applied in emergency situations.

9. Skidding happens when tires cannot grip the road; it has 4 causes: braking too hard (or using speed retarders on slippery roads), oversteering, accelerating too hard, and driving too fast for the road conditions.

10. Drive-wheel skids are the most common type of skid.

5 Transporting Cargo

Basics of Transporting Cargo

- Cargo in transport is required to be secured on or within the vehicle.
- To earn your CDL, you must understand the cargo loading and securement requirements of the FMCSA (Federal Motor Carrier Safety Administration):
    - All states have adopted these federal regulations.
    - These regulations aim to prevent or reduce cargo-related incidents.
    - Search "49 CFR 393" at www.fmcsa.dot.gov to access the regulations.
- Incorrectly loaded and/or unsecured cargo is a danger to you and others.
    - Cargo that is loose could fall off, cause traffic problems, and/or hurt or kill people, including the truck driver.
    - Overloaded cargo could damage your vehicle.
    - Steering is affected by how the cargo is loaded.
- **Regardless of who loads the cargo, drivers have 4 responsibilities:**
    1. inspecting the cargo
    2. recognizing when cargo is overloaded and/or has poor weight distribution
    3. ensuring cargo is secured properly and does not block views ahead and to the sides
    4. ensuring the loaded cargo does not prevent access to emergency equipment
- Understand the type of cargo you are transporting.
    - Hazardous materials may require vehicle placards.
    - Know whether you need a hazardous materials endorsement.
    - Specific, additional regulations apply to certain cargo (e.g., metal coils; see Chapter 14).
    - See Chapter 12 for more information on the hazardous materials endorsement.

Quick Review Question

1. What are the 4 cargo-related responsibilities that drivers must take care of?

Inspecting Cargo

- In addition to performing the 7-step vehicle inspection (see Chapter 15),
    - check that the vehicle and its cargo are not overloaded, and
    - make sure the cargo is secured and that its weight is evenly distributed.
- **Cargo should be checked and securement devices adjusted as needed**
    - **within the first 50 mi. of a trip,**
    - **when the duty status of a driver changes,**
    - **after 3 hours (or 150 mi.),**
    - **whenever a driving break is taken, and**
    - **as often as needed.**
- Always be aware of federal, state, and local regulations concerning vehicle weight and cargo.
- Be sure to have extra tie-downs and securing equipment in case adjustments are needed.

Quick Review Question

2. How often should you stop and check your cargo during a trip?

Cargo Weight and Balance

- **It is the driver's responsibility to ensure cargo is not overloaded.**
- See Table 5.1. for the definitions of weight-related terms that you must understand.

Table 5.1. Cargo Weight Terms and Definitions

Term	Definition
Gross vehicle weight rating (GVWR)	the manufacturer's specified value of the loaded weight of a single vehicle
Gross combination weight rating (GCWR)	EITHER - the manufacturer's specified value for the power unit (if the value is displayed on the Federal Motor Vehicle Safety Standard [FMVSS] certification label), OR - the GVWR sum, OR - the gross vehicle weight (GVW)* of the power unit and towed unit(s), or any such combination, that equals the highest value
Axle weight	the weight that 1 axle or 1 set of axles transmits to the ground

5. Transporting Cargo

Table 5.1. Cargo Weight Terms and Definitions

Tire load	the maximum weight a tire can safely carry at a specified pressure (stated on the side of each tire)
Suspension systems	the weight capacity rating provided by the manufacturer
Coupling device capacity	rated for the maximum weight the coupling device can pull or carry

*The GVW is only used by roadside enforcement to determine if a driver/vehicle is subject to CDL regulations; it is not used to decide if a vehicle is representative for the purposes of skills testing.

- GVWRs, GCWRs, and axle weight maximums vary by state (see Table 5.2.).
- Your weight must be within legal limits.
- Maximum axle weights are often determined by a bridge formula.
  - This formula allows less maximum axle weight for axles that are close together, which prevents bridges/roads from being overloaded.
  - The Federal Bridge Formula (FBF) determines the maximum weight allowed on interstate roadways.

Table 5.2. Commercial Truck Axle Weight Limits in the 10 Most Populous States

(listed alphabetically)

State	Single Axle	Double Axle	Tridem Axle	Gross Weight
California (CA)	20,000 lb.	34,000 lb.	undefined	80,000 lb.
Florida (FL)	20,000 lb.	40,000 lb.	per FBF	80,000 lb.
Georgia (GA)	20,340 lb.	34,000 lb.	per FBF	80,000 lb.
Illinois (IL)	20,000 lb.	34,000 lb.	42,500 lb.	80,000 lb.
Michigan (MI)	20,000 lb.	34,000 lb.	per state weight table	80,000 lb.
New York (NY)	20,000 lb.	34,000 lb.	per FBF	80,000 lb.
North Carolina (NC)	20,000 lb.	38,000 lb.	per state weight table	80,000 lb.
Ohio (OH)	20,000 lb.	34,000 lb.	per FBF	80,000 lb.
Pennsylvania (PA)	20,000 lb.	34,000 lb.	per state weight table	80,000 lb.

Table 5.2. Commercial Truck Axle Weight Limits in the 10 Most Populous States

(listed alphabetically)

Texas (TX)	20,000 lb.	34,000 lb.	N/A	80,000 lb.

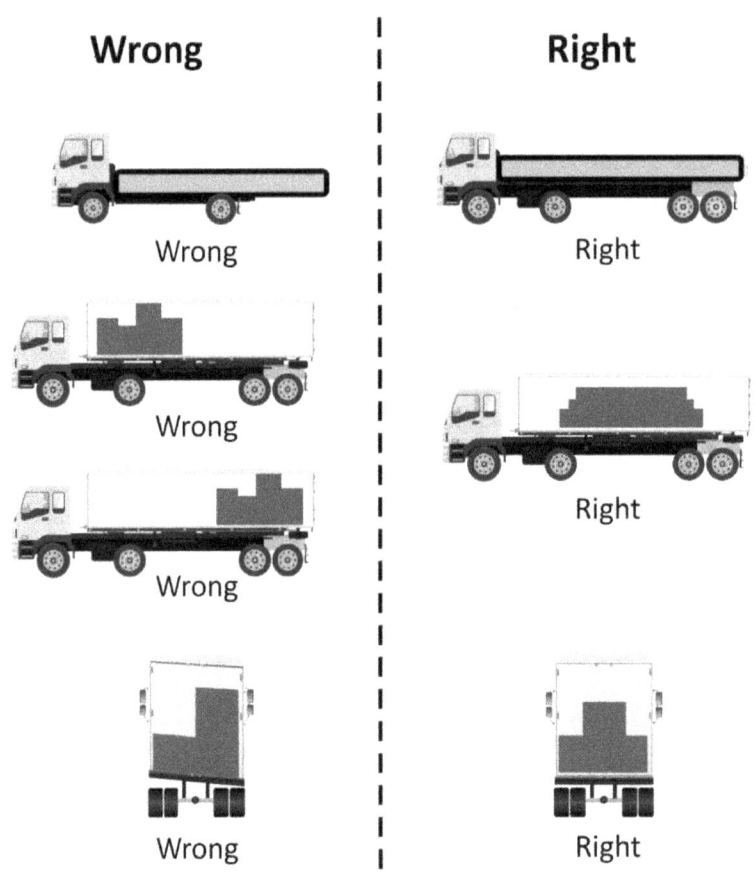

Figure 5.1. Balancing Cargo Loads

- Vehicles that are improperly balanced may not handle safely (see Figure 5.1.).
- Overloading is dangerous:
    o It can negatively affect your steering, braking, and speed control.
    o Overloaded vehicles go very slowly on upgrades.
    o Overloaded vehicles are prone to excessive speed on downgrades.
    o Overloaded vehicles increase stopping distance.
    o Overloaded vehicles can cause brakes to work too hard, leading to failure.
- Always plan ahead:
    o **The maximum cargo weight may not be safe for certain weather conditions.**
    o **The maximum cargo weight may be too dangerous for mountain driving.**

5. Transporting Cargo

- Safe handling of a vehicle depends on the height of the vehicle's center of gravity.
  - **Cargo that is piled too heavy or too high increases your chances of tipping over.**
  - A high center of gravity is especially dangerous when taking curves or swerving.
  - Always distribute cargo as low as possible.
  - Always place the heaviest parts of the cargo beneath the lightest parts.
- If there is **too much weight on the steering axle**,
  - it can be difficult to steer,
  - it can damage the steering axle, and
  - it can damage the tires.
- On the other hand, **handling with underloaded front axles is also unsafe:**
  - Weight that shifts too far to the rear can cause underloaded front axles.
  - **If the front axles are underloaded, the steering axle weight will be too light to steer safely.**
- Traction can be poor if there is not enough weight on the driving axles.
  - The drive wheels could easily spin.
  - In bad weather, underloading could prevent the vehicle from moving.
- Flatbed vehicles run the risk of cargo shifting to the sides and/or falling off.

Quick Review Questions

3. What is the difference between the GCWR and the GVW?
4. Who bears the responsibility of ensuring that cargo is properly secured?
5. Are there any situations in which the legal maximum cargo weight might not be safe? If so, what are the situations?
6. If there is not enough weight on the front axles, what could happen?

Securing Cargo

- The FMCSA requires that cargo be secured in all conditions, including when responding to an emergency.
- FMCSA rules concerning cargo securement apply to the following with a GVWR greater than 10,000 lb:
  - trucks
  - truck tractors
  - semitrailers
  - full trailers

5. Transporting Cargo

- - tractor-pole trailers
- Certain commodities require you to adhere to additional federal regulations.
  - **Additional federal regulations take precedence over general requirements.**
  - Metal coils (Chapter 14) are one example of a commodity with additional regulations.
- Cargo must be secured in such a way as to prevent it from
  - leaking,
  - spilling,
  - blowing off the vehicle,
  - falling from or through the vehicle,
  - becoming dislodged from the vehicle, or
  - swinging or shifting (which affects handling).
- The FMCSA established the minimum amount of force that cargo securement systems must withstand:
  - These amounts are based on the results of extensive testing.
  - The term *performance criteria* describes these minimum force requirements (see Table 5.3. and Figure 5.2.).
  - Performance criteria are sometimes expressed in acceleration terms (see Table 5.3. and Figure 5.2.).

Table 5.3. Performance Criteria in Each Direction

Direction	Minimum Force Requirement	Description	Performance Criteria (expressed in units of gravity)
Forward force	80% of cargo weight	when decelerating or braking while driving straight ahead	0.8 g-force deceleration (forward direction)
Rearward force	50% of cargo weight	when braking in reverse or accelerating	0.5 g-force acceleration (rearward direction)
Lateral (side-to-side) force	50% of cargo weight	when changing lanes, turning, or traveling on a ramp or curve	0.5 g-force acceleration (lateral direction)

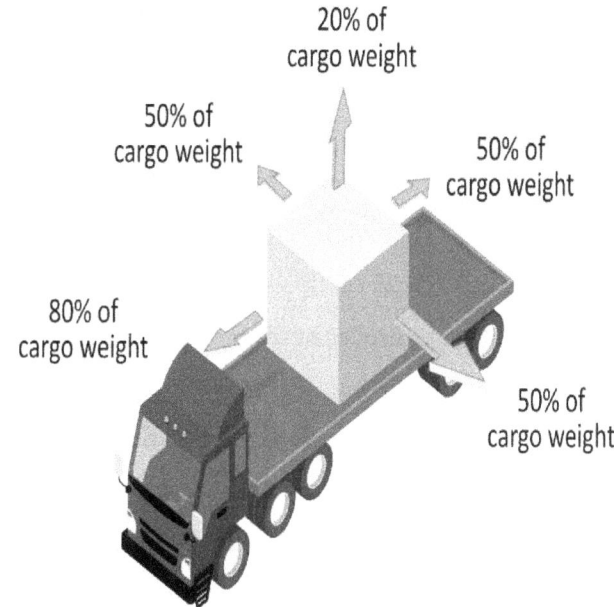

Each securement system must be able to tolerate the minimum performance criteria (force requirements) in each direction.

Figure 5.2. Cargo Securement Performance Criteria

- **The working load limit (WLL) is the maximum load that can be applied to any component of a securement system.**
    - Each part of a securement system must be within the WLL when at maximum force.
    - The WLL applies to normal service.
    - The WLL is often assigned by the component's manufacturer.
    - To determine compliance, apply each performance criteria force to the securement system separately.
- **Preventing the movement of cargo is the most important securement task.**
- Bracing and blocking are used to prevent cargo from sliding.
- **Bracing** is put on the upper portion of the cargo and extends to the floor and/or walls.
- **Blocking** is shaped to snugly fit against cargo and is secured to the cargo deck to prevent the movement of cargo.
- **The WLL of blocking systems must be at least 50% of the weight of the cargo being blocked.**
- Immobilizing cargo is the best way to prevent its forward movement.
- Cargo can be immobilized by being placed against
    - a headboard (header boarD),
    - a bulkhead,
    - stakes,
    - other vehicle structures,

- o other cargo, or
- o a void filler.
- **Void fillers**
    - o are materials that fill the space between cargo and the vehicle structure, and
    - o must have enough strength to prevent cargo from moving.
- **Tie-downs must be used to secure cargo on flatbeds or trailers without sides.**
    - o A tie-down can also be used to prevent cargo from moving forward.
    - o Tie-downs in closed vans prevent cargo from shifting, which can affect handling.
    - o Federal regulations dictate the proper strength and type of tie-downs needed.
- Per federal regulations, **securement systems/tie-downs must**
    - o **have a combined WLL that is at least one-half times the weight of the article(s) being secured,**
    - o use proper equipment, and
    - o be correctly attached to the vehicle.
- **The WLL of tie-downs is the WLL of the weakest part of the tie-down** (anchor points includeD).
- For synthetic webbing, the WLL is the WLL of the tie-down assembly OR the anchor point—whichever is less.
- Some securement components have manufacturer markings that give the WLL value as a numeral.
    - o Codes or symbols are also used by manufacturers to denote WLL values.
    - o Components with an unmarked WLL are understood to have WLLs as outlined in Tables 5.4. and 5.5.
    - o **Components with illegible WLL markings are considered unmarked.**

Table 5.4. Working Load Limit (WLL) Table for Synthetic Webbing

Diameter (in inches)	WLL (in pounds)
$1\frac{3}{4}$	1,750
2	2,000
3	3,000
4	4,000

Table 5.5. Working Load Limit (WLL) Table for Steel Strapping

Width × Thickness (in inches)	WLL (in pounds)
$1\frac{1}{4} \times .029$	1,190
$1\frac{1}{4} \times .031$	1,190
$1\frac{1}{4} \times .035$	1,190
$1\frac{1}{4} \times .044$	1,690
$1\frac{1}{4} \times .050$	1,690
$1\frac{1}{4} \times .057$	1,925
$2 \times .044$	2,650
$2 \times .050$	2,650

- Proper tie-down equipment includes
    - ropes,
    - straps,
    - chains, and
    - tensioning devices (e.g., winches, ratchets, clinching elements).
- It is critical that tie-downs are correctly attached to the vehicle using
    - hooks,
    - bolts,
    - rails, and
    - rings.
- Friction mats offer horizontal movement resistance equal to 50% of the cargo weight on the mat.
- Securement systems include vehicle structure components and securing devices (see Table 5.6.).

5. Transporting Cargo

Table 5.6. Securement System Components

Vehicle Structure Components	Securing Devices
<ul><li>floors</li><li>walls</li><li>decks</li><li>anchor points</li><li>tie-down anchor points</li><li>bulkheads</li><li>headboards</li><li>stakes</li><li>posts</li></ul>Cab shields are usually not considered part of the securement system; restraint against forward movement of cargo can be provided by a front-end structure.	<ul><li>chains</li><li>synthetic webbing</li><li>wire, manila, and/or synthetic ropes</li><li>steel strapping</li><li>clamps and latches</li><li>blocking</li><li>bracing</li><li>front-end structures</li><li>grabhooks</li><li>shackles</li><li>winches</li><li>binders</li><li>stake pockets</li><li>D-rings</li><li>pockets</li><li>webbing ratchets</li><li>friction mats</li></ul>

- **Cargo that is prevented from moving should have at least 1 indirect tie-down for every 10 ft. of cargo.**
- **Cargo that is NOT prevented from forward movement must have indirect tie-downs as described in Table 5.7.**

5. Transporting Cargo

Table 5.7. Tie-Down Requirements for Cargo NOT Prevented from Forward Movement

Cargo Measurement	Cargo Weight	Tie-Down Requirement
5 ft. or less	1,100 lb. or less	1 tie-down
5 ft. or less	over 1,100 lb.	2 tie-downs
greater than 5 ft. and less than or equal to 10 ft.	N/A	2 tie-downs
greater than 10 ft.	N/A	2 + 1 tie-down for every additional 10 ft. (or part thereof)

- See Chapter 14 for special requirements when transporting metal coils.
- Plan in advance: be sure you have enough tie-downs.
- **All cargo on a flatbed—regardless of size—should have at least 2 tie-downs.**
- Know what you're transporting:
    - Heavy pieces of metal have special securing requirements.
    - Be aware of these requirements BEFORE transporting such cargo.

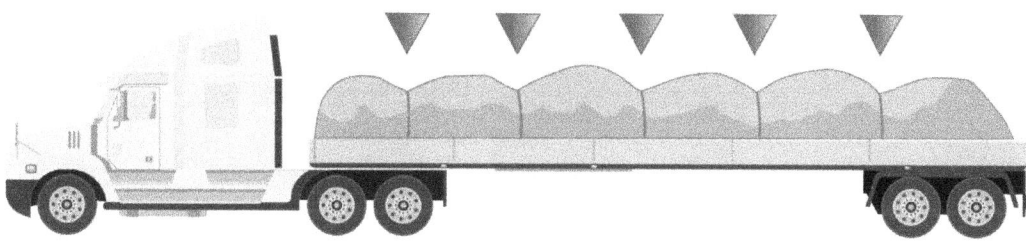

Cargo should have at least one tie-down for every 10 feet of cargo. Cargo needs at least two tie-downs, no matter the size.

Figure 5.3. Tie-Downs

Table 5.8. Direct and Indirect Tie-Downs

	Purpose/Description	Required Angles	WLL Calculations
Direct tie-downs	• to resist minimum force requirements applied to the cargo • One end of the tie-down is connected to the cargo.	• less than 45° when viewed from side of vehicle; effective against forward and rearward forces • less than 45° with the horizontal when	Aggregate WLL = • 100% of the tie-down WLL for each tie-down attached to both

Table 5.8. Direct and Indirect Tie-Downs

		viewed from the front or rear of the vehicle; effective against side-to-side forces	sides of the vehicle • 50% of the WLL for each tie-down attached to one side only of the vehicle
Indirect tie-downs	• increase frictional force (pressure) between the cargo and the deck • The tie-down goes over or through the cargo. • If cargo shifts, the tie-down has failed; direct tie-downs may be more appropriate.	• greater than or equal to 30° with the deck when viewed from the side of the vehicle; effective against side-to-side movement • Initial tension should be as high as possible (greater than or equal to 50% of its WLL). • Tension should be maintained throughout the trip.	• Any tie-down that passes over an article = 1 tie-down. • Aggregate WLL = the sum of the WLLs of each tie-down. • Example: 2 tie-downs each with a WLL of 4,000 lb. = an aggregate WLL of 8,000 lb.

Direct Tie Down:
Maximum 45°

Indirect Tie Down:
Minimum 30°

Figure 5.4. Indirect vs. Direct Tie-Down

- Gaps between cargoes can cause tie-downs to lose initial tension quickly.

- Always ensure that cargoes are placed in contact with each other and that there are no gaps.
- Cargoes stored next to each other should never be able to move toward each other.
- Transverse tie-downs are typically used on long pieces of cargo where space between items cannot be filled or blocked:
    - Transverse tie-downs are wrapped around each article.
    - Transverse tie-downs prevent side-to-side cargo movement.
- The minimum requirement is the aggregate working load (see Table 5.9.).
- Use more tie-downs than calculated for the aggregate WLLs to prevent cargo movement.

Table 5.9. Calculating Aggregate WLLs for Tie-Downs

Tie-downs from Anchor Point on Vehicle to Anchor Point on Cargo Article

one-half of the WLL of each tie-down

Tie-downs that Attach to Anchor Points, Pass Cargo (Through, Over, or ArounD), and Attach to an Anchor Point on the SAME Side of the Vehicle

one-half of the WLL of each tie-down

Tie-downs that Attach to Anchor Points, Pass Cargo (Through, Over, or ArounD), and Attach to an Anchor Point on the OTHER Side of the Vehicle

the WLL for each tie-down used

- In the event of a crash or emergency stop, front-end headboards protect you from the cargo.
- Front-end headboards are also called "headache racks."
- Forward movement of the cargo must be blocked by the front-end structure.
- Always ensure that the front-end structure is in good condition.
- Cargo that is **fully contained** means that
    - it is either placed against other cargo or a structure on the vehicle that has enough strength, and
    - it cannot tip over or shift during transportation.
- Cargo that fills a sided vehicle of appropriate strength is fully contained.
- **Covering cargo on an open bed protects both people and the cargo itself.**
    - **People are protected from cargo if it spills.**
    - **Covers protect cargo from weather conditions.**
- Be familiar with local regulations concerning spill protection safety requirements.
- Get in the habit of using your mirrors to periodically check cargo covers while driving.
    - Be on the lookout for flapping covers, which can tear loose and expose the cargo.

5. Transporting Cargo

- - If a cover tears loose, it can block your and/or others' sight.
- Cargo is packaged in containers if it will be transported by rail or ship at some point.
- Truck delivery usually occurs at the beginning and/or end of such transportation routes.
- Containers can
    - be equipped with their own tie-down devices,
    - have locks that can attach to a special frame, or
    - be loaded directly onto flatbed trailers.
- Like any cargo, containerized loads must be properly secured.
- **Since containerized loads are sealed, drivers cannot inspect them, BUT**
    - they must ensure that the **cargo does not exceed gross weight limits**, and
    - they must be sure that the **cargo does not exceed axle weight limits**.

Quick Review Questions

7. When changing lanes or driving on a curve, what is the minimum amount of force that your cargo securement system should be expected to withstand?

8. Which commercial vehicle types must comply with cargo securement regulations?

9. What does the abbreviation *WLL* stand for, and what does it mean?

10. How many tie-downs should any flatbed load have at a minimum?

11. If you are transporting a 20-ft. load on a flatbed trailer, what is the least number of tie-downs needed?

12. What are the 2 primary reasons that cargo on an open bed needs to be covered?

13. What should a driver check for before transporting cargo that is sealed in a container?

Cargo Needing Special Attention

- See Chapter 14 for guidance on preventing metal coils and similar cargo from rolling.
- Table 5.10. describes the hazards of certain cargo types and tips for their safe transport.

Table 5.10. Cargo Types Requiring Special Attention

Cargo Type	Safety Concerns	Safety Tips
Dry bulk tanks	- high center of gravity - prone to shifting during transport	Take curves and sharp turns with extreme caution.

5. Transporting Cargo

Hanging meat (refrigerated trucks)	<ul><li>an unstable load</li><li>high center of gravity</li></ul>	Avoid rollovers by taking curves and on/off ramps slowly and with extreme caution.
Livestock	<ul><li>movement of livestock during transport</li><li>livestock that lean on curves and shift the center of gravity</li><li>difficult and unsafe handling</li><li>greater likelihood of rollover</li></ul>	Use false bulkheads to keep livestock grouped together if you are not carrying a full load.

- Special transmit permits are required for
    - overlength loads,
    - over-width loads, and/or
    - overweight loads.
- Transporting oversized loads is often limited to certain times; special equipment is usually needed:
    - "wide load" signs
    - flashing lights
    - flags
- Some oversized loads require police escorts or pilot vehicles with warning signs or lights.
- Oversized loads always require the driver to take extra care when operating the vehicle.

Figure 5.5. Oversized Load

Trucks with oversized loads require special signage and may be accompanied by escort vehicles.

Quick Review Question

14. What 2 factors make transporting dry bulk tanks dangerous?

Answer Key

1. Regardless of who loads the cargo, drivers are responsible for the following: inspecting the cargo, recognizing when cargo is overloaded and/or has uneven weight distribution, making sure cargo is secured properly and does not obstruct views ahead and to the sides, and making sure that loaded cargo will not prevent emergency equipment from being accessed.

2. You must stop and check the cargo within the first 50 mi. of your trip, every 3 hours (or 150 mi.), whenever you take a driving break, and as often as needed to ensure that the load is secure.

3. The gross vehicle weight (GVW) is only used by roadside enforcement to determine if a driver/vehicle is subject to CDL regulations; it is not used to decide if a vehicle is representative for the purposes of skills testing. The gross combination weight rating (GCWR) is either 1) the manufacturer's specified value for the power unit (if the value is displayed on the Federal Motor Vehicle Safety Standard [FMVSS] certification label), OR 2) the gross vehicle weight rating (GVWR) sum, OR 3) the GVW of the power unit and towed unit(s)—or any such combination—that equals the highest value.

4. Drivers bear the responsibility of ensuring that cargo is properly secured.

5. Yes; the legal maximum cargo weight may not be safe for certain weather conditions and may be too dangerous for mountain driving.

6. Underloaded front axles could make the steering axle weight too light, resulting in unsafe steering.

7. The minimum amount of force that the cargo securement system should be expected to withstand is 50% of the cargo weight, or 0.5 g-force acceleration.

8. Trucks, truck tractors, semitrailers, full trailers, and tractor-pole trailers with a gross vehicle weight rating (GVWR) of greater than 10,000 lb. must comply with cargo securement regulations.

9. The abbreviation *WLL* stands for "working load limit," which is the maximum load that can be applied to any component of a securement system.

10. Regardless of the size of the cargo, all cargo on a flatbed should have at least 2 tie-downs.

11. At a minimum, 2 tie-downs are needed when transporting a 20-ft. load: there should be at least 1 tie-down for every 10 ft. of cargo.

12. Covers protect people from the cargo if it spills and protect the cargo from weather conditions.

13. Drivers must ensure that the cargo does not exceed gross weight limits and that it does not exceed axle weight limits.

14. Dry bulk tanks have a high center of gravity and their loads are prone to shifting.

6 The Air Brake System

Overview of Air Brakes

- Compressed air is used in air brakes to make them work.
- Air brakes are a safe way to stop large, heavy vehicles.
- Air brakes will not be reliable if they are not properly used and maintained.
- Air brakes are composed of **3 separate braking systems** (see Table 6.1.).

Table 6.1. The 3 Separate Braking Systems of Air Brakes

System Type	Description
Service brake system	applies and releases brakes when the brake pedal is used during regular driving
Parking brake system	uses a parking brake control that applies and releases the parking brakes
Emergency brake system	stops the vehicle in the event of brake system failure by utilizing parts of both the service and parking brake systems

- An air brake system is made up of many parts, including an air compressor:
    - The air compressor is connected to the engine through a *v*-belt or gears.
    - It pumps air into storage tanks, or reservoirs.

Quick Review Question

1. What are the 3 separate braking systems that make up air brakes?

Parts of the Air Brake System

Air Compressor and Governor

Air is pumped into air storage tanks, or reservoirs, by the air compressor.

- Gears or a *v*-belt connect the air compressor to the engine.

6. The Air Brake System

- Either the engine cooling system or air can cool the compressor.
- Compressors not lubricated by engine oil (i.e., that do not have their own supply) must have oil levels checked before driving.
- An air compressor governor controls when the compressor will pump air into the storage tanks.
  - **"Cut-out" level is typically around 125 psi.**
  - The governor stops the compressor when air tank pressure hits the cut-out threshold.
  - "Cut-in" pressure is typically around 100 psi.
  - The governor lets the compressor resume pumping when cut-in pressure is reached.

Quick Review Question

2. What is the approximate "cut-out" level of air tank pressure?

Air Storage Tanks and Drains

- Air storage tanks hold compressed air.
  - They hold enough air to allow the brakes to be used several times, even if the compressor no longer works.
  - Different vehicles have different amounts and sizes of air tanks.
- **Air tanks must be drained completely to ensure that water and oil are removed.**
  - Water can freeze and cause brake failure.
  - Oil can clog the air compressor.
  - Each tank has a drain valve at the bottom.
- There are 2 types of air tank drains (see Table 6.2.).

Table 6.2. Types of Air Tank Drains

Drain Type	Description
Manually operated	<ul><li>require you to pull a cable or make a quarter turn</li><li>must be drained each day after driving</li></ul>
Automatic	<ul><li>automatically release water and oil</li><li>may have electric heating elements to prevent the drain from freezing in cold weather</li></ul>

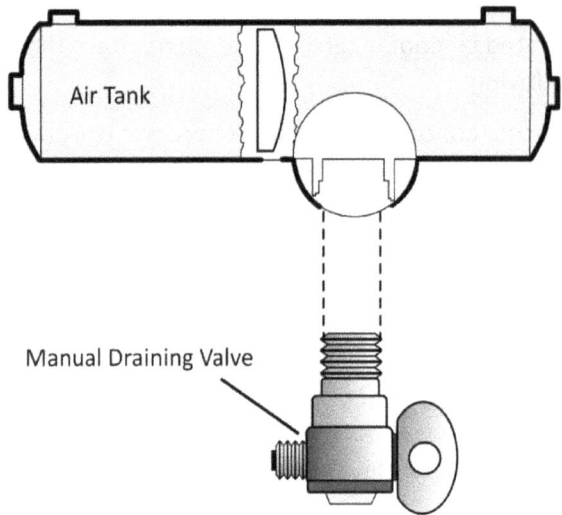

Manual draining valves on an air tank require drivers to pull a cable or make a quarter turn to empty the tank, which should be done each day after driving.

Figure 6.1. Air Tank with Manual Draining Valve

Quick Review Question

3. Why is it important to drain air tanks?

Safety Mechanisms

The alcohol evaporator releases alcohol into the air system, reducing ice formation in the air brake valves and other parts.

- The **safety release valve** protects the tank and air brake system from having too much pressure.
    - Typically, the valve is set to open at 150 psi.
    - The valve is found in the first tank into which the compressor pumps air.
    - When the valve releases air, it signals an issue that must be fixed by a mechanic.

Quick Review Question

4. What is the purpose of the alcohol evaporator?

The Brake Pedal and Foundation Brakes

Brake pedals (foot or treadle valves) activate the brakes when they are pushed down.

- The harder the brake is pushed down, the more air pressure is applied.
- Air pressure is reduced and the brakes are released when you let up on the brake pedal.
- The air compressor must compensate for the reduction in air that happens each time the brake pedal is released.

- **Do not press and release the pedal unnecessarily.**
    - Air can be released faster than the compressor can replace it.
    - If the air is released faster than it can be replaced, it leads to brake failure.
- Each wheel uses foundation brakes.
- **S-cam drum brakes** are the most common type of foundation brake (see Figure 6.2.).

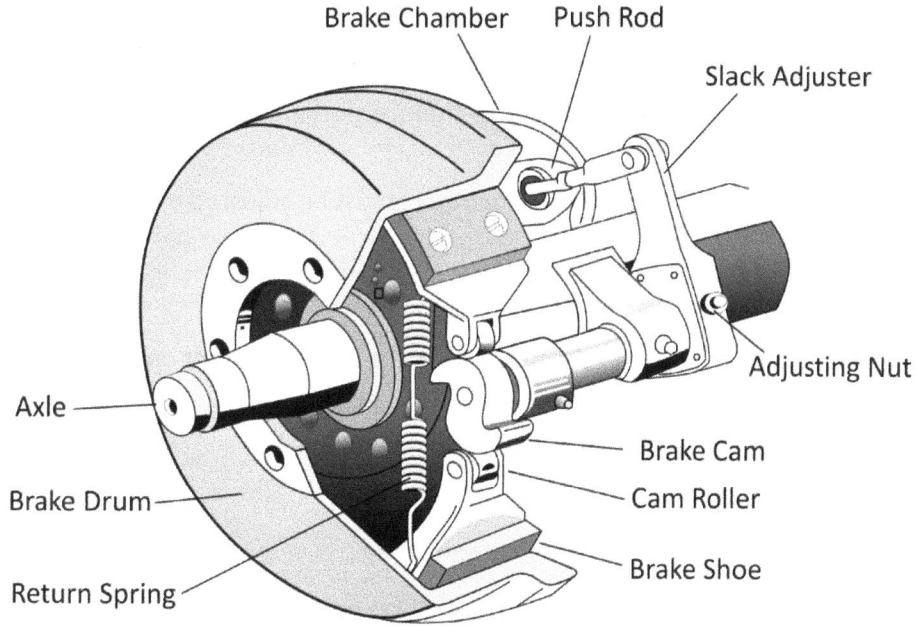

Figure 6.2. The S-Cam Drum Brake and Its Parts

- S-cam brakes release air into the brake chamber each time the brake pedal is pushed in.
    - The air pressure moves the slack adjuster by pushing the rod out (see Figure 6.2.).
    - When the slack adjuster is moved, the brake camshaft twists, which turns the S-cam.
    - The brake shoes are forced away from each other by the S-cam, which presses them against the interior of the brake drum.
    - Once the brake pedal is released, the S-cam rotates back; a spring pulls the shoes away from the drum.
    - Once the shoes are pulled away from the drum, the wheels will roll freely.
- Brake drums
    - are found on each end of a vehicle's axles,
    - are bolted to the wheels, and
    - hold the braking mechanism.
- The shoes and linings push against the inside of the drum, causing the vehicle to slow down.
- Friction and heat are generated when the shoes and linings push against the inside of the drum.
    - The amount of heat generated is determined by the force and length of braking time.

- o Too much heat can cause brake failure.
- Wedge and disc brakes (see Table 6.3.) are not as common as S-cam brakes.

Table 6.3. Wedge and Disc Brakes

Wedge Brake

- A wedge is pushed between the ends of 2 brake shoes by the brake chamber push rod.
- **The wedge pushes the shoes apart and against the brake drum's interior.**
- Some wedge brakes have a single brake chamber; others have 2 that push in wedges at both ends of the shoes.
- Some wedge brakes are self-adjusting; others must be adjusted manually.

Disc Brake

- Disc brakes use a power screw (instead of an S-cam).
- The power screw is turned by the pressure of the brake chamber on the slack adjuster.
- The disc or rotor is clamped between the brake lining pads of a caliper by the power screw, much like a large C-clamp functions.

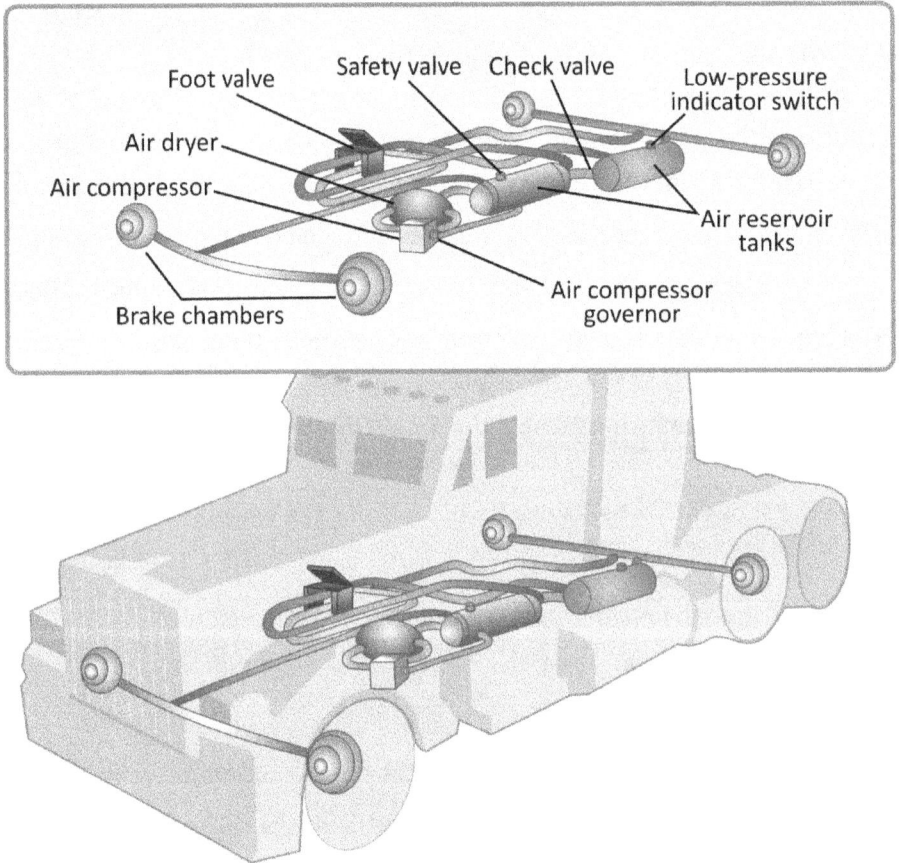

Figure 6.3. Parts of the Air Brake System

6. The Air Brake System

Quick Review Questions

5. What is the most common type of foundation brake?

6. How do wedge brakes work?

Pressure Gauges and Warnings

Supply pressure gauges indicate how much pressure is in the air tanks.

- A supply pressure gauge is connected to the air tank on all vehicles with air brakes.
- Dual air brake systems have
    - either a supply pressure gauge for each half of the system, or
    - a single gauge with 2 needles.
- An application pressure gauge indicates how much air pressure is being applied to the brakes.
    - It is not found on all vehicles.
    - Brakes are fading if increased application pressure is required to hold the same speed.
    - If increased application pressure is needed, slow down and use a lower gear instead.
- The need for increased pressure also indicates
    - air leaks,
    - mechanical problems, or
    - brakes that are out of adjustment.
- **All vehicles with air brakes must have a low air pressure warning signal.**
    - A visible warning signal must activate before the air pressure in the tanks drops under 55 psi.
    - On older vehicles, the warning signal activates at half of the governor's cut-out pressure.
    - Most warnings typically have a **red light**; some also have a buzzer.
- **Wig wag warnings** are devices that drop a mechanical arm into view when system pressure dips under 55 psi.
    - Automatic wig wags rise out of view when system pressure rises above 55 psi.
    - The device will not stay in place unless the pressure in the system is over 55 psi.
    - Manual wig wag warnings need to be put in the "out of view" position by hand.
- Large buses commonly have low pressure warning devices that activate at 80 – 85 psi.
- A **stop light switch** is activated by air pressure when the air brakes are used; it turns on your brake lights so drivers behind you know you are braking.

6. The Air Brake System

Quick Review Questions

7. What is the purpose of a supply pressure gauge?

8. Do all vehicles with air brakes need to have a low air pressure warning signal?

Brake Valves and Controls

Vehicles made prior to 1975 have a control and front brake limiting valve in their cabs.
- o The goal of limiting valves is to reduce the likelihood of having the front wheels skid in slippery conditions; instead, they reduce a vehicle's stopping power.
- o Typically, the control has "normal" and "slippery" markings.
- o When the control is in "slippery" mode, the "normal" air is cut in half by the limiting valve.
- o For normal stopping power, be sure the control is in the "normal" position.
- o **Front wheel braking works well in all conditions.**
- Automatic front wheel limiting valves are common in many vehicles.
  - o **These valves reduce air pressure to the front brakes.**
  - o An exception to this is when brake pressure is 55 psi or higher.

Quick Review Questions

9. What is the purpose of a limiting valve and what is its major drawback?

10. In what conditions can front wheel brakes be used?

Spring (Parking) Brakes and Controls

Emergency and parking brakes should be in place on all trucks, truck tractors, and buses.
- o Since air pressure can leak, these brakes are held by mechanical force.
- o **Spring brakes are the typical mechanism used for emergency/parking brakes.**
- **Spring brakes supply braking needs when air pressure leaks.**
  - o Air pressure holds back strong springs that put on the brakes when the air pressure is removed.
  - o To let the air out of spring brakes, drivers must use a parking brake control in the cab.
  - o The **parking brake control** allows the springs to apply the brakes.
  - o Air brake system leaks can also trigger the springs to put on the brakes.
- On tractors and straight trucks, spring brakes are activated when air pressure drops between 20 and 45 psi.
- **Never wait for the spring brakes to come on automatically**; stop safely while you can still control the brakes as soon as a low air pressure warning turns on.

6. The Air Brake System

- The braking power of regular brakes and parking/emergency brakes will be compromised if the brakes are improperly adjusted.
- A yellow diamond-shaped push-pull control-type knob is used to put parking brakes on in newer vehicles.
    - To put the parking/spring brakes on, pull the knob out.
    - To release the parking/spring brakes, push the knob in.
    - Some older vehicles may use a lever instead of a push-pull knob.
- **Parking brakes should be used every time you park.**
- **Never depress the brake pedal while the spring brakes are being used.**
    - **Doing this can damage the brakes** due to the dual force of the springs and the air pressure.
    - Not all braking systems are designed to prevent you from using both brakes at once.
    - Create a habit of never pressing the brake pedal while the spring brakes are activated.
- **Modulating valves** are control handles/levers that apply spring brakes gradually.
    - They are found on some—not all—dashboards.
    - These valves are spring-loaded and allow the driver to feel the braking action.
    - Spring brakes come on harder the more the control handle/lever is moved.
    - Modulating control valves give drivers better control of the spring brakes if the service brakes fail.
- The control handle/lever must be moved as far as it will go and be held in place with the locking device when parking.
- Some vehicles (e.g., buses) have a separate air tank that is used to release the spring brakes.
    - This design allows the vehicle to be moved in the event of an emergency.
    - Such vehicles use dual parking control valves: a push-pull valve to activate the spring brakes and a spring-loaded valve in the "out" position.
    - Pushing the control in lets air from the separate tank release the spring brakes.
    - Releasing the button puts the spring brakes back on.
    - Plan ahead: the separate tank only has enough air to use these valves a few times and can run out if used more than needed.

Quick Review Question

11. What are spring brakes and what is their purpose?

Dual Air Brake Systems

- For safety purposes, dual air brake systems are used on a majority of heavy-duty vehicles.
- **Dual air brakes have 2 separate air brake systems, each of which uses a single set of brake controls.**
- Each system is equipped with its own air tanks, lines, hoses, etc.
    - One system operates regular brakes on the rear axle(s).
    - The other system operates regular brakes on the front axle; sometimes it also operates them on 1 rear axle.
    - If there is a trailer, both systems supply air to it.
    - The first system is known as the primary system; the other is called the secondary system.
- Before driving, the air compressor must achieve a minimum pressure of 100 psi in both systems.
    - Observe both the primary and secondary air pressure gauges (or needles).
    - Monitor the low air pressure warning buzzer and light.
    - The warning buzzer/light should turn off once air pressure in both systems meets the predetermined value set by the manufacturer (greater than 55 psi).
- **In either system, the warning buzzer/light will be activated BEFORE the air pressure falls below 55 psi.**
    - Stop immediately and park safely if this happens while driving.
    - Very low pressure on 1 air brake system indicates that the front or rear brakes are not fully operating.
    - It will take longer to stop if the front or rear brakes are not functioning fully.
    - Arrange to have the air brake system fixed immediately.

Quick Review Question

12. Describe a dual air brake system.

6. The Air Brake System

Answer Key

1. Air brakes are composed of the service brake, parking brake, and emergency brake systems.

2. The cut-out level for air tank pressure is approximately 125 psi.

3. Air tanks must be drained to make sure that water and oil are removed: water can freeze, leading to brake failure; oil can clog the air compressor.

4. The alcohol evaporator releases alcohol into the air system, which reduces ice formation in the air brake valves and other parts.

5. S-cam drum brakes are the most common type of foundation brake.

6. A wedge is pushed between the ends of 2 brake shoes by the brake chamber push rod; it pushes the shoes apart and against the brake drum's interior.

7. A supply pressure gauge indicates how much pressure is in the air tanks.

8. Yes, all vehicles with air brakes must have a low air pressure warning signal. A visible warning signal activates before the air pressure in the tanks drops under 55 psi.

9. The limiting valve was designed to reduce front wheel skidding on slippery surfaces; its major drawback is that it reduces stopping power.

10. Front wheel braking can be used—and works well—in all conditions.

11. Spring brakes are the typical mechanism used for emergency, or parking brakes. They supply braking needs when air pressure leaks.

12. Dual air brake systems are used on a majority of heavy-duty vehicles and are composed of 2 separate air brake systems, each of which uses a single set of brake controls. The first system is known as the primary system; the other is called the secondary system. Each system has its own air tanks, lines, hoses, etc. One system operates regular brakes on the rear axle(s); the other system operates regular brakes on the front axle (or sometimes on 1 rear axle).

7 Inspecting and Using Air Brakes

Inspecting Air Brakes

- Inspecting air brakes requires following the **7-step inspection method** (Chapter 15) **AND additional checks**.
- The additional checks for air brake systems are organized below based on where the steps fall within the 7-step inspection process.
- **Step 2** (engine compartment): Check the condition and tightness of the belt in belt-driven air compressors; it should be in sound condition (e.g., no tears, cracks).
- **Step 5** (walk-around inspection): Inspect slack adjusters on S-cam brakes.
    - Slack adjusters are adjustable nuts; they are found on the backside of the brake drum and used to adjust the brakes.
    - **Slack adjusters work as a unit and rotate with the camshaft when the brakes are used; it is critical that they function properly.**
    - Chock the wheels after parking on level ground.
    - Release parking brakes in order to move the slack adjusters.
    - Using gloves, pull firmly on any slack adjusters within reach.
    - **Any slack adjuster that moves more than 1 in. at the point where it attaches to the push rod will need adjustment.**
    - Too much brake slack makes it very difficult to stop a vehicle.
    - The most common issue identified at roadside inspections is brakes that are out of adjustment.
    - Even automatic slack adjusters (mandatory in all vehicles built from 1994 on) must be inspected.
    - With automatic adjusters, when the pushrod stroke exceeds the legal brake adjustment limit, it indicates problems either with the adjuster, the related foundation brake components, or with the installation of the adjuster.
    - Adjustment should not be needed on automatic adjusters except when installing slack adjusters or during brake maintenance.
    - The need to manually adjust an automatic adjuster masks an underlying mechanical issue; it is dangerous and leads to a false sense of security.
    - **Only adjust automatic adjusters manually as a TEMPORARY solution.**

- 7. Inspecting and Using Air Brakes

  - o Routinely adjusting automatic adjusters can prematurely wear them out.
  - o Automatic adjusters in need of adjustment should be taken to a repair facility.

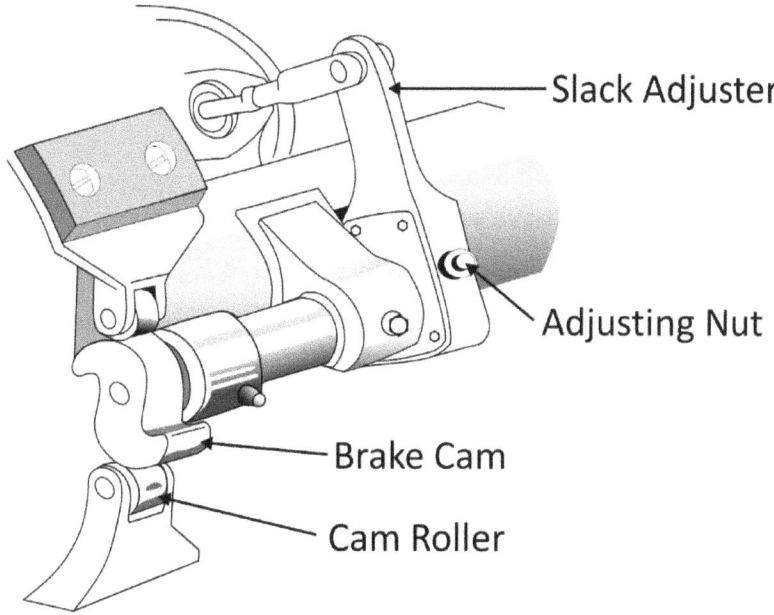

Figure 7.1. Slack Adjuster

- **Step 5** (walk-around inspection): Inspect brake drums/discs, hoses, and linings.
  - o Cracks longer than half the width of the friction area should not appear on drum brakes/discs.
  - o Friction material, or linings, should be neither loose nor soaked with grease/oil.
  - o Linings that are too thin are dangerous.
  - o All mechanical parts must be securely in place—not broken or missing.
  - o Air hoses connected to the brake chambers should not be cut or worn down (due to rubbing).
- **Step 7** (brake system check): **This is done INSTEAD OF the hydraulic brake check.**
  - o Inspect the air compressor and governor cut-in/cut-out pressures.
  - o Air compressor pumping should start at around 100 psi and stop at around 125 psi, depending on manufacturer specifications.
  - o Run the engine at a fast idle; check that the air governor cuts out the air compressor near the manufacturer's specified pressure rate. (The air pressure indicated on the gauge should stop rising.)
  - o While idling, step on and off the brake to release air tank pressure to make sure the compressor cuts in near the cut-in pressure specified by the manufacturer. (The pressure should begin to rise on the gauge.)

7. Inspecting and Using Air Brakes

- o If the above actions do not yield the results they should, the air governor likely needs to be fixed—it may not maintain enough air pressure to drive safely.
- **Step 7** (brake system check): Test the **air leakage rate**.
    - o Make sure the air system is fully charged (usually 125 psi).
    - o Turn off the engine.
    - o Release the parking brake by pushing it in.
    - o Time the drop in air pressure.
    - o **Single vehicles should have a loss rate under 2 psi per minute.**
    - o **Combination vehicles should have a loss rate under 3 psi per minute.**
    - o Shut the engine off when the air pressure builds to the governor cut-off rate (120 – 140 psi); chock the wheels and release the parking brake and tractor protection valve (on combination vehicles).
    - o After holding the foot brake for 1 full minute, observe the air gauge to see if air pressure drops.
    - o **Air pressure that drops more than 3 lb. per minute in a single vehicle is unsafe**— brake loss can occur.
    - o **Air pressure that drops more than 4 lb. per minute in a combination vehicle is unsafe**—brake loss can occur.
    - o If the air pressure drops more than it should in 1 minute, check for air leaks and make any needed repairs before driving.
- **Step 7** (brake system check): **Test the low pressure warning signal.**
    - o Once the low pressure warning signal shuts off, turn off the engine.
    - o Turn on the electrical power and reduce air tank pressure by stepping on and off the brake pedal.
    - o Before the pressure drops under 55 psi in the air tank, the low air pressure warning signal must turn on (see Figure 7.2.).
    - o In dual air systems, the tank with the lower air pressure should activate the warning signal when the pressure drops under 55 psi.

7. Inspecting and Using Air Brakes

- o Any indications that the warning signal is malfunctioning should be addressed immediately: air pressure can be unknowingly lost, resulting in limited braking action before the spring brakes are activated.

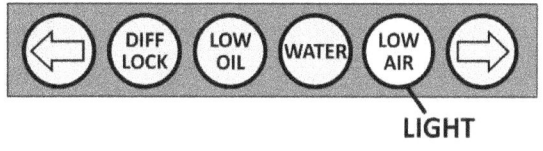

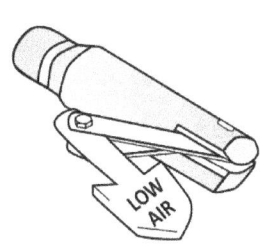

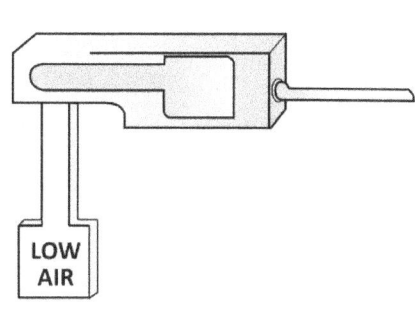

Figure 7.2. Low Air Pressure Warning Devices

- **Step 7** (brake system check): **Check that spring brakes automatically come on.**
  - o Following the steps to test the low pressure warning signal, continue to step on and off the brake pedal in order to reduce tank pressure.
  - o On tractor trailer combination vehicles, the tractor protection and parking brake valves should pop out (close).
  - o On single and other types of combination vehicles, the parking brake valve should pop out (close) when air pressure drops to 20 – 45 psi (depending on manufacturer specifications).
- **Step 7** (brake system check): Check the rate of air pressure buildup.

- o In dual air systems, the pressure in engines at operating rpm should take 45 seconds to build from 85 psi to 100 psi.
  - o Vehicles with air tanks larger than minimum size can safely have a longer buildup time—always check the manufacturer's specifications.
  - o Single-air systems from before 1975 usually have buildup requirements between 50 and 90 psi within 3 minutes while the engine idles between 600 and 900 rpm.
  - o Air pressure that does not build up quickly enough could cause pressure to drop too low while you are driving.
  - o If pressure drops too low while driving, you must stop immediately; do not drive until the issue is repaired.
- **Step 7** (brake system check): Perform parking and service brakes tests.
  - o To test the parking brake, stop the vehicle, apply the parking brake, and use a low gear to pull against it gently to be sure the brake will hold.
  - o To test the service brakes, make sure the air pressure has returned to normal before releasing the parking brake.
  - o Slowly (5 mph) move the vehicle forward.
  - o Using the brake pedal, firmly apply the brakes.
  - o Take note of any one-sided pulling, unusual feels, or delayed stopping action you may experience.
  - o Testing the service brakes allows you to be aware of any potential issues that you would otherwise not notice until the brakes are needed while driving.

Quick Review Questions

1. What are slack adjusters?
2. How can you inspect slack adjusters?
3. What are the maximum rates of air leakage for single and combination vehicles?
4. How is the low-pressure warning signal tested, and why is it important to inspect it?
5. What are the steps to check that the spring brakes come on automatically?

Normal Stops with Air Brakes

- **To stop normally with air brakes, push the brake pedal down.**
  - o To stop the vehicle smoothly and safely, control the pressure on the brake pedal.
  - o In vehicles with a manual transmission, wait until the engine's rpms are near idle stage before pushing in the clutch.
  - o Select a starting gear once you are stopped.

Quick Review Question

6. What steps are needed to stop normally with air brakes?

Emergency Stops with Air Brakes

- Use the controlled braking or stab braking techniques to make emergency stops.
- **Controlled braking** involves applying the brakes as hard as you can without locking the wheels.
    - Steering wheel movements should be small during controlled braking.
    - Release the brakes to make bigger steering wheel movements and/or if the wheels lock.
    - If you need to release the brakes for the above reasons, reapply them as soon as possible.
- **Stab braking** involves applying your brakes all the way.
    - When the wheels lock up, release the brakes.
    - Once the wheels resume rolling, fully apply the brakes again.
    - Be mindful that it can take up to 1 full second for the wheels to resume rolling after the brakes are released.
    - The vehicle will not straighten out if the brakes are reapplied before the wheels resume rolling.

Quick Review Question

7. What are the 2 braking techniques used when making emergency stops with air brakes?

Brake Lag

- Brake lag is unique to air brakes.
- Brake lag is an extra stopping delay from when the brake pedal is pushed to when the brakes actually work.
- Brake lag is the time it takes for the air to flow through the lines to the brakes.
- **Typical brake lag time is at least one half of a second.**
- Vehicles with air brake systems have a total stopping distance composed of **4 factors**:
    1. perception distance
    2. reaction distance
    3. brake lag distance
    4. braking distance
- **The sum of these factors is the total stopping distance.**

7. Inspecting and Using Air Brakes

- At 55 mph on dry pavement and with good traction, air brake lag distance adds about 32 ft. to the total stopping distance (see Figure 7.3.).

MPH	Total stopping distance	Perception Distance	Reaction Distance	Brake Lag	Braking Distance
15	72'	39'	16'	9'	17'
25	140'	65'	28'	15'	47'
35	222'	91'	39'	21'	92'
45	319'	117'	50'	27'	152'
55	419'	142'	61'	32'	216'

Figure 7.3. Stopping Distance with Brake Lag

Quick Review Questions

8. What is brake lag?

9. What is the typical brake lag time?

Braking on a Downgrade

- **Using air brakes on a downgrade supplements the braking effect of the engine.**
- After putting the vehicle in the correct low gear, follow the proper technique for using air brakes on a downgrade:
    - Only apply the brakes hard enough to notice a definitive slowdown.
    - Once you are around 5 mph below your "safe" speed, release the brakes, which should take about 3 seconds.
    - After releasing the brakes and increasing back to "safe" speed, repeat the above 2 steps until you reach the end of the downgrade.

Quick Review Question

10. When braking on a downgrade, what is important to remember about the use of air brakes?

Parking Brakes

- To use the parking brakes, pull the parking brake control knob out (see Figure 7.4.).
- To release the parking brakes, push in the parking brake control knob.

- On newer vehicles, the parking brake control knob is a yellow diamond shape (see Figure 7.4.).
- On older vehicles, the parking brake control knob is often a round blue knob (see Figure 7.4.).
- Other shapes or levers that swing (side to side or up/down) may instead appear on older vehicles.

- **With the exception of the scenarios listed below, use the parking brakes any time you park.**
  - Brakes that are hot (e.g., after going down a steep grade) can damage the parking brakes.
  - If the brakes are very wet and temperatures are freezing, the parking brakes can freeze and the vehicle will not move.
- If you experience the above conditions but need to use parking brakes, do the following:
  - Use wheel chocks (on a level surface) to hold the vehicle in place.
  - Wait for hot brakes to cool down before using the parking brakes.
  - Lightly use the brakes while driving in a low gear to heat and dry them out before using the parking brakes.

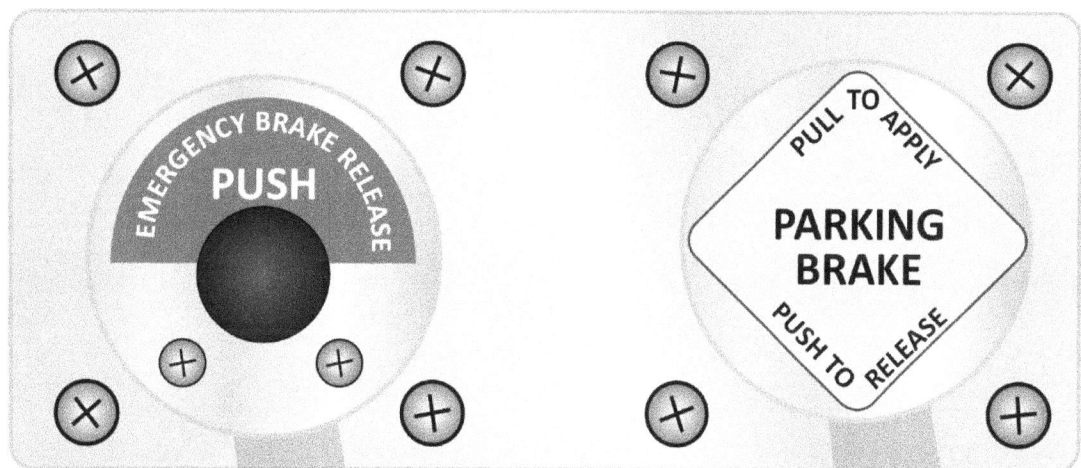

Figure 7.4. Parking Brake Knobs

- Vehicles with wheels that aren't chocked or that do not use the parking brakes can roll and cause damage and/or serious injury.
- **Always use parking brakes (or wheel chocks) when leaving your vehicle unattended.**
- Vehicles that do not have automatic air tank drains must have the tanks drained after each working day.
  - The purpose of this is to remove moisture and oil.
  - Not draining these substances can lead to brake failure.

7. Inspecting and Using Air Brakes

Quick Review Question

11. Is it ever safe to leave your vehicle unattended without the parking brakes on or the wheels chocked?

Low Air Pressure

- **If the low air pressure warning comes on, it could be a sign of an air leak in the system.**
    - If a leak is suspected, always stop while there is enough air in the tanks to use the foot brakes.
    - Air leaks can prevent controlled braking, which is only possible if there is enough air in the air tanks.
- When air pressure drops between 20 and 45 psi, the spring brakes will come on.
    - Spring brakes do not work on all axles; vehicles with heavy loads will have longer stopping distances.
    - Spring brakes can cause vehicles that are lightly loaded and/or on slick surfaces to skid out of control.

> **Helpful Hint**
>
> In most vehicles, the low air pressure warning light comes on if the air pressure is below 55 psi. On most buses, the low-pressure device is activated between 80 and 85 psi.

Quick Review Question

12. If the low air pressure warning comes on, what does that normally signal?

Answer Key

1. Slack adjusters are adjustable nuts found on the backside of the brake drum that are used to adjust the brakes.

2. Slack adjusters can be inspected by pulling firmly on any of them that are within reach after parking on level ground, chocking the wheels, and releasing the parking brakes. If any slack adjusters move more than 1 in. where they attach to the push rod, they will require adjustment.

3. Single vehicles should have a loss rate of less than 2 psi per minute; combination vehicles should have a loss rate of less than 3 psi per minute.

4. The low-pressure warning signal is tested by turning off the engine, switching on the electrical power, and reducing air tank pressure by stepping on and off the brake pedal. From there, check if the low air pressure warning signal turns on before the pressure in the air tank drops below 55 psi.

5. With the engine off and electrical power turned on, step on and off the brake pedal to reduce tank pressure. Tractor protection and parking brake valves should pop out (close) on tractor trailer combination vehicles. The parking brake valve should pop out (close) on other combination and single vehicles when the air pressure drops between 20 and 45 psi (depending on manufacturer specifications).

6. To stop normally with air brakes, push the brake pedal down and control the pressure in order to stop the vehicle smoothly and safely; once stopped, select a starting gear. For manual transmissions, the engine's rpms need to be near the idle stage before pushing in the clutch.

7. Controlled braking and stab braking are the 2 techniques used when making emergency stops with air brakes.

8. Brake lag is the extra stopping delay from when the brake pedal is pushed to when the brakes actually work.

9. The typical brake lag time is at least one half of a second.

10. It is important to remember that using air brakes on a downgrade is a supplement to the engine's braking effect.

11. It is never safe to leave your vehicle unattended without the parking brakes on or the wheels chocked. Failure to do so can cause the vehicle to roll away, resulting in damage and/or serious injury.

12. The low air pressure warning signals that there could be an air leak in the system.

8 Combination Vehicles

Controlling a Combination Vehicle

- Since combination vehicles are longer and heavier than single vehicles, more skills are required to operate them.
- **Steer gently with smooth movements when driving a combination vehicle** (pulling trailers).
    - Quick lane changes and sharp steering movements cause a dangerous effect known as "crack the whip."
    - The crack-the-whip effect can cause the trailer to turn over and is the reason that only a trailer overturns in many accidents.
    - The crack-the-whip effect is caused by rearward amplification.
- Figure 8.1. illustrates 8 types of combination vehicles and their rearward amplification in the event of a sudden lane change:
    - The top of the figure shows combination vehicles that have the least crack-the-whip effect.
    - Combination vehicles with the most crack-the-whip effect are shown at the bottom of the figure.
    - A rearward amplification of 2.0 in a double trailer means **the rear trailer has twice the chance of turning over as the tractor does**.
    - Triple trailers have a rearward amplification of 3.5, which means that the last of the trailers can roll 3.5 times as easily as a 5-axle trailer.
- Keep a following distance of at least 1 second per 10 ft. of your vehicle's length.
    - This will help prevent the need to make sudden lane changes and sharp steering maneuvers.
    - If driving over 40 mph, calculate 2 seconds of following distance per 10 ft. of vehicle length.
- Keep your eyes far enough down the road to prevent being surprised and having to make a sudden lane change.
- Drive slower at night, with headlights on, so that you can spot obstacles in time to stop gently or make a smooth lane change.

8. Combination Vehicles

- **Always slow to a safe speed before turning.**

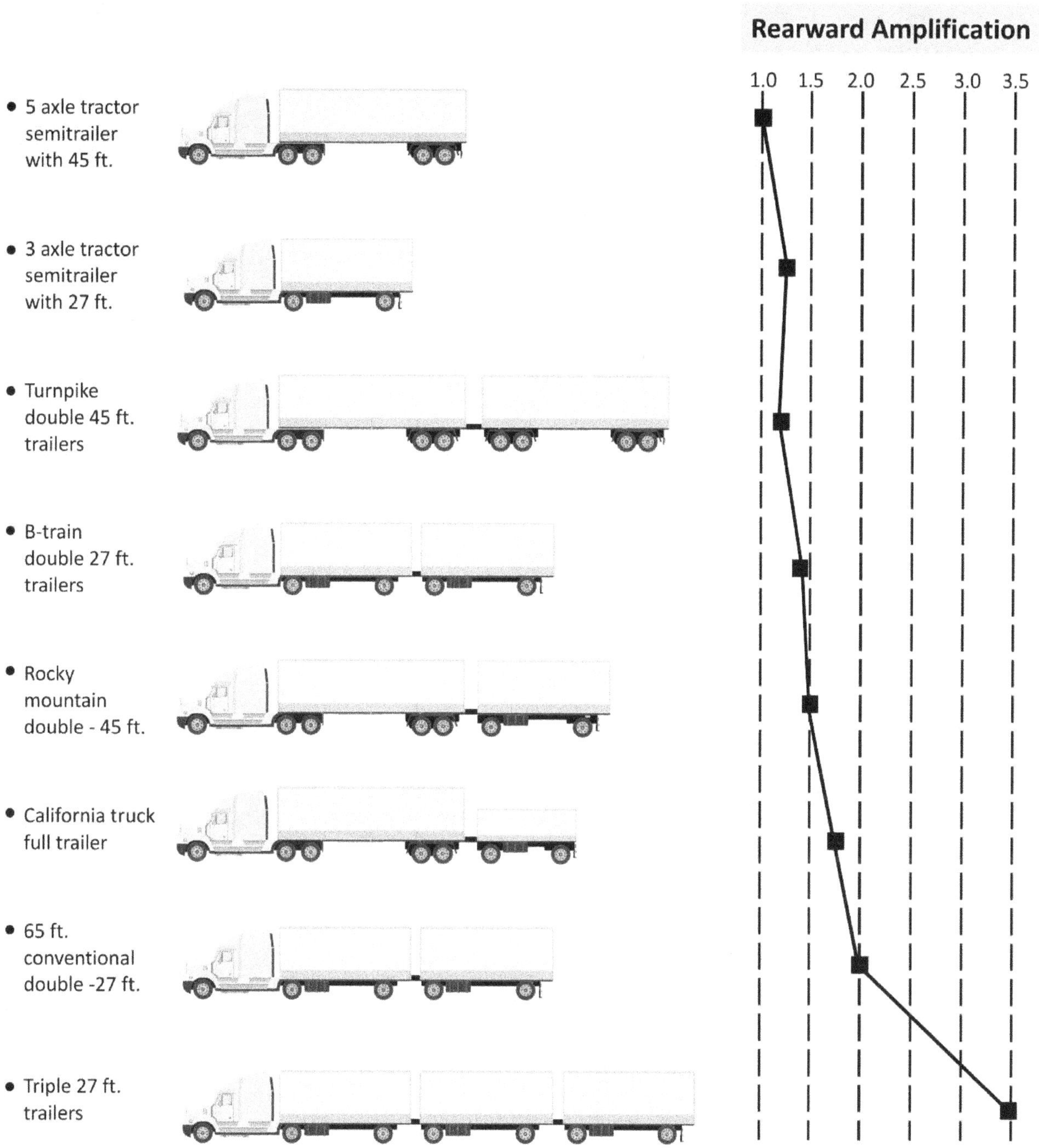

- 5 axle tractor semitrailer with 45 ft.
- 3 axle tractor semitrailer with 27 ft.
- Turnpike double 45 ft. trailers
- B-train double 27 ft. trailers
- Rocky mountain double - 45 ft.
- California truck full trailer
- 65 ft. conventional double -27 ft.
- Triple 27 ft. trailers

Figure 8.1. Rearward Amplification in Combination Vehicles

- **Always control your vehicle's speed regardless of cargo load size (including empty).**
- Empty combination vehicles take longer to stop than full ones.
    - Light (or no) loads cause the stiff suspension springs and strong brakes to create poor traction, which can result in wheel lockup.
    - Wheel lockup can cause the trailer to swing out, striking surrounding vehicles.

- - o   Wheel lockup can result in a sudden jackknife.
- Tractors without semitrailers ("bobtail" tractors) are difficult to stop smoothly and take longer to stop than fully loaded tractor semitrailers.
- **Always allow generous following distance and keep your eyes far ahead** to avoid having to make surprised or panicked maneuvers.
- Off tracking ("cheating") occurs during turns/curves.
- **In off tracking, the rear wheels follow a different path than the front wheels.**
    - o   The path of the tractor is wider than the full rig (see Figure 8.2.).
    - o   Off tracking is more common with longer vehicles: the rear wheels of the truck/tractor will off track a little; **the rear wheels on the last trailer being pulled will off track the most.**
- Follow these guidelines to safely navigate wide turns:
    - o   Steer the front end wide enough around the corner to prevent the rear from running over the curb and/or pedestrians.
    - o   Simultaneously, keep the rear of the vehicle close to the curb while steering, which will discourage drivers from passing you on the right.
    - o   Turn wide if you must enter another lane to complete the turn.
    - o   Turning wide is better than making a wide swing to the left before turning—it prevents others from passing you on the right.

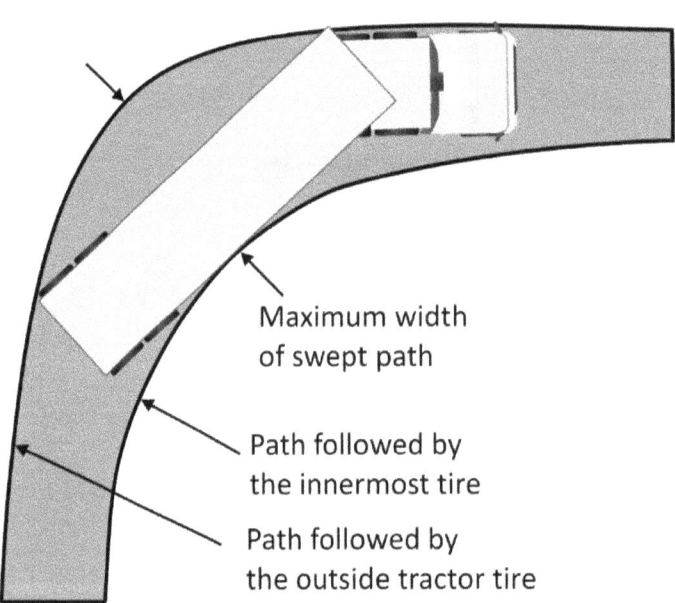

Figure 8.2. Off Tracking

- Backing a trailer differs from backing a car, bus, or straight truck:
    - o   The steering wheel must be turned in the opposite direction.
    - o   As soon as the trailer starts to turn, the wheel must be turned the other way in order to follow the trailer.

- **Whenever possible, position the vehicle to allow you to back in a straight line.**
- If backing on a curve is unavoidable, back to the driver's side for visibility (see Figure 8.3.).

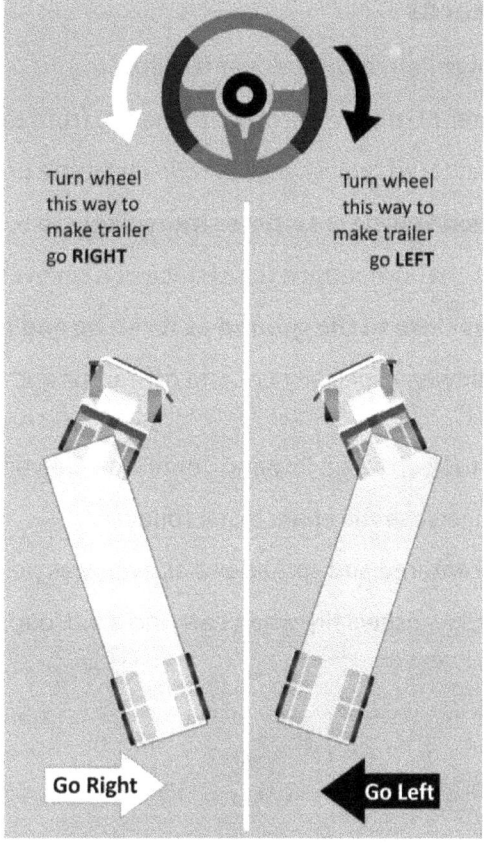

Figure 8.3. Backing a Trailer

- There are best practices for backing with a trailer:
    o Before backing, look closely at your line of travel.
    o If needed, get out to inspect clearance on the sides, overhead, in, and near your vehicle's path.
    o Frequently check the mirrors on both sides; if needed, exit the vehicle for a better view.
    o Always back slowly so that you can correct anything if necessary.
    o Immediately correct any trailer drift (going off path) by turning the top of the steering wheel in the same direction as the drift.
    o Pull forward as needed to reposition.

Quick Review Questions

1. When pulling doubles, which of the trailers is most likely to roll over?
2. Is speed control needed when driving with an empty trailer?
3. What does the term *off tracking* mean?

4. What is the best vehicle position before beginning to back?

Combination Vehicle Hazards

- Truck rollovers result in over half of truck driver fatalities.
    - The vehicle's center of gravity becomes higher up from the road as more cargo is piled up.
    - This shift in the center of gravity makes rollovers more probable.
- **A fully loaded combination vehicle is 10 times more likely to roll over than an empty one.**
- There are 2 best practices that can reduce the chance of a rollover:
    1. **Ensure cargo is as close to the ground as it can be and evenly distributed.**
    2. **Navigate turns slowly,** especially on- and off-ramps and around corners; turning too fast causes rollovers.
- It is especially important to keep cargo low and centered when driving a combination vehicle.
    - One-sided loads increase the chance of a rollover.
    - Cargo should be centered and spread out as evenly as possible (see Chapter 5).
- Avoid changing lanes quickly, especially when carrying a full load.

Figure 8.4. Vehicle Rollover

- Highway-rail crossings with low clearance are a particular hazard to combination vehicles pulling trailers.
- Two types of trailers are specifically known to get stuck on raised crossings:
    1. **Low-slung units** (lowboys, car carriers, moving vans, and possum-belly livestock trailers)
    2. **Single-axle tractors pulling long trailers with landing gear set for tandem-axle tractors**

- Follow these best practices if your vehicle gets stuck on a highway-rail crossing:
    - Exit the vehicle and move away from the tracks immediately.
    - Look for signposts or signal housing to gather emergency notification information.
    - Call 911 (or other emergency number).
    - Provide emergency personnel with the location of the crossing.
    - Provide the DOT number and any identifiable landmarks to emergency personnel.
- A trailer skid, or trailer jackknife, happens when the trailer wheels lock up and the trailer swings around (see Figure 8.5.).
- A trailer skid is especially likely to occur if the trailer is empty or has a light load.

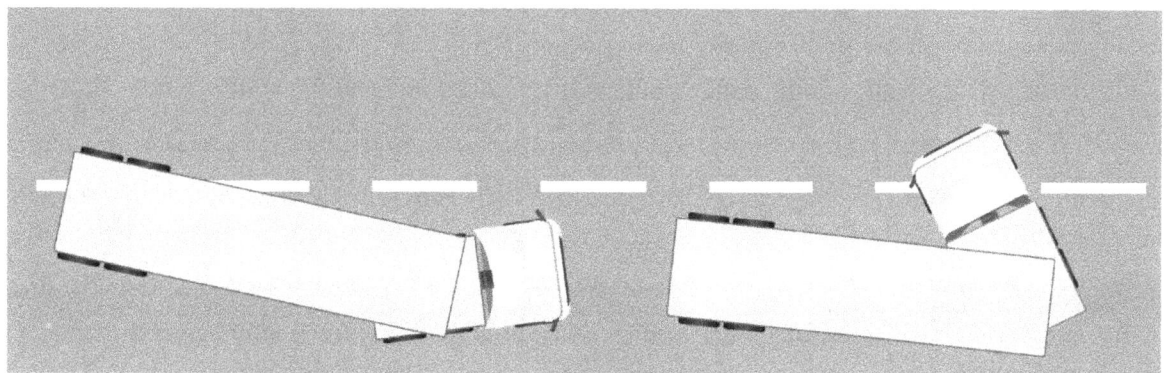

Figure 8.5. Trailer Jackknife

- **Recognizing a trailer skid is the first step to stopping it.**
    - Check your mirrors any time you brake hard, making sure the trailer stays where it should.
    - A trailer that swings out of its lane will likely lead to a jackknife.
- **Releasing the brakes is the second step in stopping a trailer skid.**
    - Releasing the brakes allows you to regain traction.
    - **Never use the trailer handbrake to straighten the rig.**
    - Since the brakes on the trailer wheels cause the skid, using the trailer handbrake will only make the situation worse.
    - As soon as the trailer wheels can grip the road again, the trailer will begin to straighten out as it follows the tractor.

Quick Review Questions

5. What are the 2 best practices that will help prevent a rollover?

6. What are the types of trailers that are most likely to getting stuck on highway-rail crossings?

7. Why is it a bad idea to use the trailer handbrake to straighten out a trailer jackknife?

Combination Vehicle Air Brakes

- In addition to the air brake components described in Chapter 6, combination vehicles have parts to control the trailer brakes.
- The trailer brakes are operated by the **trailer hand valve**, also known as the **Johnson bar** or **trolley valve**.
    - Only use the trailer hand valve to test the trailer brakes.
    - **Never use the trailer hand valve while driving; it can cause the trailer to skid.**
    - Use the foot brake instead; it sends air to all of the brakes, including the trailer brakes, and makes it far less likely to skid or jackknife.
    - **The hand valve should never be used to park**; it could cause all of the air to leak out while unlocking the brakes.
- When parking, always use the parking brakes.
    - If the trailer has no spring brakes, use wheel chocks to prevent the trailer from moving.
    - Emergency brakes are used in place of spring brakes but rely on air stored in the trailer air tank.
    - A major leak in the emergency line will cause the emergency brakes to come on.
    - **The air will eventually leak and cause brake failure, which is why using chocks is a must.**
- If a trailer breaks away or develops a serious leak, the **tractor protection valve** will keep air in the tractor or truck brake system.
- **The tractor protection valve in the cab is controlled by the trailer air supply control.**
    - On newer vehicles, the trailer air supply control is a red knob with 8 sides.
    - The air supply control lets the driver open and close the tractor protection valve.
    - The trailer air supply control is pushed in to supply air to the trailer.
    - The trailer air supply control is pulled out to turn the air off and activate the trailer's emergency brakes.
    - The air supply control knob pops out when air pressure is between 20 and 45 psi.
    - When the air supply control knob pops out, the tractor protection valve closes.
    - A closed tractor protection valve prevents any air from going out of the tractor and releases air from the trailer emergency line.
    - Releasing the air from the trailer emergency line causes the trailer's emergency brakes to come on; loss of control is possible.
- On older vehicles, the tractor protection valve controls ("emergency" valves) may not automatically operate and could use a lever instead of a knob.
    - To pull a trailer, use the "normal" position.
    - To turn the air off and activate the trailer emergency brakes, use the "emergency" position.

- All combination vehicles have 2 air lines: the service line and the emergency line.
- The 2 air lines run between each vehicle: tractor to trailer, trailer to dolly, dolly to second trailer, and so forth.
- The **service air line** is also called the control line or signal line.
    - **It carries air**, which is controlled by either the trailer handbrake or the foot brake.
    - The pressure in the service air line changes with the pressure used on the foot brake or hand valve.
    - The service air line **connects to the relay valves**, which let the driver apply the trailer brakes more quickly than usually possible.
    - Service lines are usually **blue**.
- The **emergency air line** is also called the supply line; it has 2 functions:
    1. **It supplies the air to the trailer air tanks**.
    2. On combination vehicles, it **controls the emergency brakes**.
- If the emergency line loses air pressure, the trailer emergency brakes come on.
- One cause of pressure loss is if a trailer breaks loose, resulting in the emergency air hose being torn.
- Another cause of pressure loss is a broken part, such as a hose or metal tubing.
- If the emergency line loses pressure, the tractor protection valve closes, which causes the air supply knob to pop out.
- Emergency lines are usually **red**.
- Service and emergency air lines are connected from the truck/tractor to the trailer using gladhands (hose couplers).
    - **Gladhands are coupling devices**.
    - They have a rubber seal to prevent air from escaping.
- Follow these steps to connect gladhands:
    - Clean the gladhands and rubber seals before making the connections.
    - Press the 2 seals together with the couplers, making sure the couplers are at a 90-degree angle to each other.
    - When the gladhand is attached to the hose, turn it; this will join and lock the couplers.
- Always be sure to couple the appropriate gladhands together (see Figure 8.6.).
    - Blue is usually used to indicate the service lines.
    - Red is used to indicate the emergency, or supply, lines.
    - Metal tags with either "service" or "emergency" might also be used to help make the distinction.
- If the air lines are accidentally crossed, the supply air will instead be sent to the service line.
    - This means that the supply air will not charge the trailer air tanks.

- - Air will be unavailable to release the parking, or spring, brakes on the trailer.
  - Check the air line connections if the spring brakes do not release after pushing in the trailer air supply control.
- **Crossing the air lines on trailers without spring brakes will result in no emergency brakes**; the trailer wheels will freely turn.
  - This would create an extremely dangerous situation.
  - Before driving, always use the hand valve or pull the air supply control to test the trailer brakes; pull against them gently to check the brakes.
- **Air supplies must be kept clean.**
  - "Dead end" or **dummy couplers** are used on some vehicles to help keep air supplies clean.
  - The air lines may be attached to dummy couplers when they are not being used.
  - Dummy couplers prevent water and dirt from entering the coupler and the air lines.
  - Always use dummy couplers when the air lines are unconnected to the trailer.
  - Depending on the couplings, gladhands can sometimes be locked together and used instead of dummy couplers.

The service line is blue;
the emergency line is red.

Figure 8.6. Air Lines with Gladhands

- Every converter dolly and trailer has at least 1 air tank.
- The air tanks are filled through the tractor's emergency supply line.
- Trailer air tanks supply the air pressure that is used to operate the trailer brakes.

- Relay valves send air pressure from the air tanks to the brakes.
    - Pressure in the service line dictates how much pressure the relay valves need to send to the trailer brakes.
    - Service line pressure is controlled by the brake pedal and the trailer handbrake.
- **Do not let water and oil build up in the air tanks.**
    - Water and oil buildup in the air tanks will cause the brakes to malfunction.
    - Use the drain valve on each tank daily to release moisture and oil buildup—even if the tanks have automatic drains.
- **Shut-off valves** (cut-out cocks) allow the air lines to be closed off if another trailer is not being towed.
- They are **used in the supply and service air lines at the rear of trailers used to tow other trailers**.
    - **Be sure that all shut-off valves at the back of the last trailer are closed.**
    - All other shut-off valves must be in the open position.

Quick Review Questions

8. Why is it advised to NOT use the trailer hand valve while driving?
9. Why are chocks used when a trailer without spring brakes is being parked?
10. What is the purpose of the trailer air supply control?
11. What is the purpose of the service line?
12. What is the purpose of the emergency air line?
13. What is the purpose of gladhands?
14. What is the purpose of dummy couplers?
15. Where can shut-off valves be found?
16. Which shut-off valves should be open and which should be closed?

Antilock Braking Systems (ABSs) in Combination Vehicles

- Please see Chapter 4 for the following information on ABSs:
    - what they are
    - which vehicles have them
    - braking with ABS, including skid control and recovery
- Converter dollies and trailers built prior to March 1, 1998, were not required to have antilock braking systems (ABS).

8. Combination Vehicles

- Look for the following to determine if a vehicle manufactured prior to 1998 has ABS:
  - Check beneath the vehicle for the electronics control unit (ECU) and wheel speed sensor wires.
  - The ECU and wheel speed sensor wires should come from the back of the brakes.

Quick Review Question

17. How can you determine if a vehicle manufactured prior to 1998 has ABS?

Coupling Tractor Semitrailers

- It is critical to understand how to correctly couple; failure to do so is extremely dangerous.
- Different rigs have different coupling and uncoupling requirements; be sure to understand these for the trucks you will operate.
- The general steps for coupling and uncoupling are listed below.

Step 1: Inspect the Fifth Wheel

- Look for damaged or missing parts.
- Make sure that the mounting to the tractor is secure and has no frame cracks and/or other damage.
- Check that the fifth wheel plate is adequately greased; failure to do this could cause friction between the tractor and trailer and affect steering.
- Make sure that the fifth wheel is properly positioned to be coupled:
  - The wheel should be tilted down toward the rear of the tractor.
  - The jaws should be open.
  - The safety unlocking handle should be in the automatic lock position.
  - Make sure the sliding fifth wheel (if you have one) is locked.
  - Be certain that the trailer kingpin is neither bent nor broken.

Step 2: Inspect the Area and the Chock Wheels

- Inspect to make sure that the area around the vehicle is clear.
- Make sure that the trailer wheels are chocked or that the spring brakes are on.
- Be certain that any cargo is secure against movement as a result of being coupled to the trailer.

Step 3: Position the Tractor

- Position the tractor directly in front of the trailer.
- Never back under the trailer at an angle: it could push the trailer sideways and break the landing gear.
- Use the outside mirrors and check the position by looking down both sides of the trailer.

Step 4: Back Slowly

8. Combination Vehicles

- Go slowly while backing.
- Back only until the fifth wheel just touches the trailer.
- Do not hit the trailer.

Step 5: Secure the Tractor

- Put the parking brake on.
- Shift the transmission into neutral.

Step 6: Check the Trailer Height

- Make sure that the trailer is low enough so that it is slightly raised by the tractor when the tractor backs under it.
- Raise or lower the trailer as required.
    - **Trailers that are too low could strike and damage the trailer nose.**
    - **Trailers that are too high might not couple correctly.**

Step 7: Connect the Air Lines to the Trailer

- Inspect the seals on both the emergency and service gladhands.
- Connect the tractor emergency air line to the trailer emergency gladhand.
- Connect the tractor service air line to the trailer service gladhand.
- Ensure that the air lines are safely supported to prevent them from being crushed or caught while the tractor is backing under the trailer.

Step 8: Supply Air to the Trailer

- From the cab, push in the air supply knob or adjust the tractor protection valve control from "emergency" to "normal"; doing this supplies the air to the trailer brake system.
- Stand by until the air pressure is normal.
- Do a check of the brake system to identify any crossed lines.
- Shut the engine off in order to hear the brakes.
- Apply and release the trailer brakes:
    - Listen for the sound of the trailer brakes as they are applied and released.
    - When the brakes are applied, you should be able to hear them move.
    - When the brakes are released, you should be able to hear the air escape.
- Inspect the air brake system pressure gauge for any signs of significant air loss.
- Start the engine only when you are certain that the trailer brakes are working.
- Be sure the air pressure is normal.

Step 9: Lock the Trailer Brakes

- Pull out the air supply knob or adjust the tractor protection valve from "normal" to "emergency."

Step 10: Back Under the Trailer

- Use the lowest reverse gear.
- In order to avoid hitting the kingpin too hard, back the tractor slowly under the trailer.
- When the kingpin is locked into the fifth wheel, stop backing.

Step 11: Check the Connection for Security

- Raise the trailer landing gear slightly off the ground.
- Gently pull the tractor forward with the trailer brakes still locked in order to check that the trailer is locked onto the tractor.

Step 12: Secure the Vehicle

- Shift the transmission to neutral.
- Apply the parking brakes.
- Turn off the engine.
- Take the key with you to prevent someone from moving the truck while you are under it.

Step 13: Inspect the Coupling

- Have a flashlight on hand in case it is needed.
- **Check that there is no space between the upper and lower fifth wheel.**
    - **A space indicates that something is wrong.**
    - A space could be caused by the kingpin being on top of the closed fifth wheel jaws, causing the trailer to easily come loose.
- Look into the back of the fifth wheel by going under the trailer and **be sure the fifth wheel jaws are closed around the shank of the kingpin**.
- Make sure that the locking lever is in the "locked" position.
- Check the safety latch and make sure it is in position over the locking lever; some fifth wheels require the latch to be manually put into place.
- Only drive if the coupling is correct; if it is not, it must be fixed.

Step 14: Connect the Electrical Cord and Check the Air Lines

- Plug the electrical cord into the trailer; fasten the safety latch.
- Check for signs of damage in both the air lines and the electrical line.
- Be sure that the electrical and air lines will not collide with any of the vehicle's moving parts.

Step 15: Raise the Front Trailer Supports (Landing Gear)

- If equipped to do so, use a low gear range to start raising the landing gear; shift to the high gear range once you are free of weight.
- Raise the landing gear all the way up.
- **Never drive with landing gear that is only partway up; it could catch, especially on railroad tracks.**
- Safely secure the crank handle after raising the landing gear.

- Once the full weight of the trailer is resting on the tractor, follow these steps:
  - Look to make sure there is enough clearance between the rear of the tractor frame and the landing gear.
  - Be sure that if the tractor must turn sharply it will not hit the landing gear.
  - Make sure that there is enough clearance between the trailer's nose and the top of the tractor tires.

Step 16: Remove the Trailer Wheel Chocks
- Remove the wheel chocks.
- Store the wheel chocks in a safe location.

Quick Review Questions

18. Why should you make sure that the trailer is neither too high nor too low when coupling?

19. How much space should appear between the upper and lower fifth wheel after coupling?

20. Should the fifth wheel jaws be closed around the kingpin shank?

21. Why should you be certain that the landing gear is always raised all the way up?

Uncoupling Tractor Semitrailers
- Correctly uncoupling is as important as correctly coupling; follow the steps below.

Step 1: Position the Rig
- Be certain that the parking area's surface is strong enough to support the trailer's weight.
- Line the tractor up with the trailer; avoid pulling out at an angle, which can damage landing gear.

Step 2: Ease the Pressure on the Locking Jaws
- **In order to lock the trailer brakes, shut off the trailer air supply.**
- Back up gently to ease the pressure on the fifth wheel locking jaws; doing so will help with releasing the fifth wheel locking lever.
- While the tractor is pushing against the kingpin, apply the parking brakes, which will hold the rig while pressure is off the locking jaws.

Step 3: Chock the Trailer Wheels
- If your trailer does not have spring brakes—or if you are not sure whether or not it does—use wheel chocks.
- If air were to leak out of the trailer air tank, the emergency air brakes would be released and the trailer could move if chocks are not used.

Step 4: Lower the Landing Gear
- With an empty trailer, lower the landing gear until it makes firm ground contact.

- With a loaded trailer whose landing gear has already made firm ground contact, turn the crank in low gear a few extra times.
    - Extra turns of the crank will lift some of the trailer's weight off the tractor.
        - Doing this will make unlatching the fifth wheel easier.
        - Coupling will also be easier the next time it needs to be done.

Step 5: Disconnect the Air Lines and Electrical Cable

- Disconnect the air lines from the trailer.
- Connect dummy holders at the back of the cab to the air line gladhands (or couple them together).
- To prevent moisture from entering the electrical cable, hang it with the plug facing downward.
- Be sure the air lines are supported to prevent damage while the tractor is being driven.

Step 6: Unlock the Fifth Wheel

- Start by raising the release handle lock.
- Pull the release handle so that it is in the "open" position.
- **Always keep legs and feet clear of the rear tractor wheels; this will prevent serious injury in the event the vehicle moves.**

Step 7: Pull the Tractor Partially Clear of the Trailer

- Begin pulling the tractor forward until the fifth wheel comes out from below the trailer.
- Stop when the tractor frame is under the trailer, which will prevent the trailer from falling if its landing gear sinks or collapses.

Step 8: Secure the Tractor

- Put the parking brake on.
- Shift the transmission to neutral.

Step 9: Inspect Trailer Supports

- Be certain that the ground is supporting the trailer.
- Check that the landing gear has not been damaged.

Step 10: Pull the Tractor Clear of the Trailer

- Release the parking brakes.
- Check the area around you.
- Pull the tractor forward until it clears the trailer.

Quick Review Questions

22. Why should you keep legs and feet clear of the rear tractor wheels?

23. How do you lock the trailer brakes?

Coupling a Pintle Hook

- Use the following steps to couple a pintle hook.

Step 1: Inspect the Pintle Hook

- Make sure the mount is secure and check for worn, damaged, or missing parts before operating.
- An unsecured pintle hook could separate from the vehicle, resulting in injury or death if it strikes someone.

Step 2: Unlock the Lock Pin and Open the Latch

- If there is a **tethered lock pin**, unlock and remove it.
    - Lift the lock handle away from the vehicle; **the lock should clear the lock seat on the hook body**.
    - Rotate the latch assembly up toward the vehicle to open the latch.
    - When the latch is as upright as it can be, release the lock handle.

Step 3: Lower the Drawbar

- Place the drawbar eye over the horn of the pintle hook; lower it into place.

Step 4: Lock the Pintle Hook

- Close the latch by pushing it.
- If it is locked correctly, the lock handle should rotate and move up until it and the top of the latch are flush.
- Place the tethered lock pin through the latch and lock holes.
- If applicable, close the tethered wire lock pin.
- If the latch is not locked correctly, it can separate from the trailer and vehicle, causing injury or death.

Quick Review Question

24. How do you know if the tethered lock pin has been unlocked correctly?

Uncoupling a Pintle Hook

- Make sure the trailer is parked on a firm, level surface.
- Block the trailer tires.
- Disconnect the electrical connector and breakaway brake switch lanyard.
- Disconnect the safety chains from the tow vehicle.
- Unlock the coupler; open it.
- Check that the ground surface beneath the jack is strong enough to support the tongue load before extending the jack.

8. Combination Vehicles

- **Extend the jack and transfer the weight of the trailer tongue to the jack by rotating the jack handle.**
- Raise the trailer coupler so that it is above the tow vehicle hitch.
- Drive the tow vehicle forward.

Quick Review Question

25. How do you extend the jack and transfer the weight of the trailer tongue to the jack?

Coupling a Drawbar

- Please refer to Figure 8.7. while reading the following step-by-step instructions to couple a drawbar.

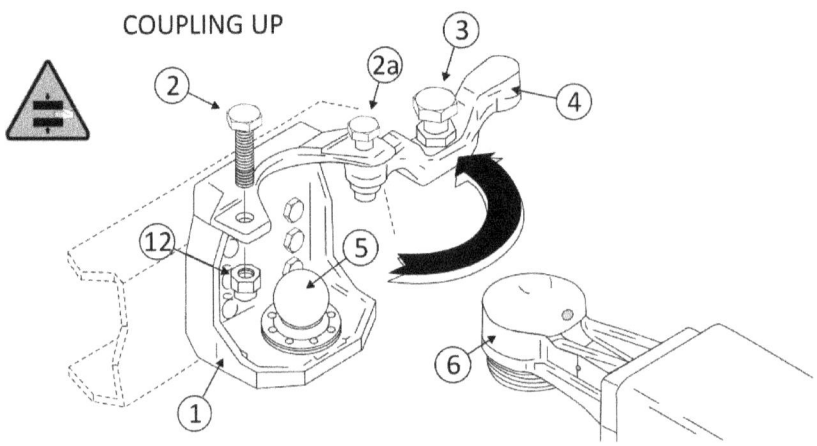

Figure 8.7. Coupling a Drawbar

Step 1: Remove the Safety Lock Screw and Rotate the Safety Cover Bar

- Take the safety lock screw (2) off.
- Take the relative self-locking nut (12) and keep it somewhere safe.
- Loosen the safety lock screw (2a).
- Turn out the adjustment screw (3)—turn at least 5 times.
- Open the safety cover bar (4) completely by rotating it outward.

Step 2: Reverse the Truck

- Put the truck in reverse; back very slowly.
- **Stop backing when the ball cup drawbar eye (6) is positioned EXACTLY above the drawbar coupling ball (5).**

Step 3: Lower the Drawbeam

- Lower the drawbeam.
- Stop lowering when the ball cup drawbar eye (6) completely covers the drawbar coupling ball (5).

Step 4: Rotate the Safety Cover Bar

8. Combination Vehicles

- The safety cover bar (4) must be rotated inward.
- Fit the safety cover bar (4) into the safety lock screw (2) with its self-locking nut.
- Tighten both lock screws (2 and 2a) with their relative self-locking nuts (12 and 12a); use a 350 – 400 N m torque wrench setting.

Step 5: Adjust the Adjustment Screw

- Make sure the adjustment screw (3) reaches a 0.3 – 0.5 mm vertical clearance between the guard disk (13) and the ball cup (6); adjust the screw as needed.
- Use the counter nut (11) to lock the setting.
- **NEVER drive if the safety cover bar (4) will not lodge perfectly into its seating.**

Step 6: Protect the Coupling Ball; Anchor the Edge onto the Ball

- Use the rubber dustproof bellows protection cover (7) to protect the visible part of the coupling ball (5).
- Anchor the edge directly onto the ball itself; this should be precise.

Step 7: Lubricate the Drawbar Eye

- Use the grease nipple (18) to directly lubricate the inside of the ball cup drawbar eye (6).

Quick Review Question

26. After coupling a drawbar, is it safe to drive if the safety cover bar fits mostly as it should into its seating?

Uncoupling a Drawbar

- Please refer to Figure 8.7. while reading the following step-by-step instructions to uncouple a drawbar.
- Before uncoupling a drawbar, make sure that the trailer brake is on.
- Take off the rubber dustproof bellows protection cover (7)
- Loosen both the counter nut (11) and the adjustment screw (3).
- Loosen the safety lock screw (2a).
- Remove the safety lock screw (2) and its self-locking nut (12).
- Completely open the safety cover bar (4) by rotating it outward.
- **Lift the trailer drawbeam; stop when the drawbar coupling ball (5) is fully visible.**
- Travel very slowly forward with the trailer.
- Lodge the safety cover bar (4) back into its housing by rotating it inward.
- Put the safety lock screw (2) back and tighten the self-locking nut (12).

Quick Review Question

27. How do you know when to stop lifting the trailer drawbeam when uncoupling a drawbar?

Coupling a Gooseneck Hitch

Step 1
- Go to the gooseneck coupler and open the clamp latch.
- Ensure that there is enough lubrication on the gooseneck ball.

Step 2
- Place the trailer coupler over the gooseneck ball.
- Put the gooseneck trailer in position by lowering it.
- Ensure the clamp is latched.

Step 3
- Put on the safety chains.
- By law, trailers must have safety chains.

Step 4
- Make the proper connections between the trailer light wires and the connector in the vehicle.
- Ensure that all lights, including brake lights, are in working order.

Step 5
- Lower the trailer jacks and put them away.
- The weight should settle onto the tow vehicle.

Quick Review Question

28. What are all trailers legally required to have?

Uncoupling a Gooseneck Hitch

Step 1
- Take out the clip and safety pin.

Step 2
- Rotate the handle to allow the trailer to be raised off of the ball.
- If done correctly, the coupler should automatically revert to the load position.

Step 3
- Put the clip and safety pin back on.

Quick Review Question

29. How will you know if a gooseneck hitch has been successfully uncoupled?

Inspecting a Combination Vehicle

- In addition to the 7-step inspection procedure described in Chapter 15, the following should also be inspected prior to operating a combination vehicle.

Coupling System Areas

Check the lower fifth wheel and be sure that

- it is securely mounted to the frame;
- it has no damaged or missing parts;
- it has enough grease;
- there is no visible space between the upper and lower fifth wheel;
- the locking jaws go around the shank, not the head of the kingpin; and
- the release arm is properly seated and the safety lock/latch is engaged.

- Check the upper fifth wheel and be sure that
    - the glide plate is securely mounted to the trailer frame,
    - the kingpin is not damaged,
    - the air and electric lines are running to the trailer,
    - the electrical cord is firmly plugged in and secured,
    - the air lines are properly connected to the gladhands,
    - the air lines have no leaks,
    - the air lines are secured correctly and **with enough slack for turns**,
    - all lines are undamaged,
    - the sliding fifth wheel is not damaged and no parts are missing,
    - the fifth wheel is properly greased,
    - all locking pins are present and locked into place,
    - there are no air leaks (if air powereD), and
    - it is not so far forward as to cause the tractor frame to hit the landing gear or the cab to hit the trailer when turning.

Quick Review Question

30. Why should the upper fifth wheel air lines have enough slack?

Landing Gear

Be sure that the landing gear is raised fully, has no missing parts, and is not broken or bent.

- Check that the crank handle is in place and secured.
- Make sure that there are no air or hydraulic leaks if power operated.

8. Combination Vehicles

Quick Review Question

31. If the landing gear is power operated, what should be checked?

Combination Vehicle Brake Check

In addition to the standard air brake system checks described in Chapter 7, use the following steps to check air brakes on combination vehicles, including double or triple trailers.

- **Make sure that air flows to all trailers:**
    - Apply the parking brake and/or use wheel chocks.
    - Wait for the air pressure to reach "normal."
    - When air pressure is normal, push in the trailer air supply knob (reD) to supply air to the emergency lines.
    - Supply air to the service line using the trailer handbrake.
    - **Go to the back of the rig and open the emergency line shut-off valve at the back of the last trailer.**
    - **Listen for the sound of escaping air**; this means that the entire system is charged.
    - Close the emergency line valve and open the service line valve.
    - **Make sure that the service pressure goes through all the trailers (the trailer handbrake or service brake pedal should be on).**
    - Close the service line valve.
- If you do not hear air escaping from the emergency and service lines, make sure that the trailer and dolly shut-off valves are in the open position.
- For all brakes to work, air must go all the way to the back.

Quick Review Questions

32. How can you be sure that air is flowing to all of the trailers?

33. What is required in order for all of the brakes to work?

Test the Tractor Protection Valve

Build air pressure up to normal; push in the air supply knob.

- Turn the engine off.
- Step on and off the brake pedal to reduce the tank's air pressure; you will need to do this several times.
- **When the air pressure falls to 20 – 45 psi (or manufacturer's specifications), the trailer air supply control should pop out ("emergency" position).**
    - If the trailer air supply control does not pop out to the "emergency" position after reducing the tank's air pressure, there may be a leak.

8. Combination Vehicles

- An air hose or trailer brake leak could drain all of the tractor's air, possibly leading to a loss of vehicle control.

Quick Review Questions

34. How is the tractor protection valve tested?

35. When testing the tractor protection valve, what is the purpose of stepping on and off the brake pedal several times?

Test Trailer Emergency and Service Brakes

Emergency Brakes

- Make sure that the trailer freely rolls after the trailer air brake system has been charged.
    - If it does: stop and pull out the trailer air supply control, or place it in the "emergency" position.
    - **Gently use the tractor to pull on the trailer to make sure that the trailer emergency brakes are on.**

Service Brakes

- Check for normal air pressure.
- Release the parking brakes.
- Slowly pull the vehicle forward.
- **Apply the trailer brakes using the hand control/trolley valve (if applicable).**
    - **If you feel the brakes come on, the trailer brakes are connected and working.**
    - Use the hand valve when checking the trailer service brakes; control the trailer brakes with the foot pedal so that air is applied to the service brakes at all wheels.

Quick Review Questions

36. How are the trailer emergency brakes tested?

37. How are the trailer service brakes tested?

Answer Key

1. The rear trailer is twice as likely to roll over when pulling doubles.

2. Controlling your speed is important regardless of whether the load is full or empty; however, empty or lightly loaded vehicles take longer to stop because the combination of stiff suspension springs and strong brakes results in poor traction and subsequent wheel lockup.

3. Off tracking describes when the rear wheels follow a different path than the front wheels.

4. The vehicle should be positioned in a way that will allow you to back in a straight line. Backing on a curved path should be avoided; if that is not possible, always back to the driver's side for better visibility.

5. The 2 best practices to help prevent a rollover are to 1) ensure that the cargo load is as close to the ground as possible and evenly distributed, and 2) turn slowly.

6. Low-slung units (lowboys, car carriers, moving vans, and possum-belly livestock trailers) and single-axle tractors pulling long trailers with landing gear set for tandem-axle tractors are most likely to get stuck on highway-rail crossings.

7. Since the brakes on the trailer wheels cause the skid, using the trailer handbrake is not recommended.

8. Using the trailer hand valve while driving can cause the trailer to skid.

9. Trailers without spring brakes rely on emergency brakes, which will fail in the event of an air leak. It is therefore critical to use wheel chocks for safety.

10. The trailer air supply control lets the driver open and close the tractor protection valve; it controls the tractor protection valve in the cab.

11. The service line carries air and connects to the relay valves.

12. The emergency air line supplies the air to the trailer air tanks and controls the emergency brakes on combination vehicles.

13. Gladhands are coupling devices that connect service and emergency air lines from the truck or tractor to the trailer; they are also known as hose couplers.

14. Dummy couplers are used on some vehicles to help keep air supplies clean; they prevent water and dirt from entering the coupler and the air lines.

15. Shut-off valves are found in the supply and service air lines at the rear of trailers that are used to tow other trailers.

16. Shut-off valves at the back of the last trailer must be closed; all others must be open.

17. To determine if a vehicle manufactured prior to 1998 has an antilock braking system (ABS), check beneath the vehicle for the electronics control unit (ECU) and wheel speed sensor wires, which should come from the back of the brakes.

18. Trailers that are too low could result in the tractor striking and damaging the trailer nose; trailers that are too high might not couple correctly.

19. There should be zero space between the upper and lower fifth wheel; having any space indicates a coupling error.

20. Yes, the fifth wheel jaws should be closed around the kingpin shank, which can be checked by going under the trailer and looking into the back of the fifth wheel.

21. You should never drive with landing gear that is only partway up; otherwise, you could risk catching it on railroad tracks or similar obstacles.

22. If the vehicle moves, keeping legs and feet clear of the rear tractor wheels will prevent serious injuries.

23. To lock the trailer brakes, shut off the trailer air supply.

24. When correctly unlocked, the lock should clear the lock seat on the hook body.

25. Rotating the jack handle will allow you to extend the jack and transfer the weight of the trailer tongue to the jack.

26. No, it is never safe to drive unless the safety cover bar fits PERFECTLY into its seating.

27. Once the drawbar coupling ball (5) is fully visible, you can stop lifting the trailer drawbeam.

28. By law, all trailers must have safety chains.

29. When successfully uncoupled, the coupler will return to the load position automatically.

30. The upper fifth wheel air lines need adequate slack for when the rig turns.

31. For landing gear that is power operated, it is important to make sure that there are no air or hydraulic leaks.

32. After applying the parking brake or using wheel chocks, wait for the air pressure to normalize and then push in the red trailer air supply knob; supply air to the service line using the trailer handbrake. Open the emergency line shut-off valve at the back of the last trailer and listen for the sound of escaping air, which indicates that the entire system is charged. Close the emergency line valve and open the service line valve; make sure that the service pressure goes through all of the trailers while the trailer handbrake or service brake pedal is on. Remember to close the service line valve when you are done.

33. In order for all of the brakes to work, air must go all the way to the back.

34. After building the air pressure up to normal, push in the air supply knob and shut off the engine. Reduce the tank's air pressure by stepping on and off the brake pedal several times. Once the air pressure falls to the manufacturer's specifications (usually 20 – 45 psi), the trailer air supply control should pop out into the "emergency" position.

35. When testing the tractor protection valve, you must step on and off the brake pedal several times in order to reduce the tank's air pressure.

36. After making sure that the trailer freely rolls after the trailer air brake system has been charged, come to a stop. Pull out the trailer air supply control (or place it in the "emergency" position); use the tractor to gently pull on the trailer to make sure that the trailer emergency brakes are on.

37. After checking for normal air pressure, releasing the parking brakes, and slowly pulling the vehicle forward, apply the trailer brakes using the hand control or trolley valve. If you can feel the brakes come on, the trailer brakes are connected and in working order.

9 Double and Triple Trailers

Safely Pulling Double and Triple Trailers

- Pulling more trailers means that more can go wrong—always take extra precautions.
- **Doubles/triples are not as stable as other commercial vehicles.**

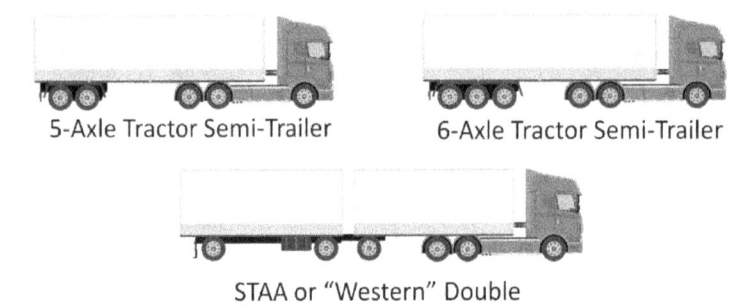

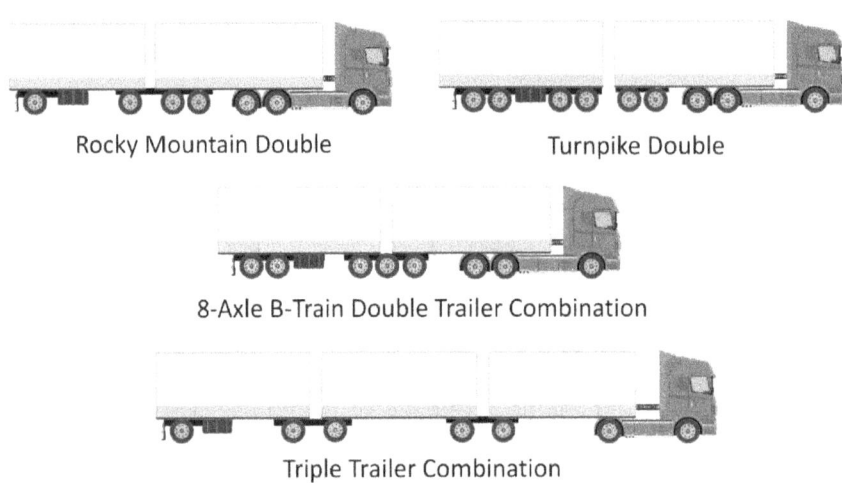

Figure 9.1. Combination and Longer Combination Vehicles

- Safe speeds for straight trucks or single-trailer combination vehicles might be too fast for doubles/triples.

- The crack-the-whip effect (see Chapter 8) makes doubles/triples and other combination vehicles more likely to roll over.
- **In a combination vehicle, the last trailer is most likely to turn over.**
- Always check the critical parts on all trailers; this is described below in "Inspecting Double and Triple Trailers."
- **Smooth driving is key to preventing rollovers in doubles and triples:**
    - Look far enough ahead.
    - Anticipate needing to slow down, change lanes, etc.
    - Steer gently.
    - Take corners, curves, and ramps slowly.
- **More following distance is needed when driving doubles/triples:**
    - They are longer and take up more space on the road.
    - They cannot be turned or stopped suddenly.
    - They require larger gaps when entering or crossing traffic.
    - Always be certain that your sides are clear before changing lanes.
- Doubles/triples are more prone to skidding and traction loss in adverse conditions.
    - Doubles/triples have added length.
    - There are more dead axles to pull with your drive axles.
- Always be aware of how parking lots are arranged and plan to take a spot you can pull straight through.
- **A converter dolly with a yellow lamp on the left side indicates that it has an antilock braking system (ABS).**

Quick Review Questions

1. Which trailer is most likely to roll over in a combination vehicle?
2. How can you tell if a converter dolly has ABS?

Coupling Twin Trailers

- Incorrect coupling is extremely dangerous.
- The steps below outline the instructions to correctly couple doubles/triples.

Secure the Second (Rear) Trailer

Apply the spring brakes on the second trailer.

- If the second trailer does not have spring brakes,
    - drive the tractor close to the trailer;
    - connect the emergency line;

- charge the trailer air tank, and then disconnect the emergency line.
- Following the steps above will set the trailer emergency brakes, provided the slack adjusters are adjusted correctly.
- Always chock the wheels if there is ever a doubt about the integrity of the brakes.
- Heavier semitrailers should be in first position behind the tractor.
- Lighter trailers should be positioned in the rear.
- **A converter dolly, or converter gear, is a coupling device composed of 1 or 2 axles and a fifth wheel.**
    - It allows a semitrailer to be coupled to the rear of a tractor trailer combo.
    - Once coupled, it creates a double-bottom rig (see Figure 9.2.).

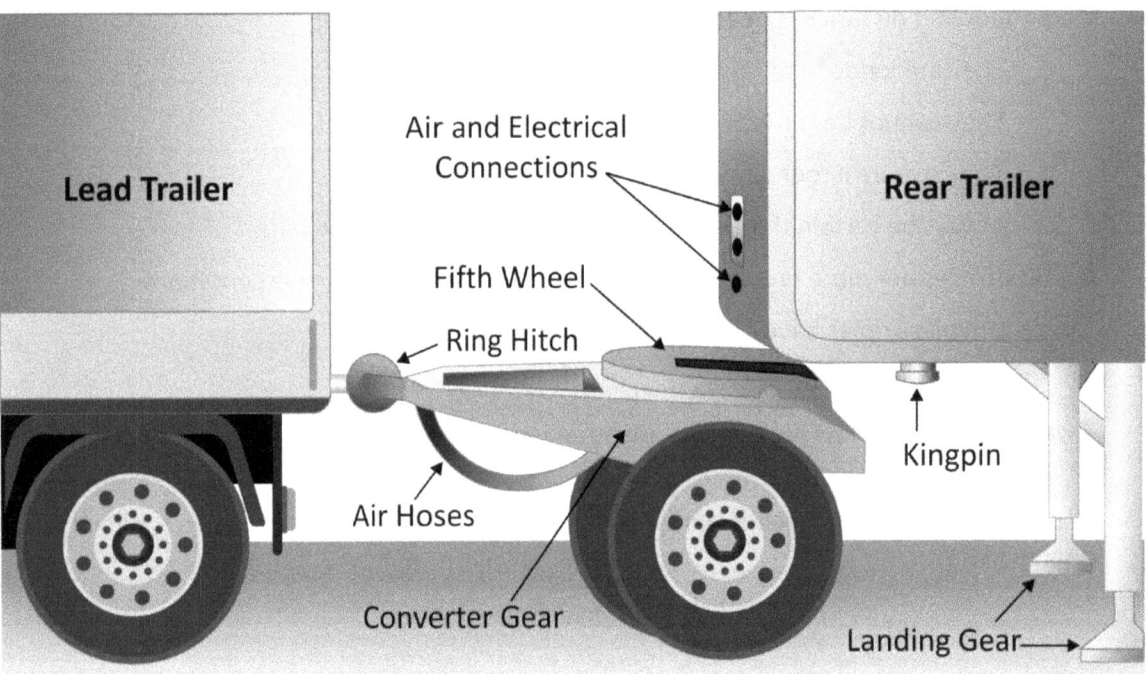

Figure 9.2. Positioning the Converter Dolly in Front of the Second (Rear) Trailer

Quick Review Questions

3. What is a converter dolly?

4. Before coupling, what are the 3 methods that can be used to secure the second (rear) trailer?

Position the Converter Dolly in Front of the Second (Rear) Trailer

Open the air tank petcock to release the dolly brakes.

- **If the dolly has spring brakes (most do not), use the dolly parking brake control to release the spring brakes.**
- Manually align the dolly to the kingpin (if the distance is not too great to do so).
- If you cannot manually align the dolly to the kingpin,

- bring the combination as close as you can to the converter dolly,
- move the dolly to the rear of the first semitrailer and couple it to the trailer,
- lock the pintle hook,
- secure the dolly support in the raised position,
- position the dolly as close as you can to the nose of the second semitrailer,
- lower the dolly support,
- unhook the dolly from the first trailer, and
- wheel the dolly into position in front of the second trailer and in line with the kingpin.

Quick Review Questions

5. What should you do if you cannot manually align the dolly to the kingpin?
6. Do converter dollies have spring brakes?

Connect the Converter Dolly to the Front Trailer

Back the first semitrailer so that it is in front of the dolly tongue.

- Hook the dolly to the front trailer.
- Lock the pintle hook.
- Secure the converter gear support in the raised position.

Quick Review Question

7. In what position should the converter gear support be secured?

Connect the Converter Dolly to the Rear Trailer

Ensure that the trailer brakes are locked and the wheels are chocked if needed.

- Check that the **trailer height** is correct:
  - **It must be a little lower than the center of the fifth wheel.**
  - **The trailer should be slightly raised when the dolly is pushed under it.**
- Back the converter dolly under the rear of the trailer.
- To prevent damage if the trailer moves, raise the landing gear slightly off the ground.
- Pull against the pin of the second semitrailer to test the coupling.
- **Visually inspect the coupling:**
  - There should be **no space between the upper and lower fifth wheel**.
  - The **locking jaws should be closed on the kingpin**.
- Connect the air hoses, light cords, and safety chains.
- Close the converter dolly air tank petcock and service and emergency shut-off valves at the rear of the second trailer.

- Open the shut-off valves at the rear of the first trailer and on the dolly (if it has them).
- Completely raise the landing gear.
- Charge the trailer brakes by pushing in the air supply knob.
    - Open the emergency line shut-off to check for air at the rear of the second trailer.
    - If there is zero air pressure, it means that something is wrong and the brakes will not work.

Quick Review Questions

8. How can you be sure that the trailer height is correct before coupling?

9. What is involved in a visual inspection of a coupling?

Uncoupling Twin Trailers

- Be sure that the rig is parked in a straight line and on firm, level ground.
- Apply the parking brakes; use wheel chocks on the second trailer if it does not have spring brakes.
- Lower the landing gear of the second semitrailer to allow some of the dolly weight to be removed.
- Close the air shut-offs at the rear of the first semitrailer and, if applicable, on the dolly.
- Disconnect and secure all of the dolly air and electric lines.
- Release the brakes on the dolly.
- Release the fifth wheel latch on the converter dolly.
- Pull the dolly out from under the rear semitrailer by slowly pulling the tractor, first semitrailer, and dolly forward.
- To uncouple the converter dolly,
    - lower the dolly landing gear and disconnect the safety chains,
    - chock the wheels or apply the converter gear spring brakes,
    - release the first semitrailer's pintle hook, and
    - slowly pull clear of the dolly.
- **Never unlock the pintle hook while the dolly is under the rear trailer.**
    - **The dolly bar could fly up and cause injury.**
    - **Recoupling could be extremely difficult.**

Quick Review Question

10. Why should the dolly be pulled out from under a trailer before it is disconnected from the trailer in front?

Coupling and Uncoupling Triple Trailers

- Couple the tractor to the first trailer as described in Chapter 8 ("Coupling Tractor Semitrailers").
- Move the converter dolly into position.
- Couple the first trailer to the second trailer as described above ("Coupling Twin Trailers").
- To uncouple the third trailer, pull the dolly out.
- Unhitch the dolly as described above for uncoupling twin trailers.
- Using the steps explained above for uncoupling double-bottom rigs, uncouple the rest of the rig.

Quick Review Question

11. How is the third trailer uncoupled?

Inspecting Double and Triple Trailers

- **Follow the 7-step inspection method** described in Chapter 15.
- During **step 5** (walk-around inspection), include the following **additional checks**:

Coupling System Areas

Inspect the lower fifth wheel:
- Make sure that it is securely mounted to the frame, has enough grease, and has no damaged/missing parts.
- Be sure that there is no visible space between the upper and lower fifth wheel.
- Check that the locking jaws are around the shank—NOT the head of the kingpin.
- Make sure that the release arm is properly seated; the safety lock should be engaged.

- **Inspect the upper fifth wheel:**
    - Make sure that the glide plate is mounted securely to the trailer frame.
    - Check that the kingpin is not damaged.

- **Inspect the trailer's air and electric lines:**
    - Make sure the electrical cord is secured and plugged in firmly.
    - Check that all lines are undamaged.
    - Be certain that the air lines are connected properly to the gladhands.
    - Make sure there are no air leaks in the lines.
    - Check that the air lines are secured properly and have enough slack for turns.

- **Inspect the sliding fifth wheel:**
    - Make sure that the slide has no damaged or missing parts.
    - Check that it has been properly greased.
    - Make sure all locking pins are there and that they are locked in place.

9. Double and Triple Trailers

- o Make sure there are no air leaks (if air powereD).
- o Be sure that the fifth wheel is not too far forward: the tractor frame should not hit the landing gear and the cab should not strike the trailer when turning.
- **Inspect the landing gear:**
    - o Make sure the landing gear is raised fully, has no missing parts, and is not bent or damaged.
    - o Check that the crank handle is in place and secure.
    - o Make sure there are no air or hydraulic leaks (if air powereD).
- **Inspect double and triple trailers:**
    - o Make sure the **shut-off valves at the rear of the front and middle trailers** are **open**.
    - o Make sure the **shut-off valves at the rear of the last trailer** are **closed**.
    - o Make sure the **converter dolly air tank drain valve** is **closed**.
    - o Check that the air lines are supported and that the gladhands are connected properly.
    - o If there is a spare tire on the dolly, make sure it is secured.
    - o **Check that the pintle-eye of the dolly is in place in the pintle hook of the trailer(s).**
    - o **Check that the pintle hook is latched.**
    - o Be certain that safety chains are secured to the trailer(s).
    - o Make sure the light cords are firmly in their sockets on trailers.

Quick Review Questions

12. What should be inspected on the converter dolly and pintle hook?

13. In which position should shut-off valves be on the rear of the last trailer, the first trailer in a set of doubles, and on the middle trailer in a set of triples?

Double and Triple Trailer Air Brakes

- Include the following checks IN ADDITION TO the brake inspection steps explained in Chapter 8.
- **Make sure that air flows to all trailers:**
    - o Hold the vehicle using the parking brake and/or wheel chocks.
    - o When the air pressure is normal, push in the red trailer air supply knob to supply the emergency (supply) lines with air.
    - o Provide air to the service line using the trailer handbrake.
    - o After going to the rear of the rig, open the emergency line shut-off valve at the rear of the last trailer.
    - o Listen for the sound of escaping air; this means the system is charged.
    - o Close the emergency line valve.

9. Double and Triple Trailers

- o Make sure the trailer handbrake or service brake pedal is on.
- o Open the service line valve and check that service pressure is going through all trailers.
- o In order for all of the brakes to work, air MUST flow all the way to the back.
- o If you do NOT hear air escaping from both lines, make sure that the shut-off valves on the trailers and dollies are in the open position.

- **Test the trailer air supply control (tractor protection valve):**
  - o Charge the trailer's air brake system by building up to normal pressure and pushing in the air supply knob.
  - o Shut off the engine.
  - o Pump the brake pedal several times to reduce air pressure in tanks.
  - o When the air pressure falls into range (typically 20 – 45 psi), the trailer air supply control should either pop out or move from the "normal" to "emergency" position.
  - o The trailer air supply control MUST be in working order: air hose or trailer brake leaks trigger the emergency brakes to come on, which could result in a loss of control.

- **Test the trailer emergency brakes:**
  - o After charging the trailer air brake system, check that the trailer rolls freely.
  - o Stop; pull out the trailer air supply control (or place it in the "emergency" position).
  - o Gently pull on the trailer with the tractor to make sure the trailer emergency brakes are on.

- **Test the trailer service brakes:**
  - o After checking for normal air pressure, release the parking brakes.
  - o Slowly move the vehicle forward.
  - o Apply the trailer brakes with the trolley valve/hand control if there is one.
  - o You should be able to feel the brakes come on, which indicates that the trailer brakes are connected and working.
  - o Remember: the trailer brakes should be tested with the hand valve but controlled with the foot pedal in normal operation.

Quick Review Question

14. How can you be sure that air is flowing to all trailers?

Answer Key

1. The last trailer is most likely to roll over in a combination vehicle.

2. A yellow lamp on the left side of the dolly indicates that it has an antilock braking system (ABS).

3. A converter dolly is a coupling device composed of 1 or 2 axles and a fifth wheel that allows a semitrailer to be coupled to the rear of a tractor trailer combo; once coupled, it creates a double-bottom rig.

4. There are 3 methods that can be used to secure the second (rear) trailer before coupling: 1) use spring brakes; 2) in second trailers without spring brakes, drive the tractor close to the trailer, connect the emergency line, charge the air tank in the trailer, and disconnect the emergency line; and 3) chock the wheels, which should be done any time there is doubt about the integrity of the brakes.

5. If you cannot manually align the dolly to the kingpin, you should perform the following steps: bring the combination as close as you can to the converter dolly; move the dolly to the rear of the first semitrailer and couple it to the trailer; lock the pintle hook; secure the dolly support in the raised position; position the dolly as close as you can to the nose of the second semitrailer; lower the dolly support; unhook the dolly from the first trailer; and wheel the dolly into position in front of the second trailer and in line with the kingpin.

6. Most converter dollies do not have spring brakes and therefore require that the air tank petcock be opened to release the dolly brakes. On dollies with spring brakes, the dolly parking brake control can be used.

7. The converter gear support should be secured in the raised position.

8. To check that the trailer height is correct, make sure that it is a little lower than the center of the fifth wheel and that the trailer is slightly raised when the dolly is pushed under it.

9. Visually inspecting the coupling involves making sure there is no space between the upper and lower fifth wheel and checking to see that the locking jaws are closed on the kingpin.

10. If the pintle hook is unlocked while the dolly is under the rear trailer, it could cause the dolly bar to fly up, resulting in injury and/or making recoupling extremely difficult.

11. The third trailer is uncoupled by pulling the dolly out.

12. You should check that the converter dolly air tank drain valve is closed, that the spare tire on the dolly is secured, and that the air lines are supported and the gladhands are properly connected. Make sure that the pintle-eye of the dolly is in place in the pintle hook of the trailer(s) and that the pintle hook is latched.

13. When pulling more than 1 trailer, all shut-off valves should be in the open position except for the last trailer: shut-off valves at the rear of the front and middle trailers should be open; shut-off valves at the rear of the last trailer should be closed.

14. To make sure that air is flowing to all trailers, use the parking brake (or chocks) to hold the vehicle in place, and then normalize the air pressure and push in the trailer air supply knob. Use the trailer handbrake to supply air to the service line. Open the emergency line shut-off valve at the rear of the last trailer and listen for the sound of escaping air to verify that the system is charged. Close the emergency line valve and make sure that the trailer handbrake or service brake pedal is on. Open the service line valve and check that service pressure is going through all trailers. If you do not hear air escaping from both lines, check that the shut-off valves on the trailers and dollies are in the open position.

10 Passengers

Vehicle Inspection

- **Drivers of vehicles that can hold 16 or more passengers (including the driver) must have a CDL and passenger endorsements.**
    - A knowledge test must be passed in order to earn the endorsement.
    - A skills test must be passed for the class of passenger vehicle you will drive.
    - Study this chapter (Passengers) and Chapter 2 (Driving Safely) when preparing for the endorsement exam.
    - Study Chapter 6 (The Air Brake System) if the vehicle you will operate has air brakes.
- Always be sure the bus is safe BEFORE you drive it.
    - Review the previous driver's inspection report.
    - Only sign the report if earlier reported defects have been certified as repaired or not in need of repairs.
    - By signing the report, you are certifying that the reported defects have been repaired.
- BEFORE driving, check that the following are all in good working order:
    - service brakes and air hose couplings (if your rig has them)
    - parking brake
    - steering mechanism
    - reflectors and lights
    - tires with front wheels that have NOT been regrooved or recapped
    - horn
    - windshield wiper(s)
    - rearview mirror(s)
    - coupling devices
    - wheels and rims
    - emergency equipment, including fire extinguishers
    - emergency reflectors (3 triangles or at least 6 fusees or 3 liquid-burning flares)
    - spare electrical fuses (unless the bus has circuit breakers)

- Check the outside of the bus: close open emergency exits (see Figure 10.2.) and open access panels (e.g., for baggage, restrooms).

Emergency exit doors and windows should always be closed during transit.

Figure 10.2. School Bus Emergency Exit Door and Window

- Unattended buses are sometimes damaged by other people; **always check the bus's interior BEFORE driving:**
    - Make sure aisles and stairwells are clear.
    - Be sure that all handholds and railings are in working condition.
    - Check that floor covers are safe and in working condition.
    - Make sure that all signaling devices are functioning properly, including the restroom emergency buzzer.
    - Check that all emergency exit handles are in working order.
    - Check that all seats are fastened securely to the bus.
- **Never drive when an open emergency exit door or window is open.** (See Figure 10.2.)
    - "Emergency Exit" signs must be clearly visible.
    - Be sure that red emergency door lights are in working order and are turned on anytime outside lights would be used.
- Some emergency roof hatches can be left partly open for fresh air.
    - Do not open these regularly.
    - Remember that an open roof hatch means a higher clearance.

- **Always wear your seatbelt.**

Always close access panels before driving.

Figure 10.3. Bus Luggage Access Panel

Quick Review Question

1. What should be checked in a bus's interior during a vehicle inspection?

Loading and Starting the Trip

- **Never allow baggage in aisles doorways.**
- Always secure baggage/freight in such a way as to
    - avoid damage,
    - allow the driver to move easily and freely,
    - allow riders to exit through any window or door in an emergency, and
    - protect passengers from injuries caused by falling or shifting carry-on luggage.

Bags should be stored out of doorways and aisles

Figure 10.4. Bus Luggage Rack

- Be on the lookout for cargo/luggage with hazardous materials.
- Refer to the federal hazard class definitions (see Table 10.1.).
    - Be on the lookout for diamond-shaped labels on luggage/cargo; these indicate the presence of a hazardous material.
    - Only transport hazardous materials if you are certain the rules allow for it.

Table 10.1. Federal Hazard Class Definitions

Class	Class Name	Examples
1	Explosives	ammunition, fireworks, dynamite
2	Gases	propane, helium, oxygen
3	Flammable	acetone, gasoline
4	Flammable Solids	fuses, matches
5	Oxidizers	ammonium, hydrogen peroxide, nitrate
6	Poisons	arsenic, pesticides
7	Radioactive	plutonium, uranium
8	Corrosives	battery acid, hydrochloric acid
9	Miscellaneous Hazardous Materials	asbestos, formaldehyde
none	Other Regulated Material-Domestic (ORM-D)	charcoal, hair spray
none	Combustible Liquids	lighter fluid, fuel oils

- **Buses ARE allowed to carry some hazardous materials:**
    - small arms ammunition labeled "ORM-D"
    - emergency hospital supplies
    - legal drugs
- **Buses are NEVER allowed to carry**
    - Division 2.3 poison gas,
    - Liquid Class 6 poison,
    - tear gas,
    - irritants,
    - more than 100 lb. of solid Class 6 poisons,

10. Passengers

- - explosives that are in the same space that is occupied by people (except for small arms ammunition),
  - materials that are labeled as radioactive and that are occupying the same space as people,
  - more than 500 total lb. of hazardous materials that ARE allowed to be transported, or
  - more than 100 lb. of allowable hazardous materials of any one class.
- Never allow riders to carry unlabeled hazardous materials, such as gasoline or car batteries.
- **Riders must stand BEHIND the standee line.**
  - A **standee line** is a 2-in. line (or similar marking) on the floor.
  - It is used on buses designed to carry standing passengers.
  - Riders are never allowed to stand ahead of the rear of the driver's seat.
- Upon arrival at a destination or intermediate stops, the following should be announced by the driver:
  - the location
  - the reason for the stop
  - the next departure time
  - the bus number
  - a reminder for riders to take their carry-ons
  - a reminder for riders to step down from seats if the aisle is on a lower level
- If driving a chartered bus, do NOT allow riders on until departure time.

Quick Review Questions

2. Are there any hazardous materials that you are allowed to transport by bus? If so, what are they?

3. Name some hazardous materials that you may NOT transport by bus.

4. What is a standee line and what is its purpose?

On the Road

- Passenger comfort and safety rules should be announced at the start of the trip and include rules about
  - smoking,
  - eating/drinking,
  - music being played, and
  - keeping heads, arms, etc. inside the bus for safety.
- Scan the bus interior as well as the sides and rear of the bus and the road ahead while driving.

- If needed, remind passengers about the rules while you are driving.
- Caution riders about watching their steps while getting on and off the bus.
- Always wait for passengers to either be seated or brace themselves before starting to drive.
- **Be sure to make starts and stops as smoothly as possible to avoid passenger injury.**
- Always ensure rider safety, including for intoxicated and/or disruptive passengers:
  - **Do not let intoxicated/disruptive passengers off at stops where they would be unsafe.**
  - If needed, drop a passenger off at a safer (e.g., better lit, more populous) stop.
  - Check with your carrier for specific guidance on dealing with intoxicated passengers.
- Bus accidents do happen—especially at intersections.
- Always use caution: do not rely solely on signals or other traffic controls.
- Always be mindful of the clearance needed for your bus.
  - Buses can hit passing vehicles or knock off side-view mirrors when they exit a stop.
  - Pay attention to poles, tree limbs, etc. at bus stops.
  - Familiarize yourself with the gap size needed to accelerate and merge the bus with other traffic.
  - Always wait for the gap to open; never assume other drivers will brake or give you needed space to pull out.
- **Always reduce speed on curves!**
  - Excessive speed on curves, especially in rain/snow, results in fatal crashes—even with good traction.
  - All banked curves have safe "design speeds."
  - Design speeds are for cars—not buses—traveling in ideal weather conditions.
  - The design speed is likely too fast for a bus.
- **Your speed is too fast if the bus leans toward the outside on a banked curve.**
- **Always stop a bus 15 – 50 ft. ahead of railroad crossings.**
- Listen and look—in both directions—for trains; open your door if needed.
- After a train passes, make sure another train isn't coming in the opposite direction BEFORE going through the crossing.
- Never change gears (on a manual transmission) while crossing railroad tracks.
- You do not need to stop, but you must slow down and carefully check for vehicles in the following situations:
  - at streetcar crossings
  - in areas where police and/or flaggers are directing traffic
  - at green traffic signals
  - at crossings labeled "exempt" or "abandoned"

- **Stop at any drawbridge that does not have a signal light or traffic control attendant.**
    - Plan to stop a minimum of 50 ft. before the draw of the bridge.
    - Always make sure the draw is closed completely before crossing.
- Slow down and check for safety on drawbridges when
    - they have traffic lights that are lit green, and
    - an attendant or traffic officer is on duty.

Quick Review Questions

5. If you encounter intoxicated or disruptive passengers, it is best to let them off as soon as possible. Is this true or false?

6. What is the recommended distance to stop a bus before a railroad crossing?

7. Under what circumstances must you always stop before crossing a drawbridge?

After-Trip Vehicle Inspection

- Always inspect the bus at the end of each shift.
- Interstate carriers require written inspection reports concerning each bus driven.
    - Such reports must list and provide details about any defects that would compromise safety and/or cause a breakdown.
    - A report is still needed if there are no defects; simply indicate that no defects were found.
    - Reporting damage allows mechanics to complete repairs before the bus goes back on the road.
- Pay attention to handholds, seats, emergency exits, and windows—passengers sometimes damage these.
- Make sure that passenger signaling devices and brake-door interlocks (see Brake-Door Interlocks section below) function as they should on all mass transit buses.

Quick Review Question

8. If no defects are found on a bus after the end of a shift, the driver does not need to write an inspection report. Is this true or false?

Prohibited Practices

- Unless there is no other option, **do not fuel the bus while passengers are on board**.
- NEVER refuel with passengers on board if you are in a closed building.
- **Avoid distractions while driving**; this includes talking with passengers.
- Unless deboarding passengers would be unsafe, **never tow or push a disabled bus with passengers on board**.

- - Tow/push the bus only far enough to safely let passengers off.
  - Consult your employer's guidance concerning towing/pushing disabled buses.

Quick Review Question

9. List the behaviors/practices that are prohibited when driving a bus.

Brake-Door Interlocks

- Some urban mass transit coaches have a brake and accelerator interlock system.
  - The interlock system is a safety feature.
  - **With the rear door open, the interlock applies the brakes and holds the throttle in idle.**
  - When the rear door is closed, the interlock releases.
- **Never use the interlock system as a replacement for the parking/emergency brake.**

Quick Review Question

10. Do you need to keep the rear door of a transit bus open in order to use the parking brake?

Answer Key

1. During a vehicle inspection of a bus's interior, drivers should check that the aisles and stairwells are clear, handholds and railings are in working condition, floor covers are safe and in working condition, signaling devices function properly, emergency exit handles work, and all seats are securely fastened to the bus.

2. There are very few hazardous materials that buses are allowed to transport: only small arms ammunition labeled "ORM-D," emergency hospital supplies, and legal drugs.

3. You may not transport Division 2.3 poison gas, Liquid Class 6 poison, tear gas, irritants, more than 100 lb. of solid Class 6 poisons, explosives that are in the same space that is occupied by people (except for small arms ammunition), materials that are labeled as radioactive and that are occupying the same space as people, more than 500 total lb. of hazardous materials that are allowed to be transported, or more than 100 lb. of allowable hazardous materials of any one class. Riders are never allowed to carry unlabeled hazardous materials, such as gasoline or car batteries.

4. A standee line is a 2-in. line on the floor of buses that carry standing passengers. It is meant to inform passengers that they must stand behind it; it exists for safety reasons.

5. This is false. You should never let intoxicated or disruptive passengers off at stops where they could be unsafe; this includes areas that are not well lit and/or that are sparsely populated. Always check with your carrier's guidelines for best practices in dealing with disruptive passengers.

6. A bus should always be stopped 15 – 50 ft. ahead of railroad crossings.

7. You must always stop at any drawbridge that does not have a signal light or traffic control attendant.

8. This is false. An inspection report is required for each interstate bus that is driven—even if there are no defects.

9. You should never fuel the bus while passengers are on board, you should avoid distractions (including talking with passengers), and disabled buses should never be towed or pushed while passengers are on board.

10. The parking brake can be applied whether the rear door is open or not; however, the rear door must be open in order for the accelerator interlock system to apply the brake and hold the throttle in idle position while the rear door is open. The accelerator interlock system should never be used as a replacement for the emergency brake.

11 Tank Vehicle

Requirements for Tank Vehicle Endorsement

- You will need to pass a knowledge test about driving a tank vehicle.
- Be sure to study the material in this chapter as well as the following chapters:
    - Chapter 2 (Driving Safely)
    - Chapter 6 (The Air Brake System)
    - Chapter 8 (Combination Vehicles)
    - Chapter 12 (Hazardous Materials)
- A tanker endorsement is needed for certain vehicles that will transport liquids or gases, even if they are not considered hazardous materials:
    - if the vehicle requires a Class A or B commercial driver's license
    - if you are transporting a liquid or certain gases in a tank with an individual rating capacity of more than 119 gal.
    - if you are transporting a liquid or certain gases in a tank with an aggregate rated capacity of 1,000 or more gal. that are permanently or temporarily attached to the vehicle or chassis
    - if the vehicle is a Class C vehicle that will transport hazardous liquid or gas materials in the rated tanks described above
- Always inspect the vehicle (see below) before driving, loading, or unloading a tanker.
    - Ensure that the vehicle can safely transport liquid or gas materials.
    - Ensure that the vehicle is safe to drive.

Quick Review Question

1. In which situations are tanker endorsements required?

Inspecting Tank Vehicles

- Use your vehicle's operator manual to be sure you understand how to inspect the tank vehicle.
    - There are special items on tank vehicles that must be checked.
    - There are a variety of types and sizes of tank vehicles, all with differing inspection needs.

- Always inspect the tanker before driving, loading, or unloading: doing so assures that the vehicle is safe enough to contain and transport its liquid or gas cargo.
- **Leaks are the most important thing to look for in an inspection.**
    - Look under and around the vehicle for any signs of leaking.
    - Make sure there are no dents or leaks on the tank's body or shell.
    - Inspect the intake, discharge, and cut-off valves: they should be in the correct positions.
    - Make sure the pipes, connections, and other hoses are not leaking, especially around joints.
    - Be certain that manhole covers and vents have gaskets and close correctly.
    - Be sure to keep vents clear so that they function properly.
- **It is a crime to carry liquids or gases in a tank that leaks.**
    - If caught transporting materials in a leaky tank, you will be cited and prevented from driving farther.
    - You could also be responsible for cleaning up any related spills.
- Make sure the following pieces of equipment function properly if your vehicle has them:
    - vapor recovery kits
    - bonding and grounding cables
    - emergency shut-off systems
    - built-in fire extinguisher
- Tank vehicles should never be driven if they have open valves or open manhole covers.
- Understand which emergency or special equipment your vehicle is required to have; be sure it works properly.

Quick Review Question

2. Why is it important to inspect a tanker before driving, loading, or unloading it?

Tank Vehicle Loads

- Movement of liquid in partially filled tanks causes liquid **surge** (wavelike movement).
- Surge can have a negative effect on how a vehicle handles.
    - When stopping, the liquid will surge back and forth.
    - When the wave of liquid hits the end of the tank, it usually pushes the truck in the same direction as the wave.
    - On slippery surfaces, the wave could push a stopped truck into an intersection.
    - Side-to-side surges could cause a rollover.

- Liquid tanker drivers must be familiar with how their vehicle handles.

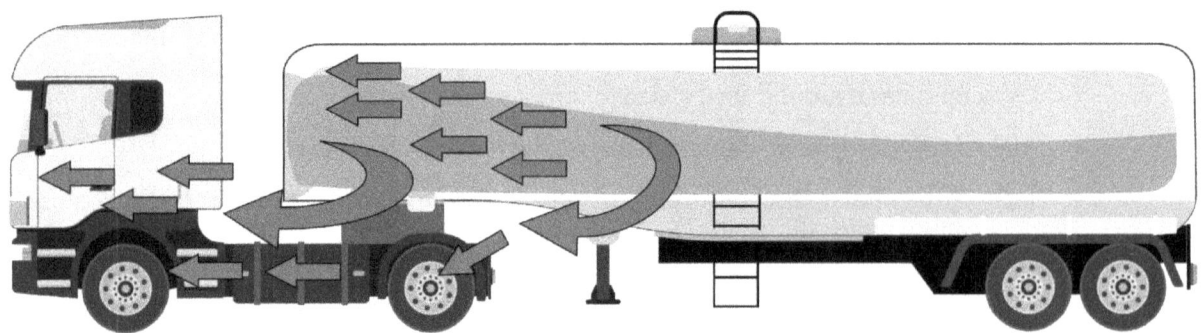

Figure 11.2. Tanker Truck Surge While Stopping

- **Bulkheads** divide liquid tanks into several smaller tanks.
    - Drivers must consider weight distribution when loading/unloading bulkheads.
    - There should never be too much weight on the front or rear of the vehicle.
- Liquid tanks with **baffles** have bulkheads with holes that allow liquid to flow through.
    - Baffles control forward and backward liquid surges.
    - Baffles do not prevent side-to-side surges.

Figure 11.3. Types of Tanker Trucks

- Unbaffled liquid tanks are also known as **"smooth bore" tanks**.
    - **They have nothing inside the tank to slow down the flow of liquid.**
    - Forward-and-back surge is highly likely with unbaffled tanks.

- - Always drive unbaffled tanks with extreme caution, especially when starting and stopping.
    - Food products (e.g., milk) are often transported in unbaffled tanks since they are easier to clean and therefore more sanitary.
  - **Outage is the expansion of liquids as they get warm.**
    - Cargo tanks should never be fully loaded; there must be room to spare for the expanding liquid.
    - Different liquids expand by different amounts.
    - Always be aware of the outage requirement for the bulk liquids you will haul.
  - Since tanks full of dense liquids can exceed the legal weight limits, those with heavy liquids are often only partially filled.
  - **Determining the amount of liquid to load in a tank** depends on
    - **legal weight limits,**
    - **the amount the liquid will expand during transit, and**
    - **the weight of the liquid.**

Quick Review Questions

3. What is the difference between bulkheads and baffles?

4. How does driving a smooth bore tanker differ from driving a tanker with baffles?

5. What are the 3 determining factors for how much liquid can be loaded in a tanker?

6. What does the term *outage* mean?

Safely Driving Tank Vehicles

- A high center of gravity means that the majority of a load's weight is high up from the road.
- Liquid tankers have a high center of gravity.
  - A high center of gravity makes a vehicle top heavy and easy to roll over.
  - Tankers have been proven to roll over when traveling at the posted speed limit on curves.
  - **Always take all curves and ramps at well below the posted speed limits, which are often too fast for tankers.**

- **Special care is needed to drive a tanker due to its high center of gravity and surge of liquid.**
- Always start, slow down, stop, change lanes, and turn as smoothly as possible.
- **Do the following to control surge:**
  - Keep steady pressure on the brakes and do not release them prematurely.

11. Tank Vehicle

- - Increase following distance and brake far enough in advance.
  - Use controlled or stab braking (see Chapter 7) if a quick stop is needed to prevent a crash.
  - Never steer quickly while braking; the vehicle could roll over.
- Always slow down before taking curves; accelerate lightly through the curve.
- Be mindful of the amount of space needed to stop the vehicle.
  - Normal stopping distance is doubled on wet roads.
  - It can take longer to stop an empty tank vehicle than a full one.
- Skidding is caused by
  - oversteering,
  - overaccelerating, and
  - over braking.
- Tank trailers can jackknife if the drive or trailer wheels start to skid.
- Always try to restore wheel traction if a vehicle starts to skid.

> **Helpful Hint**
>
> The center of gravity on a tanker is usually between 60 and 78 in. high; on a car, the center of gravity is typically between 18 and 24 in. high.

Quick Review Questions

7. It is recommended that tank vehicles take curves, on ramps, and off ramps at the posted speed limit. Is this true or false?

8. How can drivers control surge?

9. What are the 2 main reasons why special care is needed when driving a tanker?

Answer Key

1. Tanker endorsements are required if the vehicle requires a Class A or B commercial driver's license, if you are transporting a liquid or certain gases in a tank with an individual rating capacity of more than 119 gal., if you are transporting a liquid or certain gases in a tank with an aggregate rated capacity of 1,000 or more gal. that are permanently or temporarily attached to the vehicle or chassis, and if the vehicle is a Class C vehicle that will transport hazardous liquid or gas materials in the rated tanks described above.

2. Inspecting a tanker before driving, loading, or unloading it helps assure that the vehicle is safe enough to contain and transport its cargo.

3. Bulkheads divide liquid tanks into smaller tanks; baffles are bulkheads with holes in them that allow liquid to flow through them.

4. Smooth bore tankers are unbaffled and therefore have nothing to slow down the flow of liquid. Since forward-and-back surge is likely with unbaffled tankers, smooth bore tankers must be driven with extreme caution, especially when starting and stopping.

5. Legal weight limits, the amount the liquid will expand during transit, and the weight of the liquid all determine how much liquid can be loaded in a tanker.

6. Outage is the expansion of liquids as they warm up.

7. This is false. Posted speeds for curves and ramps are often too fast for tank vehicles; always slow down before taking curves and on/off ramps.

8. To control surge, drivers must keep steady pressure on the brakes, avoid releasing the brakes prematurely when stopping, increase following distance and brake far enough in advance, use controlled or stab braking if a quick stop is needed, and never steer quickly while braking.

9. A tanker's high center of gravity and surge of the liquid it transports are the 2 main reasons why special care is needed when driving such vehicles.

12 Hazardous Materials

Introduction to Hazardous Materials

Government regulations concerning the hauling of hazardous materials change constantly; it is not possible to ensure that the regulations described below will be accurate by the time you are reading this. It is critical that you consult an up-to-date copy of the "49 CFR Parts 100 – 185" (https://www.ecfr.gov/current/title-49) and the "Federal Motor Carrier Safety Regulations" (https://www.ecfr.gov/current/title-49/subtitle-B/chapter-III/subchapter-B/part-390).

- Hazardous materials are those that pose a risk to safety, health, and property during transport.
    - The term *hazmat* is short for "hazardous materials" and appears on road signs.
    - The abbreviation *HM* is often used in government regulations.
- Parts 171 – 180 of Title 49 of the *Code of Federal Regulations* (*CFR*) contain the **hazardous materials regulations (HMR)**.
- The *CFR*, specifically **49 CFR 383.5**, defines hazardous materials as "any material that has been designated as hazardous under 49 U.S.C. 5103 and is required to be placarded under subpart F of 49 CFR part 172 or any quantity of a material listed as a select agent or toxin in 42 CFR part 73."[1]
    - Copies of the *CFR* can be found at your local Government Printing Office bookstore.
    - Various CDL-related publishers and union/company offices usually have copies as well.
    - **Be sure to find out where you can get your own copy of these regulations.**
- Hazardous materials include the following:
    - explosives
    - various types of gas
    - solids
    - combustible and flammable liquids
    - other materials
- The *CFR* contains a Hazardous Materials Table that lists many of these items.
    - The list is NOT all-inclusive.
    - A material's characteristics can determine whether it qualifies as a hazardous material.
    - The shipper may also decide whether a material should be considered hazardous.

---

[1] United States Department of Transportation, "How to Comply with Federal Hazardous Materials Regulations," Federal Motor Carrier Safety Administration, last updated July 18, 2022, https://www.ecfr.gov/current/title-49/subtitle-B/chapter-III/subchapter-B/part-383/subpart-A/section-383.5

12. Hazardous Materials

- **The handling of hazardous materials is regulated by all levels of government.**
- In order to transport hazardous materials, you must have a CDL with a hazardous materials endorsement.
- To earn this endorsement, you must pass a written test concerning the regulations and requirements.
- Passing the test will require you to
    - be able to identify hazardous materials,
    - understand how to safety load shipments,
    - know how to properly placard your vehicle according to the associated rules, and
    - understand how to properly transport shipments.
- Passing the written exam is only the start of becoming a driver of hazardous materials.
    - Once on the job, you will need to be aware of many more regulations.
    - Be sure to attend hazardous materials training courses.
    - Make a point of reading—and understanding—federal and state rules concerning the transport of hazardous materials.
- You must learn all of the rules and follow them to reduce the chance of injury.
- It is not only unsafe to take shortcuts and break rules—it can also result in fines or jail time.
- The regulations require that drivers be trained and tested to transport hazardous materials.
    - Your employer (or your employer's representative) must provide this training and testing.
    - Employers dealing with hazardous materials must keep training records for any employee who works with hazardous materials.
    - The records must be maintained for the duration of time the employee works with the hazardous materials, plus 90 days.
    - Hazardous materials employees must be trained and tested AT LEAST once every 3 years.
- You must be trained to understand the security risks of transporting hazardous materials and how to respond to security threats.
- Special training is required if you will transport certain flammable gas materials and/or highway route-controlled radioactive materials.
- Specialized training is required if you will transport cargo tanks and portable tanks.
- You must be aware of the permits, exemptions, and special routes required in the locations you will drive through.
    - Some areas require permits for certain explosives or bulk hazardous waste.
    - Some states and counties require drivers to follow special routes when transporting hazardous materials.
    - The federal government may require special exemptions or permits for certain hazardous materials cargo, such as rocket fuel.
- The type and amount of hazardous materials may require the display of placards during transport.

Quick Review Question

1. What are hazardous materials?

12. Hazardous Materials

Purpose of Hazmat Regulations

- It is risky to transport hazardous materials.
- Hazmat regulations (HMR) serve 3 purposes:
    1. to contain the material
    2. to communicate the risk posed by the materials
    3. to ensure that both drivers and equipment are safe
- These regulations protect you, those around you, and the environment.
- **Containment rules**
    - inform shippers how to safely package materials; and
    - inform drivers how to safely load, transport, and unload materials.
- **Shippers must warn drivers and others about a material's hazards to communicate the risk.**
- To communicate the risk of hazards, shippers must
    - use hazard warning labels on packages,
    - make sure the proper shipping papers are provided, and
    - provide emergency response information and placards.
- Your vehicle should be inspected before and during each trip.
- Be prepared for law enforcement to stop and check the following:
    - your vehicle
    - shipping papers
    - vehicle placards
    - the hazardous materials endorsement on your CDL
    - your knowledge of hazardous materials and how to transport them

Quick Review Question

2. Why do shippers package materials?

Hazmat Transportation Roles

Shippers

- Shippers send products from one place to another by way of rail, truck, airplane, or vessel.
- Hazardous materials regulations are used by shippers to determine a product's
    - identification number,
    - correct shipping name,
    - hazard class,
    - packing group,
    - correct packaging,
    - correct markings and labels, and
    - correct placards.
- Shippers are in charge of
    - packaging, marking, and labeling materials;
    - preparing shipping papers;
    - providing emergency response information;
    - supplying placards; and
    - certifying on the shipping papers that the shipment is properly prepared based on the rules.

160

12. Hazardous Materials

- An exception to certifying the shipping papers is if the cargo tanks are supplied by you or your employer.

Carriers

- Carriers take a shipment from the shipper to the destination.
- Carriers check that the shipper prepared the shipment correctly (as described above).
- Carriers make the decision to refuse shipments that have been improperly prepared.

Drivers

- Drivers perform another check of the shipper's work (as described above).
- Drivers refuse leaking packages and shipments.
- When required, drivers place placards on the vehicle during the loading process.
- Drivers transport the shipment safely and on time.
- Drivers understand and follow all special rules related to transporting hazardous materials.
- Drivers ensure shipping papers and emergency response information are stored properly.
- Drivers report any incidents to the appropriate government agency while the shipment is under their control.

Quick Review Questions

3. What responsibility do drivers have with regard to shipping papers and emergency response information?

4. Are there any exceptions when it comes to certifying shipping papers?

5. What are the 3 main responsibilities of carriers?

Classifying Hazardous Materials

- **There are 9 hazardous materials classes.**
- The hazard class of a material is a reflection of its associated risks.

Table 12.1. Hazardous Materials Classes

Class	Division	Class or Division Name	Examples
1	1.1	mass explosion	dynamite
	1.2	projection hazard	flares
	1.3	fire hazard	display fireworks
	1.4	minor explosion	ammunition
	1.5	very insensitive	blasting agents
	1.6	extremely insensitive	explosive devices
2	2.1	flammable gases	propane
	2.2	nonflammable gases	helium
	2.3	poisonous/toxic gases	fluorine, compressed
3	N/A	flammable liquids	gasoline

Table 12.1. Hazardous Materials Classes

4	4.1	• flammable solids	• ammonium picrate, wetted
	4.2	• spontaneously combustible	• white phosphorous
	4.3	• dangerous when wet	• sodium
5	5.1	• oxidizers	• ammonium nitrate
	5.2	• organic peroxides	• methyl ethyl ketone peroxide
6	6.1	• poison (toxic material)	• potassium cyanide
	6.2	• infectious substances	• anthrax virus
7	N/A	radioactive	uranium
8	N/A	corrosives	battery fluid
9	N/A	• miscellaneous hazardous materials	polychlorinated biphenyls (PCB)
None	N/A	• other regulated material-domestic (ORM-D) • combustible liquids	• food flavorings (ORM-D) • medicines (ORM-D) • fuel oil (combustible)

Quick Review Question

6. How many hazardous materials classes are there?

12. Hazardous Materials

Hazmat Placards

- Placards are signs placed on the outside of vehicles and bulk packages.
- **Placards warn others about hazardous materials.**
- Placards identify the class of the cargo being transported.
- Vehicles with placards must display 4 identical placards.
- Placards are placed on
  - the rear of the vehicle,
  - the front of the vehicle, and
  - both sides of the vehicle.

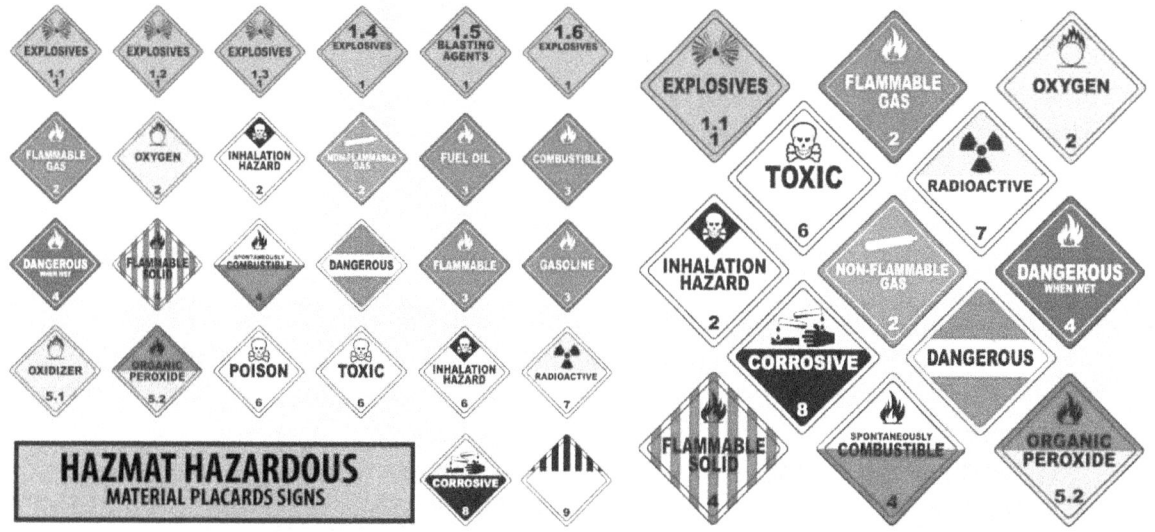

Hazmat placards must be at least 250 millimeters (9.84 in.) square, square-on-point, and shaped like a diamond.

Figure 12.1. Hazmat Placards

- You must be able to read a placard from all 4 sides of the vehicle.
- Placards must be
  - at least 250 mm (9.84 in.) square,
  - square-on-point, and
  - shaped like a diamond.
- **The identification number of the contents of bulk packaging, such as cargo tanks, is displayed on**
  - **placards, and**
  - **orange panels or white square-on-point displays of equal size to placards.**
- First responders use identification numbers to identify hazardous materials.

- Identification numbers consist of a 4-digit code.

Figure 12.2. Hazmat Placard With Identification Number (Flammable Liquid – Gasoline)

- Identification numbers are preceded by the letters *NA* or *UN*.
- A list of chemicals and their assigned identification numbers can be found in the United States Department of Transportation's *Emergency Response Guidebook* (*ERG*).
- Shippers, drivers, and carriers rely on 3 lists to identify hazardous materials:
    1. Section 172.101 of the Hazardous Materials Table
    2. Appendix A to Section 172.101 (List of Hazardous Substances and Reportable Quantities)
    3. Appendix B to Section 172.101 (List of Marine Pollutants)
- The relevant placard(s) must be attached to the vehicle before driving.
- Improperly placarded vehicles may be moved during an emergency ONLY.
- Placards must
    o be on both sides of the vehicle,
    o be on both ends of the vehicle,
    o be seen easily from the direction they face,
    o be placed so that the numbers/words are level and legible from left to right,
    o be at least 3 in. away from all other markings,
    o be kept clear of devices or attachments (e.g., ladders, tarps),
    o remain clean and undamaged (i.e., color format, message on placarD),
    o be placed on a background of a contrasting color,
    o not contain slogans (e.g., "Drive Safely"), and
    o be placed on the front of the tractor or trailer (if a front placarD).
- **To determine the correct placard to use**, drivers must know
    o **the hazard class** of the materials being transported,
    o **the amount** of hazardous materials being transported, and
    o **the total weight** (of all classes) of the materials being transported.
- Placard Table 1 and Placard Table 2 (Tables 12.2. and 12.3.) should each be consulted when determining whether a placard is needed.

Table 12.2. Placard Table 1—Applies to Any Amount of Hazardous Materials

Cargo Contained in Vehicle	Required Placard
1.1 Mass Explosives	Explosives 1.1
1.2 Project Hazards	Explosives 1.2
1.3 Mass Fire Hazards	Explosives 1.3
2.3 Poisonous/Toxic Gases	Poison Gas
4.3 Dangerous When Wet	Dangerous When Wet
5.2 (Organic Peroxide, Type B, liquid or solid, temperature-controlleD)	Organic Peroxide
6.1 (only Inhalation Hazard Zones A and B)	Poison/toxic inhalation
7 (Radioactive Yellow-III label only)	Radioactive

Table 12.3. Placard Table 2—Applies to Hazardous Materials of 1,001 lb. or More

Material Category (hazard class/division number and additional description as needeD)	Placard Name
1.4 Minor Explosion	Explosives 1.4
1.5 Very Insensitive	Explosives 1.5
1.6 Extremely Insensitive	Explosives 1.6
2.1 Flammable Gases	Flammable Gas
2.2 Nonflammable Gases	Nonflammable Gas
3 Flammable Liquids	Flammable
Combustible Liquid	Combustible*
4.1 Flammable Solids	Flammable Solid
4.2 Spontaneously Combustible	Spontaneously Combustible
5.1 Oxidizers	Oxidizer
5.2 (other than organic peroxide, Type B, liquid or solid, temperature-controlleD)	Organic Peroxide
6.1 (other than Inhalation Hazard Zones A or B)	Poison
6.2 Infectious Substances	(none)
8 Corrosives	Corrosive
9 Miscellaneous Hazardous Materials	Class 9**

12. Hazardous Materials

| ORM-D | (none) |

*The "FLAMMABLE" placard may be used in place of a "COMBUSTIBLE" placard on cargo or a portable tank.

**The "CLASS 9" placard is not required for domestic transportation.

- Materials listed in Placard Table 1 (Table 12.2.) must be placarded whenever they are transported.
- Materials listed in Placard Table 2 (Table 12.3.)—EXCEPT bulk packaging—only need placarding if the total amount being transported is at least 1,001 lb.
    - The 1,001-lb. minimum threshold includes the weight of the package.
    - To determine the total weight amount for Placard Table 2 materials, add the amounts listed on the shipping papers.
- "DANGEROUS" placards may be used in place of separate placards for each Placard Table 2 hazard class as follows:
    - when there is at least 1,001 lb. of materials from 2 or more Placard Table 2 hazard classes that require different placards
    - when 2,205 lb. or more of any Placard Table 2 material have not been loaded at any one place (in which case a placard for the specific material must be useD)
- The option to use a "DANGEROUS" placard, as described above, is only an option—not a requirement; the materials can be placarded instead.
- If a shipping paper has "INHALATION HAZARD" on it, the following placards must be displayed:
    - "POISON GAS"
    - "POISON INHALATION"
    - any other placards required based on the product's hazard class
- The 1,000-lb. exception does not apply to materials deemed to be inhalation hazards.
- Some materials have a secondary "dangerous when wet" hazard:
    - A "DANGEROUS WHEN WET" placard must be displayed when transporting these types of materials.
    - Any other placards required by the material's hazard class must also be displayed.
    - The 1,000-lb. exception concerning placarding does not apply to these types of materials.
- Sometimes placards identify the primary or subsidiary hazard class of a material:
    - These placards must have the division number or hazard class displayed in the placard's lower corner.
    - If a permanently affixed subsidiary hazard placard does not have the hazard class number, it may be used as long as color specifications are followed.
- Placards can be displayed even if they are not required; the placard must identify the type of hazmat that is being transported.
- Bulk packaging is defined as a single container with a capacity that is greater than 119 gal.
- Both bulk packages AND the vehicles that transport them must be placarded:
    - This applies even if there is only hazmat residue.
    - Some bulk packages only need placards on the 2 opposite sides (or have labels displayed insteaD).
    - Any other bulk package must have placards on all 4 sides.

Quick Review Questions

7. Why do drivers placard their vehicles?

8. In order to determine whether you need placards on your vehicle, what 3 things do you need to know?

9. In addition to appearing on cargo tanks and other bulk packaging, in which 2 places must the hazardous materials identification number appear?

Identifying Hazardous Materials

- Table 12.4. provides a sample of a 49 CFR 172.101 Hazardous Materials Table.

Table 12.4. 49 CFR 172.101 Hazardous Materials Table

Symbols	Hazardous Materials Description & Proper Shipping Names	Hazard Class or Division	Identification Numbers	PG	Label Codes	Special Provisions (172.102)	Packaging (CFR part 173)		
							Exceptions	Nonbulk	Bulk
(1)	(2)	(3)	(4)	(5)	(6)	(7)	(8A)	(8B)	(8C)
A	acetaldehyde ammonia	9	UN1841	III	9	IB8, IP3, IP7, T1, TP33	155	204	240

- Column 1 of the Hazardous Materials Table concerns the shipping description, including which shipping mode the entry affects.
- The other columns list each material's
    - shipping name,
    - hazard class (or division),
    - identification number,
    - packaging group, and
    - required labels.
- **Column 1** could include 6 different symbols, as described in Table 12.5.

Table 12.5. Symbols Appearing in Column 1 of the Hazardous Materials Table

Symbol	Description
+	indicates which shipping name, hazard class, and packing group to use; material may not necessarily meet the terms of the hazard class definition
A	indicates that the item appearing in Column 2 only needs to follow hazmat regulations if meant for air transportation (exception: hazardous material or waste)
W	indicates that the item in Column 2 only needs to follow hazmat regulations if meant for water transportation (exception: hazardous material, waste, or marine pollutant)
D	indicates that the correct shipping name may differ if the item will be transported internationally

Table 12.5. Symbols Appearing in Column 1 of the Hazardous Materials Table

I	indicates that the correct shipping name may differ if the item will be transported *only* domestically
G	indicates a generic shipping name is being used for the item described in Column 2 and must include a technical name on the shipping paper
	(Note: The specific chemical that makes a product hazardous is used as the technical name.)

- **Column 2** provides proper shipping names and descriptions of regulated materials.
    - It is organized alphabetically.
    - The proper shipping names appear in regular type.
    - Some name are written in italics; these are NOT proper shipping names.
- Shipping papers are required to show the proper shipping names—not the ones that appear in italics.
- **Column 3** contains the hazard class/division of a material or the word *forbidden*.
- Never transport materials listed as "forbidden."
- Hazardous materials shipments should be placarded based on the material's quantity and hazard class/division.
- There are 3 factors to determine which placards to use:
    1. the material's hazard class
    2. the amount being shipped
    3. the amount of all hazardous materials of all classes on your vehicle
- **Column 4** contains the identification number of each proper shipping name.
- The following letters precede identification numbers:
    - UN (United Nations)
    - NA (used only within the US and to/from Canada and as associated with the proper shipping names)
    - ID (associated with proper shipping names recognized by the International Civil Aviation Organization's [IACO] technical instructions for air transportation)
- Identification numbers are required to appear on shipping papers and packages as part of the shipping description.
- Identification numbers are also required to appear on cargo tanks/bulk packaging.
- **Column 5** indicates, using Roman numerals, the packing group assigned to a material.
- **Column 6** indicates which hazard warning label(s) shippers must use on packages containing hazardous materials.
    - Some products contain multiple hazards.
    - Products with more than 1 hazard require more than 1 label.
- **Column 7** contains any additional (special) provisions concerning the hazardous material.
    - Refer to the federal regulations for details whenever entries appear in this column.
    - Numbers 1 – 6 in this column indicate a poison inhalation hazard (PIH), which has certain shipping paper, marking, and placard requirements.
- **Column 8** consists of 3 parts that show the section numbers concerning each hazardous material's packaging requirements.
- **Columns 9 and 10** do not apply to transportation that takes place by highway.

12. Hazardous Materials

Quick Review Question

10. Which column of the Hazardous Materials Table includes the shipping description and shipping mode?

The List of Hazardous Substances and Reportable Quantities (Appendix A to 49 CFR 172.101)

Appendix A lists the spilled quantities of hazardous materials that must be reported to the United States Department of Transportation (DOT) and the United States Environmental Protection Agency (EPA).

- When at least the **reportable quantity** (RQ) is being transported, the letters *RQ* must be displayed on the shipping paper and package.
- These letters might appear before or after the basic product description.
- If any of these materials spill in a reportable quantity, a report must be submitted by you or your employer.
- The words *inhalation hazard* on a shipping paper or package require 1 of the following placards, as appropriate:
    - "poison inhalation hazard"
    - "poison gas"
- These placards are used IN ADDITION TO other displayed placards.
- These placards should be used regardless of the amount of the substance.

The List of Marine Pollutants (Appendix B to 49 CFR 172.101)

This appendix lists chemicals deemed toxic to marine life.

- For highway transportation, appendix B is used only for certain chemicals:
    - those in a 119-gal. (or more) capacity container
    - those without a label/placard, as outlined in the HMR
- Marine pollutants in bulk packages are required to display the marine pollutant marking (see Figure 12.3.).
    - The marine pollutant marking is not a placard.
    - The marine pollutant marking is required to be displayed on the outside of the vehicle.
- Shipping papers must also contain a "marine pollutant" notation near the material's description.

Figure 12.3. Marine Pollutant Marking

Quick Review Question

11. What does the abbreviation *RQ* stand for, and what does it mean?

Hazmat Shipping Papers

- **Shipping papers describe the hazardous materials that are being transported.**
- Shipping papers include
    - shipping orders,
    - bills of lading, and
    - manifests.
- Locating shipping papers after an accident can be the difference between life and death.
- Emergency personnel MUST be able to quickly identify the hazardous materials.
- **You have a few options as to where to keep hazardous materials shipping papers:**
    - in a pouch on the driver's side door
    - in clear view and within immediate reach while you are buckled in
    - on the driver's seat (when you are out of the vehicle)
- Hazardous materials shipping papers must include
    - page numbers (if more than 1 page);
    - an indication on the first page of the total number of pages (e.g., "1 of 5");
    - proper shipping descriptions for each hazardous material; and
    - the shipper's certification and signature, indicating that the shipment was prepared according to regulations.
- When shipping papers include both hazardous materials and nonhazardous materials, certain guidelines apply:
    - Enter the hazardous materials' names first.
    - Highlight the hazardous materials in contrasting colors from the nonhazardous materials.
    - Instead of highlighting, the letter *X* can be put before the shipping description in the "HM" column.
    - The letters *RQ* (reportable quantity) can be used instead of the letter *X* if applicable.
- The basic description of hazardous materials includes the following information in the order in which it is listed:
    - the identification number
    - the proper shipping name
    - the hazard class (or division)
    - the packing group (if any; it is displayed in Roman numerals and often preceded by the letters *PG*)
- Unless otherwise specified in the HMR, the identification number, shipping name, and hazard class must NOT be abbreviated.
- Hazardous materials descriptions must also include the following:
    - the total quantity and unit of measure
    - the number and type of packages (e.g., "7 drums")
    - if a reportable quantity, the letters *RQ*
    - the name of the hazardous substance (if it is not part of the shipping name and if the letters *RQ* appear)
    - the technical name of the hazardous substance (if the letter *G*—for "generic"—appears in column 1)
- Unless there is an exception, an **emergency response phone number** must be listed on shipping papers.
    - The shipper is responsible for including this information.
    - Emergency personnel use this number to gather information about hazardous materials that have been involved in a spill or fire.

12. Hazardous Materials

- Emergency response phone numbers must include 1 of the following:
  - the number of the shipper/supplier of the hazardous material being transported
  - the number of an agency/organization that can accept responsibility for and share emergency response information (ERI) of the materials
- The name, contact number, or other unique identifier of the person registered with the ERI provider must be on the shipping papers.
- ERI must be provided by the shipper to the motor carrier for EACH hazardous material being shipped.
- The ERI must include information on how to safely handle incidents with the material.
- The ERI must be able to be used away from the motor vehicle that is transporting it.
- ERI is required to include the following information:
  - the basic technical name and a description of the hazardous material
  - immediate health hazards
  - fire and/or explosion risks
  - needed immediate precautions should an accident/incident occur
  - immediate ways in which to handle fires
  - preliminary methods to handle spills/leaks with no fires present
  - initial measures for first aid
- ERI can appear on the shipping papers, another document that has the basic description and technical name of the material, or in a guidance book.
  - The Emergency Response Guidebook (ERG) can be offered by motor carriers to assist shippers.
  - Drivers are required to provide ERI to any local, state, or federal authority that responds to or investigates incidents involving hazardous materials.
- Either before or after the basic description, the total quantity of materials, number, and type of packages must appear.
- Packaging types and units of measurement can be abbreviated (e.g., 12 ctns. UN1263, Paint, 3, PG II, 600 lb.).
- The word *waste* must appear before the proper shipping name on the shipping papers/hazardous waste manifest (e.g., UN1090, Waste Acetone, 3, PG II).
- A hazard class or identification number may NOT be used to describe nonhazardous materials.
- A copy or electronic image of shipping papers for nonhazardous materials must be kept by shippers for 2 years after being accepted by the initial carrier.
- A copy or electronic image of shipping papers for hazardous materials must be kept by shippers for 3 years after being accepted by the initial carrier.
- Carrier-only services must keep copies or images of shipping papers for 1 year.
- Always refer to the Code of Federal Regulations, Title 49, Parts 175 – 185, for the complete regulatory requirements to transport hazardous materials.
- Shippers packaging hazardous materials certify that the package is prepared in accordance with the regulations.
- The shipper's signed certification is on the original shipping papers.
- There are some exceptions to having a signed shipper's certification:
  - when shippers are private carriers transporting their own products
  - when the package (e.g., a cargo tank) is provided by the carrier
- Drivers may accept shippers' certifications as long as the package is safe and complies with the HMR.
- Always familiarize yourself with your employer's rules concerning accepting shipments.

- Always look at the shipping papers; familiarize yourself with how to spot a hazardous materials shipment:
    - Do the shipping papers have the proper shipping name, hazard class, and identification number?
    - Are there highlighted entries, or any entries with the letters *X* or *RQ* in the hazardous materials column?
- Other clues can also alert you to the possibility of hazardous materials:
    - What type of business is the shipper in (e.g., paint, explosives, pest control)?
    - Do the shipper's tanks have diamond-shaped labels or placards?
    - Is the package a cylinder or drum? (These are often used to ship hazardous materials.)
    - Does the package have a hazard class label, proper shipping name, or identification number?
    - Does the shipment contain any handling precautions?
- A **Uniform Hazardous Waste Manifest** must be hand-signed and carried with you while transporting hazardous wastes.
- The manifest must include
    - the name of each shipper and carrier,
    - the EPA registration number of each shipper and carrier, and
    - the destination.
- The manifest must be prepared, dated, and signed by the shippers.
- When transporting waste, the manifest should be treated like a shipping paper.
- Waste shipments must only be given to other registered carriers or disposal/treatment facilities.
- Each carrier involved in waste transport must hand-sign the manifest.
- After a waste shipment is delivered, a copy of the manifest should be kept and include
    - all required signatures (including that of the person to whom the waste is delivereD), and
    - all dates, including the delivery date.

Quick Review Question

12. Where must shipping papers that describe hazardous materials be kept?

Hazmat Package Labels

- Diamond-shaped hazard warning labels (see Figure 12.4.) are used by shippers on most hazardous materials packages to inform others that the package is hazardous.

12. Hazardous Materials

- When the label will not fit on the package itself, it can be put on a tag that is securely affixed to the package (e.g., gas cylinders, which could also use tags or decals).

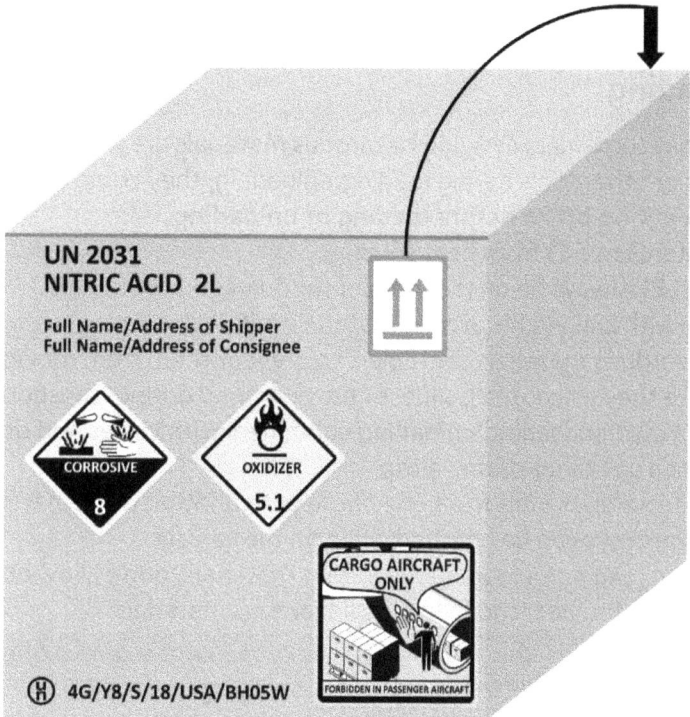

Figure 12.4. Package with Hazmat Labels

- Required markings are printed directly onto the package, an attached label, or a tag.
- The name of the hazardous material is a very important package marking; it is the same name used on the shipping papers.
- Different package sizes and materials have different marking requirements.
- Shippers include the following package markings, as required:
    - the name and address of the shipper or consignee
    - the shipping name and identification number of the hazardous material
    - required labels
- Always compare the shipping papers to the markings and labels:
    - The shipping papers should contain the correct basic description.
    - Make sure the shipper verifies that the proper labels appear on the packages.
    - Ask the shipper to contact your employer's office if you are unfamiliar with the material.
- Packages should contain the following markings, if required:
    - pollutant
    - biohazard
    - hot
    - inhalation hazard
- Packages with liquid-filled containers have orientation markings to indicate the upright direction.
- The product's hazard class is always reflected on the package labels.
- Packages needing more than 1 label must have the additional labels close together and near the proper shipping name.

Quick Review Question

13. What are the required package markings that shippers must include?

Loading and Unloading

- Always ensure that containers carrying hazardous materials are protected.
- Never use hooks or other tools during loading/unloading; they could damage containers.
- **Always set the parking brake before loading or unloading.**
- Load/unload materials away from heat sources.
- LEAKS = TROUBLE! Always be on the lookout for damaged containers.
- Moving a vehicle with leaking hazardous materials is illegal.
- Always brace hazardous materials containers to prevent them from moving during transport.
    - Make sure they will not fall, slide, or move around during transport.
    - Use extra caution loading/unloading containers with valves and other fittings.
    - Never open packages during a trip.
    - Never transfer materials from one package to another while in transport.
    - Only cargo tanks can be emptied while on the vehicle.
- Never smoke when loading/unloading hazardous materials; don't allow others to smoke nearby.
- Never smoke or have fire near the following hazardous materials:
    - Class 1 (explosives)
    - Division 2.1 (flammable gas)
    - Class 3 (flammable liquids)
    - Class 4 (flammable solids)
    - Class 5 (oxidizers)
- Special cargo heater rules are in place for loading the following:
    - **Class 1 (explosives)**
    - **Division 2.1 (flammable gas)**
    - **Class 3 (flammable liquids)**
- **Using cargo heaters, including automatic and heat/AC units, is usually forbidden.**
- Read all related rules before loading these products in cargo spaces with heaters.
- The following materials must be loaded into a closed cargo space with no overhang/tailgate:
    - Class 1 (explosives)
    - Class 4 (flammable solids)
    - Class 5 (oxidizers)
- An EXCEPTION to the list above is packages that are fire and water resistant or covered with a fire- and water-resistant tarp.

Quick Review Question

14. Trailers with heated and/or air-conditioned units should not transport hazardous materials from which 3 hazardous materials classes?

Loading Precautions for Specific Materials

- Precautions are in place for specific hazards:
    - Class 1 (explosives)
    - Class 2 (compressed gases)

12. Hazardous Materials

- Class 4 (flammable solids)
- Class 5 (oxidizers)
- Class 7 (radioactive materials)
- Class 8 (corrosive materials)
- Division 2.3 (poisonous gases)
- Division 6.1 (poisonous materials)

Class 1 (Explosives)
- Turn the engine off before loading/unloading explosives.
- Check the cargo space:
  - Make sure cargo heaters are disabled.
  - Disconnect the drain heater fuel tanks and heater power sources.
- Check that there are no sharp objects that could damage cargo.
- Floor linings must be used with Division 1.1, 1.2, and 1.3 cargo:
  - Make sure the floor linings are tight.
  - **Floor linings cannot be made of metallic or ferrous (iron or iron alloy) materials.**
- Take extra precautions to protect explosives:
  - Never use metal tools or hooks.
  - Never throw, drop, or roll packages.
  - Ensure such packages are safe from cargo that could cause damage.
- Never transfer Division 1.1, 1.2, or 1.3 cargo between vehicles on public roadways.
  - Transfers may be done in emergency situations only.
  - Red warning reflectors, flags, or electric lanterns must be set out if a transfer is needed.
- Damaged explosives packages should never be transported.
- Never accept packages that appear damp and/or have oily stains.
- Never transport Division 1.1 or 1.2 cargo in combination with marked or placarded cargo tanks.
- Never transport Division 1.1 or 1.2 cargo if a vehicle in the combination contains
  - Division 1.1 A (initiating explosives) materials,
  - packages containing Class 7 (radioactive materials) with a "Radioactive Yellow-III" label,
  - Division 2.3 (poisonous gases) Hazard Zone A or B,
  - Division 6.1 (poisonous materials) Hazard Zone A, or
  - hazardous materials on a DOT Spec 106A, 110A tank, or portable tank.

Class 2 (Compressed Gases); Includes Cryogenic Liquids
- Racks inside the vehicle are ideal for holding cylinders.
- **If your vehicle does not have racks, cylinders must be placed on a flat cargo space floor.**
- Cylinders must always be
  - upright,
  - in boxes to prevent them from turning over or in racks fastened to the vehicle, and
  - loaded horizontally (if designed for the relief valve to be in the vapor space).

Class 4 (Flammable Solids) and Class 5 (Oxidizers)
- Class 4 materials are solids.
- They can react spontaneously to water, heat, and/or air.
- Class 4 reactions include fire and explosion.
- Always fully enclose Class 4 and 5 materials in a vehicle or cover them securely.
- Class 4 and 5 materials are dangerous and unstable when wet.
- Always keep Class 4 and 5 materials dry while in transit, loading, and unloading.
- Class 4 and 5 materials must be in vehicles that have sufficient ventilation.

Class 7 (Radioactive Materials)

12. Hazardous Materials

- **The transport index is a number that appears on some Class 7 packages.**
    - The transport index informs you of the degree of control needed during transport.
    - A single vehicle may not exceed a total transport index sum of 50 for all packages.
- Class 7 packages are labeled "Radioactive Yellow-II" or "Radioactive Yellow-III" by the shipper.
- A package's transport index is printed on the label.
- Class 7 packages are surrounded by radiation that passes through nearby packages.
    - For this reason, the number of packages loaded together must be controlled.
    - The proximity of these packages to people, animals, and unexposed film must be controlled.
- See Table 12.6. for guidance on how closely Class 7 materials can be loaded to other things and people.

Table 12.6. Radioactive Separation Table

Total Transport Index	Minimum Distance (in Ft.) from Nearest Undeveloped Film					Minimum Distance from People or Cargo Compartment Partitions
	0–2 hours	2–4 hours	4–8 hours	8–12 hours	Over 12 hours	
None	0	0	0	0	0	0
0.1–1.0	1	2	3	4	5	1
1.1–5.0	3	4	6	8	11	2
5.1–10.0	4	6	9	11	15	3
10.1–20.0	5	8	12	16	22	4
20.1–30.0	7	10	15	20	29	5
30.1–40.0	8	11	17	22	33	6
40.1–50.0	9	12	19	24	36	

Class 8 (Corrosive) Materials

- When hand loading, load breakable containers with corrosive liquids one by one.
- Keep containers with corrosive materials right side up.
- Never drop or roll containers with corrosive materials.
- Always load corrosive material containers onto an even floor surface.
- Only stack carboys if the lower layers can safely hold the weight of the upper layers.
- Never load nitric acid above any other products.
- Charged storage batteries should be kept right side up to prevent spilling.
- Be sure other cargo will not fall against or short-circuit charged storage batteries.
- Corrosive liquids should never be loaded next to or above materials from
    - Division 1.4 (explosives C),
    - Division 4.1 (flammable solids),
    - Division 4.3 (dangerous when wet),
    - Class 5 (oxidizers),
    - Division 2.3, Hazard Zone B (poisonous gases),

12. Hazardous Materials

- Division 4.2 (spontaneously combustible materials), or
- Division 6.1, PGI, Hazard Zone A (poison liquids).

Division 2.3 (Poisonous Gas) or Division 6.1 (Poisonous Materials)

- These materials can never be transported in containers with interconnections.
- Packages labeled "poison" or "poison inhalation hazard" must never be loaded
  - in the driver's cab,
  - in the driver's sleeper, or
  - with food meant for human or animal consumption.
- Special training is needed to load/unload Class 2 materials in cargo tanks.

Quick Review Questions

15. Materials from which class or division can never be transported in containers with interconnections?

16. When is it safe to stack carboys of Class 8 (corrosive) materials?

17. Are stainless steel floor linings required for Division 1.1 or 1.2 materials?

18. What is 1 of the hazard classes that uses transport indexes to determine how much of a material can be loaded in a single vehicle?

Mixed Loads

Some products must be loaded separately (see Table 12.7.).

- The CFR Segregation Table for Hazardous Materials lists additional materials that must be kept separate during transport.

Table 12.7. Items That Cannot Be Loaded Together

Material	Items Material Cannot Be Loaded With
Division 6.1 or 2.3 (poison or material with "Poison Inhalation Hazard" label)	food for human or animal consumption (unless poison is in approved packaging); includes anything that can be swallowed EXCEPT mouthwash, toothpaste, and skin creams
Division 2.3 (poisonous gases) Hazard Zone A or Division 6.1, PGI, Hazard Zone A (poison liquids)	materials from Division 1.1, 1.2, 1.3 (explosives); Division 5.1 (oxidizers); Class 3 (flammable liquids); Class 8 (corrosive liquids); Division 5.2 (organic peroxides); Division 1.5 (blasting agents); Division 2.1 (flammable gases); or Class 4 (flammable solids)
Charged storage batteries	Division 1.1 materials
Class 1 (detonating primers)	any other explosives (except for those in authorized packages/containers)
Division 6.1 (cyanides or cyanide mixtures)	acids, corrosive materials, or other acidic materials that can release hydrocyanic acid (e.g., cyanides, inorganic,

Table 12.7. Items That Cannot Be Loaded Together

Material	Items Material Cannot Be Loaded With
	not otherwise specified, silver cyanide, and sodium cyanide)
Nitric acid (Class 8)	other materials (unless the nitric acid is not loaded on top of or above any other materials)

- The Segregation Table for Hazardous Materials lists materials that must be kept apart during transportation.
    - Such products must not be loaded together in the same cargo space.
    - Radioactive packages labeled "Yellow-II" or "Yellow-III" must not be left near people, animals, or film for longer than shown in the Radioactive Separation Table (Table 12.6.)

Quick Review Question

19. If you are currently transporting 100 lb. of dry silver cyanide and you are given shipping papers for 100 cartons of battery acid, what precautions will you need to take?

Bulk Packaging

- **A cargo tank is a bulk package that is permanently attached to a vehicle.**
    - Cargo tanks stay on vehicles during loading/unloading.
    - The most common cargo tanks are MC306 (liquids) and MC331 (gases).
- **Portable tanks are also bulk packages; they are not permanently attached to a vehicle.**
    - They are taken off the vehicle for loading/unloading.
    - Portable tanks are placed on vehicles for transportation.
    - They must show the name of the owner (or lessee).
    - Portable tanks must display the shipping name and contents on 2 opposite sides.
    - Shipping name letters must be at least 2 in. tall if the capacity is over 1,000 gal.
    - Shipping name letters must be at least 1 in. tall if the capacity is under 1,000 gal.
    - Identification numbers must be visible once the tank is loaded on a vehicle.
    - If the numbers are not visible, they must be placed on both ends and sides of the vehicle.
- Bulk packaging holding at least 1,000 gal. must have identification numbers on each side and each end.
- Bulk packaging holding less than 1,000 gal. must have identification numbers on 2 opposing sides.
- A material's identification number must be displayed on bulk packaging.
- Column 4 of the Hazardous Materials Table shows the identification numbers.
- Rules for bulk packaging markings include the following:
    - Black 100-mm (3.9-in.) numbers must appear on orange panels, on placards, or against a white, diamond-shaped background.
    - Retest date markings must appear on specification cargo tanks.
- Bulk packages not required to have the owner's or shipping name are called intermediate bulk containers (IBCs).
- A qualified person must always supervise the loading/unloading of cargo tanks.
- The person in charge of loading/unloading is responsible for making sure someone is there to supervise.

- The qualified person supervising the loading/unloading must
  - be alert,
  - be able to clearly view the cargo tank,
  - be within 25 ft. of the tank,
  - understand the hazards of the materials being loaded/unloaded,
  - understand the required procedures should an emergency arise, and
  - have the ability to move the cargo tank and the authority to do so.
- Cargo tanks that transport propane and anhydrous ammonia have special attendance rules.
- Before moving hazardous materials tanks, always close all manholes and valves.
  - Close these regardless of the amount in the tank and the distance that the tank is being moved.
  - Closing manholes and valves prevents leaks.
  - **Moving cargo tanks with open valves or manhole covers is illegal.**
- Always shut the engine off before loading/unloading flammable materials.
- The engine should only be run if needed to operate a pump.
- Make sure a cargo tank is grounded correctly before filling it through a fill hole.
- Make sure the tank is grounded before opening the fill hole.
- Be sure the tank remains grounded until after the fill hole is closed.
- Liquid discharge valves on a compressed gas tank should be kept closed (except when loading/unloading).
- Turn off the engine unless it is running a pump for product transfer.
  - If the engine is used, turn it off after the product transfer.
  - It should be turned off before the hose is unhooked.
- Before coupling, uncoupling, or moving a cargo tank, unhook all loading/unloading connections.
- Be sure trailers and semitrailers are chocked to prevent movement after being uncoupled.

Quick Review Questions

20. What is the definition of the term *cargo tank*?

21. How do cargo tanks differ from portable tanks?

22. After a delivery of compressed gas during which your engine runs a pump, when should you turn the engine off: before or after unhooking the hose?

Parking

Parking with Division 1.1, 1.2, or 1.3 Explosives

Never park within 5 ft. of the road when transporting Division 1.1, 1.2, or 1.3 explosives.

- Do not park within 300 ft. of the following EXCEPT for short periods out of necessity (e.g., fueling):
  - bridges, tunnels, or buildings
  - gathering places for people
  - open fire
- Do not park on private property unless the owner understands the danger.
- A parked vehicle must always be watched by the driver; it can only be watched by others if it is
  - on the shipper's property,

- on the carrier's property, or
- on the consignee's property
- Vehicles may be left unattended in a **safe haven**.
  - These are approved places for vehicles carrying explosives.
  - Local authorities typically designate authorized safe havens.

Quick Review Questions

23. What does the term *safe haven* mean as it applies to commercial vehicles?

24. When transporting Division 1.3 materials, how close to the traveled part of the roadway may you park? How close to a tunnel may you park with the same materials?

Parking Placarded Vehicles (Not Transporting Division 1.1, 1.2, or 1.3 Explosives)

Park placarded vehicles without explosives within 5 ft. of the traveled roadway.
- This should be brief.
- Parking this way must only be done if necessary for your work.
- A person must watch the vehicle when it is parked on a roadway or shoulder.
- Never uncouple a trailer with hazardous materials and leave it on a public street.
- Never park within 300 ft. of an open fire.

Quick Review Question

25. When can a placarded vehicle without explosives be parked within 5 ft. of the traveled roadway?

Attending Parked Vehicles and Using Flares

The person authorized to watch a parked vehicle must
- be awake,
- be in the vehicle (not in the sleeper berth),
- be within 100 ft. of the vehicle (if not inside it),
- have a clear view of the vehicle (if not inside it),
- understand and be aware of the hazardous materials in the vehicle,
- understand what to do in the event of an emergency, and
- know how to move the vehicle if needed.
- Never use flares, fusees, or other burning signals for a stopped vehicle that
  - is a tanker—loaded or empty—used for Class 3 (flammable liquids) materials,
  - is carrying Division 2.1 (flammable gases) materials—loaded or empty, or
  - is carrying Division 1.1, 1.2, or 1.3 explosives.

Quick Review Question

26. Flares or fusees can be used for stopped vehicles that carry Division 2.1 materials as long as the vehicle is empty. Is this true or false?

Driving

Route Restrictions

Permits may be required in some jurisdictions when transporting hazardous materials or waste.

- Certain jurisdictions limit allowable routes for transporting hazardous materials or waste.
- The rules about routes and permits change often.
    - You are responsible for knowing whether permits and/or special routes must be used.
    - Always make sure you have all of the necessary paperwork BEFORE driving.
- Ask carrier dispatchers about route restrictions and permits.
- Independent truckers must check with state agencies concerning special routes and permits.
- Be aware that some jurisdictions forbid hazardous materials to be transported
    - through tunnels,
    - over bridges, or
    - over certain other roadways.
- ALWAYS check which permits are needed and any other special rules.
- If the vehicle is placarded, avoid the following and look for alternate routes:
    - areas that are heavily populated
    - crowds
    - narrow streets
    - tunnels
    - alleys
- Placarded vehicles should never be driven near open flames unless you can pass through safely and without stopping.
- Written route plans are required when transporting Division 1.1, 1.2, or 1.3 explosives.
    - Written route plans must be followed.
    - Route plans are prepared by carriers and given to the driver.
- You may plan routes yourself if explosives are picked up someplace other than your employer's terminal.
    - The plan must be written out ahead of time.
    - The plan must be kept on you while transporting explosives.
- Shipments of explosives can only be delivered to authorized people or left in locked rooms designed to store such materials.
- The safest route must be selected for transporting placarded radioactive materials.
    - The carrier must inform you about the radioactive materials.
    - The carrier must show you the route plan to transport radioactive materials.

Quick Review Questions

27. How can independent truck drivers determine if special routes or permits are required?

28. Are there any situations in which placarded vehicles can be driven near open flames?

Smoking, Refueling, and Fire Extinguishers

Never carry or smoke anything within 25 ft. of vehicles carrying the following materials:

- Class 1 (explosives)
- Class 3 (flammable liquids)

- o Class 5 (oxidizers)
- o Division 2.1 (gases)
- o Division 4.1 (flammable solids)
- o Division 4.2 (spontaneously combustible materials)
- Always shut off the engine when refueling vehicles with hazardous materials.
- Make sure someone remains at the nozzle and controls the fuel flow.
- Power units of placarded vehicles are required to have extinguishers with **UL ratings of 10 B:C or greater**.

Quick Review Questions

29. Which hazard classes require that you never smoke around them?

30. Placarded vehicles must carry which type of fire extinguisher?

Checking Tires

Always be sure that tires are properly inflated.

- **Examine each tire (including dual tires),**
    - o **at the start of every trip, and**
    - o **each time you park the vehicle.**
- Using a tire pressure gauge is the only acceptable way to check pressure.
- Never drive with tires that are leaking or flat (except to the nearest safe area to fix them).
- Remove any tires that have overheated.
    - o Place overheated tires a safe distance from the vehicle.
    - o Correct the cause of the overheated tire before driving again.
- The rules about parking and attending placarded vehicles also apply to
    - o checking tires,
    - o repairing tires, and
    - o replacing tires.

Quick Review Questions

31. What is the only acceptable way to check tire pressure?

32. How often should dual tires on a placarded trailer be checked?

Shipping Papers, Emergency Response Information, and Special Equipment

The following information is IN ADDITION TO the guidance above concerning shipping papers:

Papers for Division 1.1, 1.2, and 1.3 Explosives

- Carriers must give drivers of these materials a copy of FMCSR[2] Part 397 and written instructions on what to do if delayed or in an accident.
- Written instructions must include
    - o names and phone numbers of contact persons, including carriers and shippers;

---

[2] Federal Motor Carrier Safety Regulations

12. Hazardous Materials

- o an account of which types of explosives are being transported; and
- o precautions that must be taken in emergencies.
- Drivers are required to sign receipts for the above-mentioned documents.
- Drivers must possess and be familiar with
    - o shipping papers,
    - o written instructions for emergencies,
    - o written route plans, and
    - o the FMCSR, Part 397.

Special Equipment for Transporting Chlorine

- Drivers transporting chlorine must have the following:
    - o approved gas masks in the vehicle
    - o an emergency kit to control leaks in a cargo tank's dome cover plate fittings

Quick Review Question

33. What must be included on written instructions for drivers of Division 1.1, 1.2, and 1.3 explosives?

Railroad Crossings

Always stop BEFORE a railroad crossing if

- o **your vehicle is placarded,**
- o **you are transporting any amount of chlorine, or**
- o **your vehicle has cargo tanks for hazardous materials (empty or not).**
- Always stop 15 – 50 ft. BEFORE the nearest rail.
- Start driving ONLY when you are certain there are no oncoming trains.
- Start driving ONLY when you can clear the tracks without having to stop.
- Never shift gears while crossing railroad tracks.

Quick Review Question

34. Do you need to stop before a railroad crossing if you are hauling 100 lb. of materials that are dangerous when wet (Division 4.3)?

Emergencies Involving Hazardous Materials

- The Emergency Response Guidebook is published by the United States Department of Transportation (USDOT).
    - o It informs workers about how to protect themselves and others from hazardous materials.
    - o It is indexed by proper shipping name and identification numbers, since these are what emergency personnel look for.
- You have certain responsibilities in the event of emergency incidents:
    - o Make sure people are kept away from the scene.
    - o Limit the spread of material (if it can be done safely).
    - o Alert emergency personnel to the danger of the material(s).
    - o Give responders the shipping papers and emergency response information.
- The following checklist should be followed in the event of an incident:

- Make sure your driving partner is OK.
- Be sure the shipping papers are kept with you.
- Keep others upwind and far away.
- Warn others about the danger.
- Call for assistance.

Quick Review Question

35. If an incident involving hazardous materials occurs, what are the checklist items that you should follow?

Fires

Minor truck fires may need to be controlled on the road.

- Hazardous materials fires require training and equipment.
- Do not fight hazardous materials fires if you are not trained and equipped.
- Protective gear is needed to fight hazardous materials fires.
- Call for help as soon as you notice a fire.
- Extinguishers may be used to prevent fires from spreading to cargo before help arrives.
- Do not open trailer doors that are hot; they could signal a cargo fire.
- Air makes fires flare up; do not open doors.
- Many fires smolder without air, causing less damage.
- Do not fight cargo fires; it is unsafe.
- Always keep shipping papers on you.
- Warn others about the fire and keep them away.

Quick Review Question

36. Why should doors not be opened during a fire?

Leaks

Use shipping papers, labels, or package location to identify what is leaking.

- **NEVER touch leaking materials.**
- Do not rely on smell to identify or find the source of a leak.
- Gases that are toxic
  - may not have a smell,
  - can destroy your sense of smell, and
  - can injure and/or kill you.
- NEVER eat, drink, or smoke near a leak or spill.
- Never move a vehicle with spilled or leaking materials unless required to do so for safety.
  - Moving off the road and away from gathering places is allowed for safety purposes.
  - Never move the vehicle if it could hurt you or others.
- STOP DRIVING if hazardous materials are leaking from your vehicle.
  - This includes driving to a phone and/or to find help.
  - Carriers pay for cleanup: lengthy contamination trails cost a fortune.
- **Follow these steps if hazardous materials are leaking from your vehicle:**
  - Park the vehicle.

12. Hazardous Materials

- Secure the area.
- Stay where you are.
- **Call or send someone for help.**
- The person who calls for help needs to know
  - how to describe the emergency,
  - the exact location and direction of travel,
  - your name,
  - the name of the carrier,
  - the name of the location where your terminal is located,
  - the proper shipping name,
  - the hazard class, and
  - the identification number.
- This information should be written down and given to the person seeking help.
- Having this information allows responders to find you and bring the needed equipment.

Quick Review Question

37. If you have no access to a phone and notice that the hazardous materials you are transporting are slowly leaking from the vehicle, what should you do?

Required Notification

The National Response Center aids in coordinating emergency responses to chemical hazards.

- It maintains a 24-hour toll-free line: **(800) 424-8802**.
- The center serves as a resource for police and firefighters.
- You or your employer must call the center if any of the following takes place as a result of a hazardous materials incident:
  - Someone is killed.
  - Someone is injured and requires hospitalization.
  - Property damage could exceed $50,000.
  - The general public needs to be evacuated for more than 1 hour.
  - At least 1 transportation artery or facility must be closed for 1 hour or more.
  - Breakage, spillage, fire, or suspected radioactive contamination takes place.
  - Breakage, spillage, fire, or suspected infectious substance contamination happens.
  - More than 119 gal. of liquid marine pollutants are released.
  - More than 882 lb. of solid marine pollutants are released.
  - A continuing danger to life or similar situation exists that the carrier deems reportable.
- When calling the National Response Center, be prepared to share the following:
  - the name of the person calling
  - the name and address of the carrier
  - the phone number where the caller or carrier can be reached
  - the location, date, and time of the incident
  - the extent of any injuries
  - the classification, name, and quantity of materials involved
  - the type of incident and nature of the involved materials
  - whether a continuing danger to life is present
  - for reportable quantities: the name of the shipper and the quantity of the discharged substance

12. Hazardous Materials

- The information listed above should also be given to your employer.
- Carriers involved in incidents must submit detailed, written reports within 30 days.
- The Chemical and Transportation Emergency Center (**CHEMTREC**)
  - provides responders with technical information concerning a material's physical properties;
  - has a 24-hour toll-free line: **(800) 424-9300**; and
  - coordinates closely with the National Response Center.
- If you call CHEMTREC, they will alert the National Response Center.
- If you call the National Response Center, they will alert CHEMTREC.

Quick Review Question

38. Under what circumstances must you or your employer call the National Response Center?

Emergency Responses to Specific Materials

Class 1 (Explosives)

Warn others of the danger if your vehicle breaks down/has an accident while carrying these.

- Ensure bystanders are kept away from your vehicle.
- Never allow smoking or open flames near the vehicle.
- If there is a fire, alert those around you to the possibility of explosion.
- In a collision, remove all explosives before separating the involved vehicles.
- Explosives should be kept at least 200 ft. from vehicles and occupied buildings.
- Maintain a safe physical distance from the explosives.

Quick Review Question

39. How far away should explosives be kept from vehicles and occupied buildings?

Class 2 (Compressed Gases)

Warn others about the danger if compressed gas leaks from your vehicle.

- Only those allowed to remove the hazard or wreckage are allowed to be close to the vehicle.
- Notify the shipper if any accidents involve compressed gas.
- Do not transfer flammable gas from tank to tank on a public road unless
  - you are fueling machinery, and/or
  - the gas is to be used in road construction or maintenance.

Quick Review Question

40. In the event of an emergency incident, who is allowed to be close to a vehicle transporting Class 2 materials?

Class 3 (Flammable Liquids)

Prevent bystanders from gathering near your vehicle if you have an accident or breakdown.

- Warn others of the danger.
- Do not allow anyone to smoke or have open flames nearby.

- Leaking cargo tanks should never be transported farther than needed to reach safety.
- In the event of a leak, safely leave the roadway if it is possible.
- Unless it is an emergency, never transfer flammable liquids between vehicles on public roadways.

Quick Review Question

41. How far can a leaking cargo tank be transported?

Class 4 (Flammable Solids) and Class 5 (Oxidizing Materials)

Others must be warned of the fire hazard if these materials spill.

- Never open packages of flammable solids that are smoldering.
    - It is better to remove these packages if you can safely do so.
    - If it will decrease the fire hazard, remove unbroken packages too.

Quick Review Question

42. How should smoldering packages be handled?

Class 6 (Poisonous Materials and Infectious Substances)

Many products in the poison class can also be flammable.

- It is your responsibility to protect others from harm from these materials.
- Take necessary precautions if you suspect that the following are flammable:
    - Division 2.3 (poison gases)
    - Division 6.1 (poison materials)
- Never allow smoking, open flames, or welding near these materials.
- Warn others of the following hazards with these materials:
    - fire
    - vapor inhalation
    - coming into contact with the poisonous material
- Vehicles involved in leaks with poison must be checked for stray poison before being used again.
- If Division 6.2 (infectious substances) packages are damaged during handling or transport,
    - contact your supervisor right away, and
    - never accept packages that are damaged or show signs of leakage.

Quick Review Question

43. Before being driven again, what needs to be done with vehicles that were involved in leaks of Class 6 materials?

Class 7 (Radioactive Materials)

Dispatchers or supervisors must be notified immediately if these materials are leaking or in broken packages.

- Do not touch or inhale any materials involved in a spill or whose container is damaged.
- The vehicle cannot be used until it is cleaned and passes inspection with a survey meter.

Quick Review Question

44. For vehicles involved in leaks of Class 7 materials, what must happen before the vehicle can be put back in service?

Class 8 (Corrosive Materials)

Handle containers with spilled or leaking corrosives carefully to prevent injury.

- Use water to wash vehicle parts that have been exposed to corrosive materials.
- Wash the vehicle's interior after unloading as soon as possible before reloading.
- Leave the road if transporting leaking corrosives would be unsafe.
- If you can do so safely, contain any material that is leaking from the vehicle.
- Prevent bystanders from coming near the material and its fumes.
- Do whatever you can do to prevent injuring yourself and/or others.

Quick Review Question

45. What should be used to wash vehicle parts that have been exposed to spilled or leaking Class 8 materials?

Answer Key

1. Hazardous materials are those which pose a risk to safety, health, and property during transport.

2. Shippers package materials so that they can communicate any risks associated with the materials.

3. Drivers must make sure that all shipping papers and emergency response information are stored properly.

4. Yes. An exception to certifying the shipping papers is if the cargo tanks are supplied by you or your employer.

5. Carriers are responsible for 1) taking a shipment from the shipper to the destination, 2) checking that the shipper prepared the shipment correctly, and 3) making the decision to refuse shipments that have been improperly prepared.

6. There are 9 hazardous materials classes.

7. Drivers placard their vehicles in order to warn others about a hazardous materials risk.

8. In order to determine whether you need placards, you must know 1) the hazard class of the material, 2) the amount that is being shipped, and 3) the total amount of all hazardous materials of all classes that you are transporting.

9. The hazardous materials identification number must appear on placards and either on orange panels or white square-on-point displays of equal size to the placards.

10. Column 1 of the Hazardous Materials Table includes the shipping description and mode.

11. The abbreviation *RQ* stands for "reportable quantity." The spilling of any material that has the letters *RQ* on its packaging must be reported to the United States Department of Transportation (DOT) and the United States Environmental Protection Agency (EPA).

12. Shipping papers that describe hazardous materials must be kept in a place where they can be quickly and easily located by you and/or emergency personnel; these places are 1) in a pouch on the driver's side door, 2) in clear view and within immediate reach while you are buckled in, or 3) on the driver's seat (when you are out of the vehicle).

13. The required package markings that shippers must include are the name and address of the shipper (or consignee), the shipping name and identification number of the hazardous material, and required labels.

14. It is usually forbidden to use cargo heaters, including automatic and heat/air-conditioning units, when transporting the following hazardous materials classes: 1) Class 1 (explosives), 2) Division 2.1 (flammable gas), and 3) Class 3 (flammable liquids).

15. Materials from Division 2.3 (poisonous gas) or Division 6.1 (poisonous materials) can never be transported in containers with interconnections.

16. Carboys of Class 8 (corrosive) materials can only be stacked if the lower layers can safely hold the weight of the upper layers.

17. While floor linings are required for Division 1.1, 1.2, and 1.3 cargo, they cannot be made of metallic and/or ferrous (iron or iron alloy) materials.

18. Some Class 7 packages use transport indexes to determine how much of a material can be loaded in a single vehicle.

19. You should not load battery acid with dry silver cyanide since it could release hydrocyanic acid. If asked to transport both, you should refuse to do so and inform your supervisor of the situation.

20. A cargo tank is a bulk package that is permanently attached to a vehicle; it stays on vehicles during loading/unloading.

21. Portable tanks are bulk packages that are not permanently attached to a vehicle; they are taken off for loading/unloading.

22. The engine should be turned off before the hose is unhooked and after the product is transferred/delivered. Unless the engine is running the pump to transfer product, it should be turned off.

23. A safe haven is an approved place where vehicles carrying explosives may be left unattended. Safe havens are typically authorized by local authorities.

24. When transporting Division 1.2 or 1.3 materials (explosives), you should never park within 5 ft. of the road or within 300 ft. of bridges, tunnels, buildings, gathering places, or open fires.

25. A placarded vehicle without explosives can be parked within 5 ft. of the traveled roadway only when doing so is necessary for the driver's work.

26. This is false. Flares or fusees can never be used for Division 2.1 materials—even if the vehicle is empty.

27. Independent truckers must check with state agencies concerning special routes and permits.

28. Placarded vehicles can only be driven near open flames if you are certain that the vehicle can pass through safely and without stopping.

29. The following hazard classes require that you never smoke around them: Class 1 (explosives), Class 3 (flammable liquids), Class 5 (oxidizers), Division 2.1 (gases), Division 4.1 (flammable solids), Division 4.2 (spontaneously combustible materials).

30. Placarded vehicles must carry extinguishers with UL ratings of 10 B:C or greater.

31. A tire pressure gauge is the only acceptable way to check tire pressure.

32. Dual tires on a placarded trailer should be checked at the start of every trip and each time the trailer is parked.

33. Written instructions for drivers of Division 1.1, 1.2, and 1.3 explosives must include the names and phone numbers of contact persons, including carriers and shippers; an account of which types of explosives are being transported; and the precautions that must be taken in emergencies.

34. Since vehicles transporting Division 4.3 materials require placards, you must stop before a railroad crossing.

35. If an incident involving hazardous materials occurs, you should ensure that your driving partner is OK, ensure that the shipping papers are with you, ensure that others are kept far away and upwind from the incident, warn others about the danger, and call for assistance.

36. Since air makes fires flare up, doors should not be opened during a fire.

37. Unless required for safety (e.g., to move away from people), you should never move a vehicle that is leaking materials. After parking the vehicle and securing the area, stay where you are. If you do not have access to a phone, you should send someone for help. The person you send for help must be able to describe the emergency and must know your exact location and direction of travel, your and the carrier's names, where your terminal is located, the proper shipping name, the hazard class, and the identification number.

12. Hazardous Materials

38. You or your employer must call the National Response Center if one of the following happens as the result of a hazardous materials incident: someone is killed; someone is injured and requires hospitalization; property damage could exceed $50,000; the general public needs to be evacuated for more than 1 hour; at least 1 transportation artery or facility must be closed for 1 hour or more; breakage, spillage, fire, or suspected radioactive contamination takes place; breakage, spillage, fire, or suspected infectious substance contamination happens; more than 119 gal. of liquid marine pollutants are released; more than 882 lb. of solid marine pollutants are released; there is a continuing danger to life; and/or a similar situation exists that the carrier deems reportable.

39. Explosives should be kept at least 200 ft. from vehicles and occupied buildings.

40. In the event of an emergency incident, only those allowed to remove the hazard or wreckage are allowed to be close to a vehicle carrying Class 2 materials.

41. Leaking cargo tanks should never be transported farther than is needed to reach safety.

42. Smoldering packages from Class 4 and Class 5 materials should never be opened; they should be removed if it is safe to do so, and unbroken packages should also be removed if the fire hazard will be decreased.

43. Before being driven again, vehicles involved in leaks with poison must be checked for stray poison.

44. Vehicles involved in leaks of Class 7 materials must be cleaned and pass inspection with a survey meter before they can be used again.

45. Water should be used to wash vehicle parts that have been exposed to spilled or leaking Class 8 materials.

13 | School Bus

Danger Zones

- The area on all sides of the bus where children have the highest likelihood of being struck is called the **danger zone**.
- Danger zones
    - extend up to 30 ft. from the front bumper (the first 10 ft. are the most dangerous),
    - extend 10 ft. from the left and right sides of the bus, and
    - extend 10 ft. behind the bus's rear bumper.
- Because of passing cars, **the area to the left of the bus is always dangerous**.

> **Helpful Hint:**
> Local and state laws regulate many school transportation options and vary widely. It is critical to be aware of and understand the regulations where you will be driving.

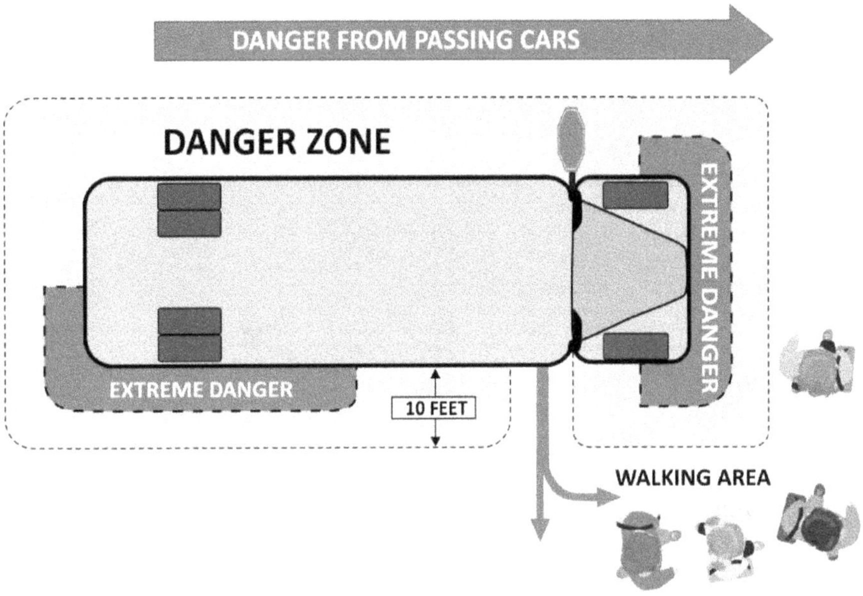

Figure 13.1. School Bus Danger Zones

Quick Review Question

1. What is the danger zone, and how far should it extend around the bus?

Mirrors

Adjusting Mirrors

- Safe school bus operation depends on properly adjusting and using all mirrors:
    - You should be able to see the danger zones around the bus.
    - You should be able to notice traffic, students, and other objects.
    - Always check each mirror BEFORE operating the bus; adjust as needed.
    - Make sure the maximum viewing area is visible.

Right Side Flat and Outside Left Mirrors

- Right side flat and outside left mirrors are mounted
    - at the side or front of the windshield, and
    - at the left and right front corners of the bus.
- These mirrors serve 3 purposes:
    1. to monitor traffic
    2. to check clearances at the sides and rear of the bus
    3. to check for students at the sides and rear of the bus
- These mirrors have blind spots:
    - One is immediately below and in front of each mirror.
    - Another is directly in back of the rear bumper.
    - Behind the bus, a blind spot can extend 50 – 400 ft. depending on the bus's length and width.
- **These mirrors must be adjusted to allow you to see**
    - **200 ft. or 4 bus lengths behind the bus,**
    - **along the sides of the bus, and**
    - **the rear tires making contact with the ground.**

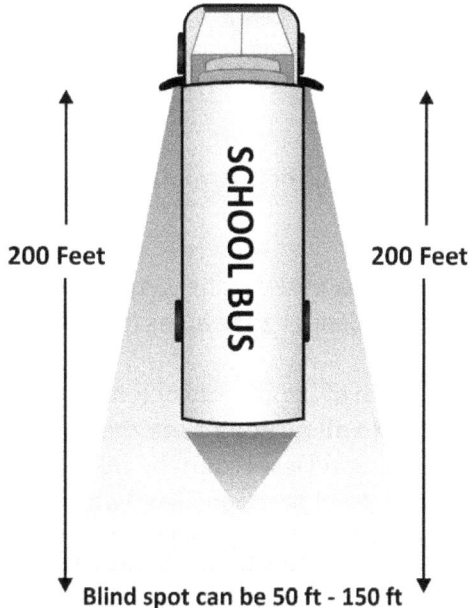

Figure 13.2. School Bus Flat Mirrors

Outside Left and Right Side Convex Mirrors

- Convex mirrors are found below the outside flat mirrors.

- They monitor the left and right sides of the bus at a wide angle.
- They offer a view of traffic, clearances, and students at the side of the bus.
- They distort the actual size of people and objects and their distances from the bus.
- **These types of mirrors should be positioned so as to allow you to see**
    - **the entire side of the bus (up to the mirror mounts),**
    - **the front of the rear tires making contact with the ground, and**
    - **a minimum of 1 traffic lane on either side.**

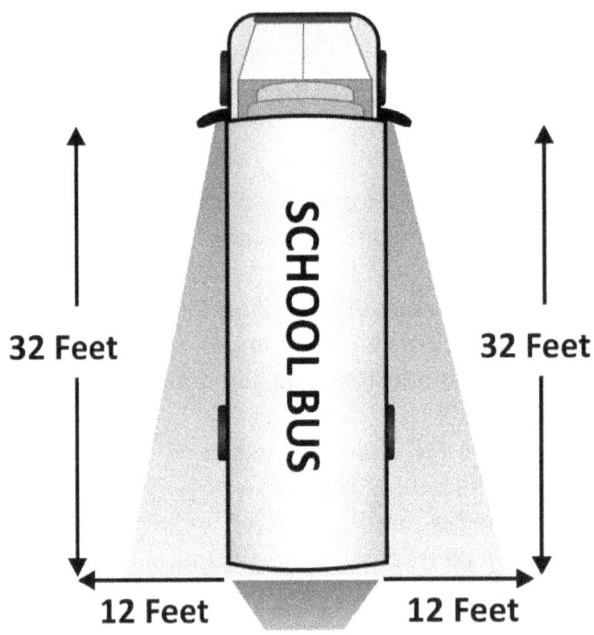

Figure 13.3. School Bus Convex Mirrors

Outside Left and Right Side Crossover Mirrors

- Outside left and right side crossover mirrors are mounted on both the left and right front corners of the bus.
- They are used to
    - observe the danger zone area of the front bumper, and
    - view the left and right side danger zone areas (including the service door and front wheel area).
- These mirrors distort the actual size of people and objects and their distance from the bus.
- **These mirrors must be adjusted to allow you to see the entire area in front of the bus:**
    - You must be able to see ground level from the front bumper.
    - You must be able to see a point at ground level where direct vision is possible.
    - There should be overlap between the direct vision and mirror-view vision.
    - You must also be able to see the front left and right tires touching the ground.
    - You must be able to see the area extending from the front of the bus to the service door.

- View crossover, convex, and flat mirrors in a logical sequence to make sure children or objects are not in danger zones.

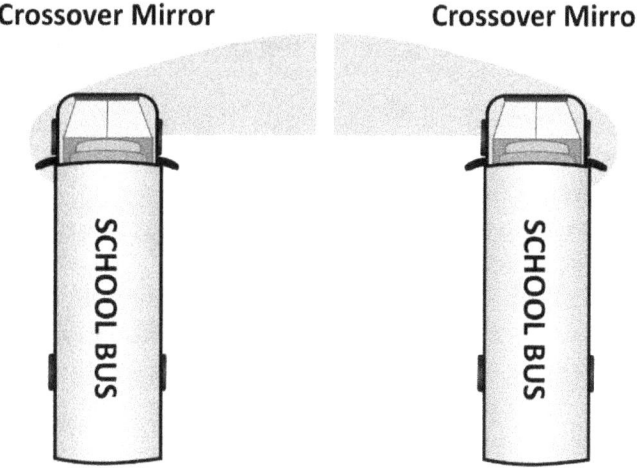

Figure 13.4. School Bus Crossover Mirrors

Overhead Inside Rearview Mirror

- The overhead inside rearview mirror is on the driver's side area of the bus, mounted directly above the windshield.
- It is used to observe passenger activity inside the bus.
- If the bus has a glass-bottomed rear emergency door, this mirror can offer limited visibility behind the bus.
- These mirrors have 2 blind spot areas:
    1. right behind the driver's seat
    2. beginning at the rear bumper and extending up to at least 400 ft. behind the bus
- Always use exterior side mirrors to check for traffic in areas with blind spots.
- The overheard inside rearview mirror should be positioned in such a way as to allow you to see
    - the top of the rear window in the top of the mirror, and
    - all students/passengers, including the heads of those directly behind you.

Quick Review Questions

2. When the outside flat mirrors are properly adjusted, what should you be able to see?

3. When the outside convex mirrors are properly adjusted, what should you be able to see?

4. When the crossover mirrors are properly adjusted, what should you be able to see?

Loading Students

Student fatalities are greater while getting on or off a bus than while riding inside one; it is imperative to know what to do before, after, and during student loading/unloading. The guidance which follows for loading and unloading students is not definitive: **always learn and understand local laws and regulations**.

- All bus stops and routes should be approved by the school district.
- Never change a bus stop location without prior written approval from district officials.

13. School Bus

- Approach all bus stops with extreme caution: these are demanding situations.
- You must understand all state and local regulations that concern approaching a bus stop:
    - the proper use of mirrors
    - alternating flashing lights
    - moveable stop signal and crossing control arms (if equippeD)
- When **approaching a stop**
    - use a slow speed and approach the stop cautiously;
    - check for pedestrians, traffic, and objects before, during, and after stopping;
    - check all mirrors constantly;
    - **activate any flashing amber warning lights at least 200 ft. (or about 5 – 10 seconds) before the stop, as required by law;**
    - about 100 – 300 ft. (3 – 5 seconds) before pulling over, turn on the right turn signal;
    - keep checking mirrors regularly to monitor danger zones; and
    - move as far to the right of the traveled portion of the roadway as you can.
- Follow these steps when **stopping the bus:**
    - Bring the bus to a complete stop.
    - Make sure the front bumper is a minimum of 10 ft. from students at the stop.
    - The 10-ft. buffer forces students to walk to the bus, ensuring that you can see them.
    - Put the transmission in "park."
    - If a "park" shift point does not exist, put the transmission in "neutral."
    - Always set the parking brake at each stop.
    - Ensure the stop arm is extended when traffic is at a safe distance from the bus.
    - Turn on the alternating red lights when traffic is at a safe distance from the bus.
    - Be sure that all traffic has stopped BEFORE opening the door and allowing students on.
- **Loading procedures** are as follows:
    - Stop safely (as described above).
    - Make sure students know to wait in a designated location, facing the bus.
    - Be sure that students only load the bus when signaled to do so by you.
    - Continuously monitor all mirrors.
    - Count the number of students at the bus stop; make sure they all board.
    - Try to learn the students' names; it will make it easier to ask about a missing student.
    - Make sure students board the bus slowly.
    - Students should board in single file and use the handrail.
    - If it is dark, ensure that the dome light is on.
    - Do not move the bus until students are seated and facing forward.
    - Check all mirrors: be certain that no one is running to catch the bus.
- If a student outside the bus cannot be accounted for inside the bus,
    - make sure the bus is secure,
    - take the key with you,
    - check all around the bus, and
    - check underneath the bus.
- When you have accounted for all of the students, you may prepare to leave:
    - Close the door.
    - Engage the transmission.
    - Release the parking brake.
    - Turn the alternating flashing red lights off.
    - Put the left turn signal on.
    - Check all of the mirrors.

13. School Bus

- - Let congested traffic disperse first.
  - Move the bus, enter traffic, and continue the route when it is safe to do so.
- These steps are usually the same wherever students are loaded, except on the school's campus.
- When loading students at a school's campus,
  - turn off the ignition switch,
  - remove the key (if you are leaving the driver's compartment), and
  - position yourself so that you can supervise loading as required by local regulations.

Quick Review Question

5. When should the alternating flashing amber warning lights be activated along a route?

Unloading Students

Unloading on the Route

- **Unloading** procedures are as follows:
  - Stop safely (as described above).
  - Ensure students remain seated until told to exit.
  - Check all mirrors.
  - Confirm students' locations by counting how many are unloading before pulling away.
  - **Inform students to exit and walk at least 10 ft. from the side of the bus.**
  - After they leave the bus, you should be able to clearly see the students.
  - Check all mirrors again: there should be no students around or returning to the bus.
  - Account for all students.
  - If not all students are accounted for, secure the bus, take the key, and check all sides of the bus and beneath it.
- After all unloaded students have been accounted for, prepare to leave:
  - Close the door.
  - Engage the transmission.
  - Release the parking brake.
  - Turn the alternating flashing red lights off.
  - Turn on the left turn signal.
  - Check all mirrors again.
  - Let congested traffic disperse first.
  - Move the bus, enter traffic, and continue the route when it is safe to do so.
- If you miss a student's unloading stop, DO NOT BACK UP; follow local procedures.
- Additional procedures exist for students who must cross roadways after unloading.
- It is important to remember that students may not always do as they are told.
- Students who must cross roadways after exiting the bus should
  - **keep away from the bus while walking to a place at least 10 ft. in front of the bumper's right corner, and**
  - **position themselves so that the you can see them,**
  - stop at the roadway's edge so that you can see their feet.
- After students reach the roadway's edge, they should
  - stop, look in all directions, and ensure the roadway is clear and safe;
  - make sure that the red flashing lights are still flashing; and
  - wait for your signal before crossing the roadway.
- Once you signal that students can cross the road, students should

- - - cross in front of the bus, far enough away that you can see them;
    - stop at the left edge of the bus and look for your signal to cross;
    - check for traffic in all directions and make sure the roadway is clear; and
    - cross the roadway while continuing to check in all directions for safety.
  - You should enforce applicable local regulations regarding student actions outside the bus.

Unloading at School

- Unloading at a school differs from unloading students on a route.
- You must familiarize yourself with and understand local regulations.
- Follow these steps when unloading at a school:
  - Stop safely (as described above).
  - Turn the ignition switch off.
  - Remove the key (if exiting the driver's compartment).
  - Ensure students remain seated until given the signal to exit.
  - Ensure you are positioned to supervise unloading (as required by local regulations).
  - Prompt students to exit in an orderly fashion.
  - Make sure all exiting students promptly leave the unloading area.
  - Do a walk-through of the bus: look for hiding/sleeping students and forgotten items.
  - Check all mirrors: ensure that no students are returning to the bus.
  - Account for all students.
  - If students are unaccounted for, secure the bus, take the key, and check all sides of and beneath the bus.
- After all students have been accounted for, you may prepare to leave:
  - Close the door.
  - Fasten your safety belt.
  - Start the engine.
  - Engage the transmission.
  - Release the parking brake.
  - Turn the alternating flashing red lights off.
  - Put the left turn signal on.
  - Check all mirrors.
  - Allow congested traffic to disperse first.
  - Pull away from the unloading area when it is safe to do so.

Special Loading and Unloading Dangers

- Students may drop or forget belongings:
  - Always watch students as they approach the bus.
  - Be aware of any students who disappear from your sight.
- Students may attempt to retrieve items dropped near a bus:
  - They may stop to pick an item up or return to the bus; this is extremely dangerous.
  - Stopping or returning to the bus may prevent you from seeing the students.
- Instruct students to leave any dropped items and move away from danger zones.
- Instruct students to try to get your attention in order to retrieve the items.
- Getting clothing, accessories, or body parts caught on handrails or in doors can be fatal.
- Closely watch all students as they exit.
- Make sure students are in a safe location before moving the bus.

Inspecting the Bus After the Trip

- Always conduct an inspection after your route or school activity is done.

- **Do a walk-through and be on the lookout for the following:**
    - items left on the bus
    - students who are sleeping or hiding
    - doors and windows that are open
    - damage
    - vandalism
- Also check for any mechanical or operational issues, including issues with
    - mirror systems,
    - flashing warning lamps, or
    - stop signal alarms.
- Report issues or special situations to supervisors or school authorities immediately.

> **Did You Know?**
>
> The school bus endorsement is separate from the passenger endorsement; you must earn the

Quick Review Questions

6. After you unload students along the route, where should they walk after exiting the bus?

7. Why should you do a walk-through of the bus after unloading students at school?

8. Before crossing a roadway, in what position should students be while they are in front of the bus?

Emergency Exit and Evacuation

- No one is immune from the various emergency situations that can arise.
- Understanding what to do before, after, and during emergencies is imperative.
- Recognizing a hazard is the first and foremost consideration.
- Call your dispatcher (if time permits) BEFORE evacuating to explain the situation:
    - A decision can be made whether it is best to evacuate the bus or not.
    - **It is generally best to keep students on the bus, if possible.**
    - The decision to evacuate must be made quickly.
- Consider the following when deciding to evacuate:
    - Is there a fire or an imminent danger of one?
    - Do you smell raw or leaking fuel?
    - Could the bus be struck by other vehicles?
    - Is the bus in the path of rising waters or a confirmed tornado?
    - Are downed power lines nearby?
    - If students are evacuated, will they be exposed to dangerous traffic or other conditions?
    - If students are evacuated, would moving them exacerbate any sustained injuries?
    - Is a hazardous spill involved? (It may be safer to remain on the bus.)
- **Always be prepared and plan ahead.**
    - If possible, assign older, responsible students to each emergency exit.
    - Teach these students how to help their peers off the bus.
    - Assign another student the duty of helping others reach a "safe place" after evacuating.
- Always explain emergency procedures to all students:
    - There may not be any who are old enough to help.
    - The students should know how to operate all emergency exits.

- Explain to the students the importance of following your instructions.
  - A **"safe place"** must be determined:
    - **It should be at least 100 ft. off the road.**
    - It should be in the direction of oncoming traffic.
    - If there is a fire, lead the students upwind.
    - Lead the students as far as possible from railroad tracks but in the direction of any oncoming trains.
    - If there is a spilled hazardous materials risk, lead the students at least 300 ft. upwind from the bus.
  - When evacuating due to a sighted tornado, find shelter in a building, if possible.
  - If sheltering in a building is not possible
    - bring the students to the nearest safe ditch or culvert,
    - instruct the students to lay face down,
    - tell the students to cover their heads with their hands, and
    - make sure the safe place is far enough away to prevent the bus from falling on anyone.
  - Always avoid areas that are prone to flash flooding.

General Evacuation Procedures

- **In some instances, evacuating a bus is mandatory:**
  - when the bus is on fire or a fire is imminent
  - when the bus is stalled on or adjacent to a highway-rail crossing
  - when the position of the bus could change, increasing danger
  - if a collision is imminent
  - when a hazardous materials spill requires passengers to evacuate quickly
- As with unloading and loading, procedures exist for safely evacuating.
- Secure the bus:
  - Put the transmission in park (or neutral if there is no shift point).
  - Set the parking brakes.
  - Shut the engine off.
  - Remove the ignition key.
  - Activate the hazard warning lights.
- Alert the dispatch office (if time allows).
  - Inform them of your evacuation location.
  - Describe the conditions.
  - Describe the type of assistance needed.
- If the radio microphone works, dangle it from the driver's side window.
  - This is so you can use it later.
  - If there is no working radio, ask a passing motorist or resident to call for help.
  - Dispatch two older, responsible students—this should be done as a last resort.
- Order the evacuation and evacuate the students.
- For students who may have sustained neck or spinal injuries
  - to prevent further injury, avoid moving them,
  - only move them if their lives are in imminent danger, and
  - be aware of special procedures to move students with such injuries.
- Instruct any student assistants to lead their peers to the nearest safe space.
- Do a walk-through of the bus:
  - Make sure no students are still on the bus.
  - Grab any emergency equipment.

- Join the students who are waiting.
- Account for all students and check their safety.
- Set out appropriate emergency warning devices to protect the scene.
- Prepare any information needed for emergency responders.

Quick Review Questions

9. What are the conditions under which a school bus must be evacuated?

10. Where should a working radio microphone be placed in the event of an evacuation?

Railroad Crossings

Please review the railroad crossing information discussed in Chapter 2. You must have a solid understanding of that information as well as the information in this section.

- Regulations concerning how school buses operate at highway-rail crossings vary by state; you must understand and obey all state laws and regulations.
- Generally, buses must stop at all crossings and ensure that it is safe to cross before doing so.
- Despite the overall safety of school buses, they are no match for a collision with a train.
    - The size and weight of trains prevents them from being able to stop quickly.
    - There are no emergency escape routes when dealing with a train.

The following procedures aim to prevent collisions with school buses and trains:

- Approach the crossing slowly:
    - Shift into a lower gear (in a manual transmission bus).
    - Test your brakes.
    - **Turn your hazard lights on about 200 ft. before the crossing.**
    - Make your intentions known.
    - Do a scan of your surroundings; check if there is traffic behind you.
    - If possible, stay to the right of the roadway.
- When you reach the crossing
    - **do not stop closer than 15 ft. from the nearest rail or more than 50 ft. from the nearest rail** (this will give you the best view of the tracks),
    - put the transmission in park (or neutral if no shift point for park),
    - push down on the service brake or set the parking brake,
    - ensure all passengers remain silent,
    - shut off all radios and/or other noisy equipment,
    - open the service door,
    - open the driver's side window, and
    - listen and look for an approaching train.
- When you decide to cross the tracks,
    - double-check the crossing signals before proceeding,
    - only stop before the first set of tracks at multiple-track crossings,
    - proceed across all tracks only when you are certain that no trains are approaching,
    - use a low gear to cross the tracks, and
    - never change gears while crossing.
- If a crossing gate comes down before you clear the tracks, drive through it (break the gate if you have to).

- Special situations sometimes arise when crossing tracks.
- If a bus stalls or is trapped on the tracks
    - evacuate everyone from the bus and the tracks immediately, and
    - usher everyone far from the bus at an angle (your direction of movement should be away from the tracks and toward the train).
- If there is a police officer at a crossing, obey all directions.
- If there is not a police officer and the signal isn't working properly
    - call your dispatcher to report the situation, and
    - ask the dispatcher for instructions about proceeding.
- If your view of the tracks is obstructed, follow these guidelines:
    - Try to avoid this by planning your route so you have maximum sight distance.
    - Never try to cross tracks unless you can see far enough to confirm there are no trains.
    - **Take extra precautions at passive crossings** (i.e., those with no traffic control devices; see Chapter 2).
    - Always look and listen for trains, regardless of whether a crossing is active or passive.
- Be sure the bus has an adequate containment or storage area to fully clear the tracks on the other side.
    - Remember the saying, "If it won't fit, do not commit!"
    - Be aware of the length of your bus.
    - Be aware of containment area sizes at crossings on any routes that you will take.
- If there is a stop sign/signal on the other side of the tracks,
    - make sure the bus has the needed containment/storage area to fully clear the tracks, and
    - plan to add 15 ft. of length to your bus (this is a decent amount of containment/storage area).

Quick Review Questions

11. At what distance from the nearest rail should you stop at a highway-rail crossing?

12. What are passive highway-rail crossings, and why should you take extra precautions at these types of crossings?

Managing Students

- Always focus on driving: do not address behavioral issues while driving.
- Never take your eyes off what is happening outside of the bus.
- Do not divert your attention when loading/unloading students.
- If behavior issues need to be addressed
    - wait until students are safely loaded/unloaded;
    - if unloading, wait until students are off and have moved a safe distance away; and

- if needed, pull the bus over to address the issue.

Figure 13.5. Kids Fighting on School Bus

- Serious issues with students may arise:
  - Follow the school's discipline protocols or refusal of privileges to ride the bus.
  - Stop the bus.
  - Park off the road in a safe location (e.g., a driveway or parking lot).
  - Secure the bus.
  - If you leave your seat, take the ignition key with you.
  - Stand up.
  - Speak respectfully to any offenders.
  - Speak courteously—but firmly.
  - Remind offenders of behavior expectations.
  - Never show anger; instead, let the offenders know that you mean business!
  - If appropriate, tell the student to move to a seat closer to you.
- Never remove students from the bus or drop them elsewhere than their designated stop.
- If the behavior prevents you from safely operating the bus
  - call an administrator, or
  - if required, call the police to remove the student.
- If assistance with a behavior issue is needed, follow your state/local protocols.

Quick Review Question

13. What should be done if a student's behavior is preventing you from safely operating the bus?

Special Safety Considerations

- Some school buses have white strobe lights mounted to the roof; use these when visibility is limited.
- Limited visibility means that you cannot see around the school bus easily (i.e., in front, behind, and on either side); it includes slightly limited or near-zero visibility.
- Always follow state and local regulations, regardless of the extent of the limited visibility.

13. School Bus

- **Windy conditions affect how a school bus handles!**
- The sides of school buses behave like sails on a boat:
    - Strong winds can push buses sideways or off the road.
    - Extreme winds could cause buses to tip over.
- When driving with strong winds
    - maintain a firm grip on the steering wheel;
    - anticipate gusts as much as you can;
    - slow down, since this lessens the effect of the wind;
    - pull off the roadway and wait, if possible; and
    - contact the dispatcher for further information on how to proceed.
- It is highly discouraged to back a school bus: it is dangerous and increases collision possibilities.
    - Backing should happen only when there are no other safe alternatives.
    - School buses should never be backed when students are outside.
- If backing is your only option, use the following procedures:
    - Assign a lookout.
    - The lookout should warn you of obstacles (e.g., persons, vehicles).
    - The lookout should never give backing instructions.
    - Signal for all passengers to be quiet.
    - Check all mirrors and rear windows constantly.
    - Back smoothly; back slowly.
- If there is no one serving as a lookout,
    - set the parking brake,
    - turn the motor off,
    - take the keys with you, and
    - walk to the rear of the bus to make sure the way is clear.
- If backing is required at a student pick-up point,
    - ensure that all students are loaded onto the bus BEFORE backing, and
    - always be on the lookout for any students who may be running late.
- Always unload students at drop-off points AFTER backing.
- Keep in mind that school buses can have upwards of a 3-ft. tail swing.
- Monitor the tail swing by checking all mirrors before and during any turning movements.
- If your bus is equipped with an **antilock braking system (ABS)**
    - **brake as you normally would**, and
    - do not use more than the braking force needed to stop safely.
- **If emergency braking is needed on a bus with ABS, do NOT pump the brakes.**
- Always monitor your bus while slowing down; safely back off the brakes as needed to maintain control of the vehicle.

Quick Review Question

14. If you are driving a school bus that is equipped with ABS, how should you use the brakes?

Answer Key

1. The danger zone is the area on all sides of the bus where children have the highest likelihood of being struck. Danger zones extend up to 30 ft. from the front bumper (with the first 10 ft. being the most dangerous), 10 ft. from the left and right sides of the bus, and 10 ft. behind the bus's rear bumper.

2. When the outside flat mirrors are properly adjusted, you should be able to see 200 ft. (or 4 bus lengths) behind the bus, along the sides of the bus, and the rear tires making contact with the ground.

3. When the outside convex mirrors are properly adjusted, you should be able to see the entire side of the bus (up to the mirror mounts), the front of the rear tires making contact with the ground, and a minimum of 1 traffic lane on either side.

4. When the crossover mirrors are properly adjusted, you should be able to see the entire area in front of the bus, which includes the ground level from the front bumper, a point at ground level where direct vision is possible, and an overlap between the direct vision and mirror-view vision. You must also be able to see the front left and right tires touching the ground and the area extending from the front of the bus to the service door.

5. Flashing amber warning lights should be activated at least 200 ft. (or about 5 – 10 seconds) before the pickup stop, as required by law.

6. After you unload students along the route, they should walk at least 10 ft. from the side of the bus.

7. After unloading students at school, you should do a walk-through of the bus to make sure there are no hiding/sleeping students or forgotten items.

8. While in front of the bus and waiting to cross the roadway, students should position themselves so that you can see them.

9. The following conditions require that a school bus be evacuated immediately: 1) when the bus is on fire or a fire is imminent; 2) when the bus is stalled on or adjacent to a highway-rail crossing; 3) when the position of the bus could change, increasing danger; 4) if a collision is imminent; and 5) when a hazardous materials spill requires passengers to quickly evacuate.

10. In the event of an evacuation, a working radio microphone should be dangled from the driver's side window so that it can be used later.

11. When stopping at a highway-rail crossing, you should stop no closer than 15 ft. and no farther than 50 ft. from the nearest rail.

12. Passive highway-rail crossings are those that have no traffic control devices. You must take extra precautions while crossing these since you must rely on yourself to recognize these types of crossings and check for yourself whether a train is approaching.

13. If a student's behavior prevents your safe operation of the bus, an administrator from the school should be called. If needed, the police can be called to remove the student.

14. When driving a school bus with an antilock braking system (ABS), you should brake as you normally would and only use the force needed to safely stop and maintain control of the vehicle. Do not pump the brakes in an emergency.

14 Metal Coils

The Securement and Application of Metal Coils

- Securement systems must be used to immobilize metal coils.
- Securement systems prevent coils from rolling, tipping, and/or sliding.
- Ensure that you comply with the specific securement method regulations.

Table 14.1. Metal Coils Securement Application

Metal Coil(s) and Weight	Cargo Securement Requirements	License Requirements
metal coil shipments weighing greater than or equal to 5,000 lb. (individually or bundled together)	metal-coil-specific securement rules	in New York State (NYS): metal coil endorsement (M)
metal coil shipments weighing less than 5,000 lb. (individually or bundled together)	general cargo securement rules	in NYS: CDL (M endorsement not requireD)

At the time of publication, a metal coil endorsement is only required for drivers holding a CDL from New York State. Drivers from other states are not required to have this endorsement even if they will be going through New York while transporting metal coils.[1]

- Tie-downs are combinations of securement devices.
    - They are used to restrain cargo.
    - They can be attached to themselves by way of passing through points on the vehicle.
    - They can be attached directly to anchor points on the vehicle.
    - They include chains, steel strapping, wire rope, cordage, and synthetic webbing.
- **Direct tie-downs are attached to both the cargo and the vehicle.**
    - In some cases, direct tie-downs pass through or around a cargo item and are attached to both sides of the vehicle.
    - They provide direct resistance against forces on the cargo.
- **Indirect tie-downs are attached to the vehicle but pass over the cargo instead of through and around it.**
    - They create a downward force.
    - The downward force boosts the friction effect between the deck and the cargo, and the friction helps hold the cargo in place.
- All tie-downs and their components are required to be in working condition.

[1] New York Department of Motor Vehicles, "Driver's Manual for the Safe Securement of Metal Coils and Other Cargo," https://dmv.ny.gov/forms/mv79.pdf, May 2022

14. Metal Coils

- They cannot have knots.
- Any repairs to tie-downs must be made in accordance with manufacturer recommendations or CFR standards.
- With the exception of steel strapping, tie-downs must be designed in such a way as to be tightened by the driver.
- Tie-downs must be securely attached in such a way as to prevent any unfastening or loosening while cargo is being transported.
- On trailers with rub rails and carrying loads that do not extend past the rub rails, tie-downs and related components must be positioned inboard of the rub rails.
- The packages of cargo must be strong enough and not collapse under the pressure of the tie-downs.
- If the shipper packs the cargo; the driver must inform shipper if the packaging is inadequate.

Quick Review Question

1. When transporting 1 or more metal coils—bundled together or individually—that weigh at least 5,000 lb., which load securement requirement must you comply with?

Securement Requirements and Orientation

- The orientation of the eye of the coil on the vehicle determines the securement requirements.
- There are 3 coil eye orientations:
    1. eyes vertical
    2. eyes crosswise
    3. eyes lengthwise

Quick Review Question

2. How many types of coil eye orientations are there, and what are they?

Single Metal Coil with Eyes Vertical

This section describes securement requirements for metal coils that are transported on
- flatbeds,
- van-type vehicles, and/or
- intermodal containers with anchor points.
- Pallets upon which coils are fastened must be strong and not collapse (see Chapter 5).
- **To prevent coils from tipping (forward, rearward, or laterally), arrange tie-downs as follows:**
    - A minimum of 1 indirect tie-down should be attached diagonally from the left side of the vehicle, across the coil eye, and to the right side of the vehicle.
    - A minimum of 1 indirect tie-down should be attached diagonally from the right side of the vehicle, across the coil eye, to the left side of the vehicle.
    - A minimum of 1 indirect tie-down should be attached side-to-side over the coil eye.
    - **Direct tie-downs, friction mats, or either blocking or bracing should be used to prevent forward-rearward movement.**
- To increase friction between the pallet and the deck, place a friction mat under the pallet.
- Secure the coil to the pallet in order to withstand the performance criteria forces (described in Chapter 5).

- **Ensure that the sum of the working load limits (WLLs) from all tie-downs is greater than or equal to 50% of the coil weight.**

Figure 14.1. Eyes Vertical Orientation

Quick Review Questions

3. What devices or structures are used to prevent longitudinal movement of the coil in the forward direction?

4. What percentage of the coil weight must the sum of the WLLs from all tie-downs be?

Row of Metal Coils with Eyes Vertical

This section describes securement requirements for metal coils that are transported on
- flatbeds,
- van-type or sided vehicles, and/or
- intermodal containers with anchor points.
- Coils transported in rows have certain securement requirements.
- There must be a minimum of 1 direct tie-down against the front of the row of coils.
  - The direct tie-down(s) must restrain against forward motion.
  - If possible, the tie-down must make an angle less than or equal to 45° with the floor.
- There must be a minimum of 1 direct tie-down against the rear of the row of coils.
  - The direct tie-down(s) must prevent rearward motion.
  - If possible, it must make an angle less than or equal to 45° with the floor.
- There must be a minimum of 1 indirect tie-down over the top of each coil or side-by-side row of coils.
  - The indirect tie-down(s) must prevent vertical motion.
  - Keep indirect tie-down(s) that go over the top of the coil as close to the coil eye as possible.
- Always arrange direct tie-downs, blocking, or bracing so that they prevent tipping and/or shifting in ALL directions.
- If there are more than 2 coils in the front and rear rows
  - ensure the direct tie-down runs outside some sort of channel that bears against all coils in both the front and rear rows;

14. Metal Coils

- o use a friction mat under each pallet to increase the friction between the pallet and the deck; and
- o always use a friction mat when the coil or deck is soaked with oil.

Quick Review Question

5. How are tie-downs used to secure coils with eyes vertical on flatbed vehicles or intermodal containers with anchor points?

Metal Coils with Eyes Crosswise

This section describes securement requirements for metal coils that are transported on
- o flatbeds,
- o van-type or sided vehicles, and/or
- o intermodal containers with anchor points.
- There are 3 steps to secure metal coils with eyes crosswise.

Step 1: Support the Coil

- Support the coil above the deck to prevent rocking.
- Ensure the coil supports are held in place; they should not become loose during transport.
- Timbers, chocks, or wedges must be held in place by coil bunks (or similar devices); they should be prevented from coming loose.
- Do NOT use nailed blocking or cleats as the only means with which to secure timbers, wedges, or chocks.
- Prevent the cradle from sliding by
  - o putting **friction mats** under the timbers and coil bunks,
  - o using nailed wood blocking or cleats against the front timber, or
  - o placing a direct tie-down around the cradle's front.
- A direct tie-down used around the front of the cradle does NOT count toward the aggregate WLL for tie-downs through the coil eye.

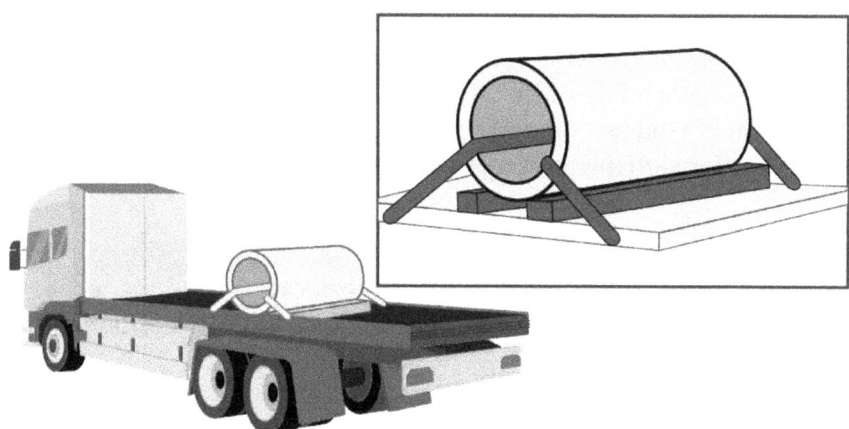

Figure 14.2. Eyes Crosswise Orientation

Step 2: Prevent Forward Movement from the Coil

- At least 1 direct tie-down is required through the coil's eye to restrict forward motion.

Step 3: Prevent Rearward Movement from the Coil

- To restrict rearward motion, at least 1 direct tie-down is required.
- If more than 2 chains are needed, place them symmetrically on either side of the coil.
- If an odd number of chains is needed, ensure the last chain is to the rear.
- **It is prohibited to attach direct tie-downs diagonally through the coil eye, forming an X pattern** (see Figure 14.3.).

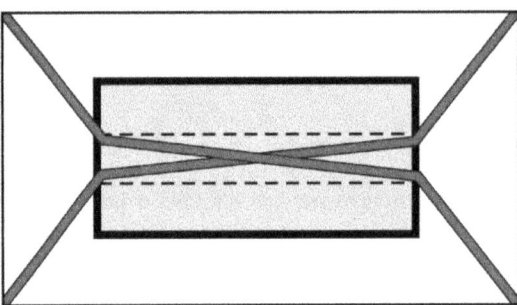

Figure 14.3. Prohibited X Pattern with Direct Tie-Downs

Quick Review Question

6. If an odd number of chains is needed in order to prevent rearward movement from the coil, where should the last chain be positioned?

Individual Metal Coils with Eyes Lengthwise

This section describes securement requirements for metal coils that are transported on

- flatbeds,
- van-type or sided vehicles, and/or
- containers with anchor points.
- You have 3 options to safely secure individual coils loaded with their eyes lengthwise.

Securement Option 1

- **Step 1:** To prevent the coil from rolling, support it above the deck.
- **Step 2:** At an angle less than or equal to 45° with the floor of the vehicle viewed from the side, attach a minimum of 1 direct tie-down on each diagonal through the coil eye.
- **Step 3:** A minimum of 1 indirect tie-down should be attached side-to-side over the top of the coil.
- **Step 4: To prevent forward movement, use friction mats or blocking.**

Securement Option 2

- To prevent the coil from rolling, support it above the deck.
- Follow the same steps described in Securement Option 1 EXCEPT position the direct tie-downs straight (not diagonally).

14. Metal Coils

Securement Option 3

- To prevent the coil from rolling, support it above the deck.
- Attach 2 indirect tie-downs over the front and rear parts of the coil.
- Prevent forward movement by using friction mats or blocking.

Figure 14.4. Eyes Lengthwise Orientation

Quick Review Question

7. In what situation is it recommended to use a friction mat?

Row of Metal Coils with Eyes Lengthwise

This section describes securement requirements for metal coils that are transported on

- flatbeds,
- van-type or sided vehicles, and/or
- intermodal containers with anchor points.
- When at least 3 coils are loaded in like mode and in a line, it is considered a row of coils.
- Securing a row of coils has similar requirements to Securement Option 3 for individual metal coils with eyes lengthwise (as discussed above).

Step 1

- To prevent them from rolling, support the coils above the deck.
- Whatever is used to support the coils CANNOT become loose or unfastened during transport.

Step 2

- Attach at least 2 indirect tie-downs over each side-by-side row or coil.

Step 3

- To prevent front-to-back forward movement, use friction mats or blocking.

Quick Review Question

8. When securing metal coils with eyes lengthwise, what are the requirements?

Metal Coils in Sided Vehicles or Intermodal Containers without Anchor Points

This section describes securement requirements for metal coils transported in sided vehicles or intermodal containers WITHOUT anchor points.

- An **anchor point** is part of the attachment, fitting, or structure on a piece of cargo or on a vehicle to which tie-downs are attached.
- In sided vehicles and intermodal containers without anchor points
    - the coil itself forms the anchor point, OR
    - a tie-down attached to itself forms the anchor point (e.g., an indirect securement can be formed by having a tie-down travel through the vehicle structure and attach to itself around the coil).
- You must prevent coils from tipping or having horizontal movement by using
    - friction mats,
    - blocking and bracing systems,
    - blocking and tie-downs, or
    - bracing and tie-downs.
- It is the responsibility of the driver/carrier to make sure the securement system meets the performance criteria specifications outlined in Chapter 5.

Quick Review Question

9. What is an anchor point?

Roll Prevention

- Metal coils (and similar cargo) must be prevented from rolling.
- Timbers, chocks, wedges, or a cradle can be used to prevent coils from rolling.
    - The prevention method must support the coil off the deck.
    - The prevention method should be incapable of loosening or becoming unfastened during transport.
    - Timbers, chocks, and wedges require coil bunks (or similar) to hold them in place and prevent them from loosening.
    - It is prohibited to use nailed blocking or cleats as the only securement method for timbers, chocks, or wedges.
- At least 1 tie-down should go through the eye of the coil to **restrict both forward and rearward movement**.
    - In both cases, the tie-down should create an angle that is 45° or less with the vehicle's floor when viewed from the side.
    - The same guidance applies to intermodal containers.
- **Cradles are especially effective at preventing rolling.**
    - Those with angles of 45° offer the most restraining force.
    - The restraining force decreases as the cradle angle falls below 45°.
- Multiple coils or similar cargoes positioned against each other are prone to rocking.
    - Control this by placing tie-downs through the 2 end articles and pulling the articles together.
    - **NEVER attach tie-downs diagonally through the coil's eye to form an X pattern** (when viewed from above the vehicle).

Quick Review Question

10. Which device or structure is considered especially effective in preventing metal coils from rolling?

Answer Key

1. You must follow the metal coil-specific securement rules when transporting 1 or more metal coils—bundled together or individually—that weigh at least 5,000 lb.

2. There are 3 types of coil eye orientations: 1) eyes vertical, 2) eyes crosswise, and 3) eyes lengthwise.

3. Either direct tie-downs, friction mats, blocking, or bracing are used to prevent forward-rearward (longitudinal) movement.

4. The sum of the working load limits (WLLs) from all tie-downs must be greater than or equal to 50% of the coil weight.

5. First, ensure that the pallets on which the coils are fastened are strong enough and will not collapse per performance criteria. Next, arrange the tie-downs to prevent the coils from tipping in any direction: at least 1 indirect tie-down should be attached diagonally from the left side of the vehicle, across the coil eye, and to the right side of the vehicle; at least 1 indirect tie-down should be attached diagonally from the right side of the vehicle, across the coil eye, to the left side of the vehicle; and at least 1 indirect tie-down should be attached side-to-side over the coil eye. Direct tie-downs, friction mats, or either blocking or bracing must be used to prevent forward-rearward movement. Secure the coil to the pallet in order for it to withstand the performance criteria forces (described in Chapter 5) and ensure that the sum of the working load limits (WLLs) from all tie-downs is greater than or equal to 50% of the coil weight.

6. If an odd number of chains is needed in order to prevent rearward movement from the coil, the last chain must be positioned to the rear.

7. Friction mats are used to prevent tipping, forward, backward, and/or horizontal movement; to prevent the cradle from sliding; and to increase the friction between the pallet and the deck. They must always be used when the coil or deck is soaked with oil.

8. There are similar requirements for securing both individual metal coils with eyes lengthwise and rows of metal coils with eyes lengthwise. When securing individual or rows of metal coils with eyes lengthwise, the coil(s) must always first be supported above the deck to prevent it/them from rolling. After first supporting the coil above the deck to keep it from rolling, you have 3 options to choose from to secure an individual coil: 1) At an angle less than or equal to 45° with the floor of the vehicle viewed from the side, attach at least 1 direct tie-down on each diagonal through the coil eye. Then, ensure that at least 1 indirect tie-down is attached side-to-side over the top of the coil; use friction mats or blocking to prevent forward movement. 2) After supporting the coil above the deck to prevent it from rolling, follow the same steps as described in the first securement option, but position the direct tie-downs straight (not diagonally). 3) After supporting the coil above the deck to prevent it from rolling, attach 2 indirect tie-downs over the front and rear parts of the coil and use friction mats or blocking to prevent forward movement.

9. An anchor point is part of the attachment, fitting, or structure on a piece of cargo or on a vehicle to which tie-downs are attached.

10. Cradles are especially effective at preventing rolling: those with angles of 45° provide the most restraining force, which decreases as the cradle angle falls below 45°.

15 Vehicle Safety Inspection

- The primary reason to inspect your vehicle is to help ensure your safety and the safety of others.
- Spotting defects during the inspection can prevent problems down the road.
- Inspecting your vehicle is both a state and federal requirement.
    - Inspectors from state and federal agencies reserve the right to inspect your vehicle.
    - If an inspector deems your vehicle to be unsafe, it will be placed "out of service" until the problem is resolved.

Quick Review Question

1. What is the primary reason for vehicle inspections?

Specific Issues to Look For

- **Vehicle inspections let you identify issues that could cause a breakdown or crash.**
- Specific things must be checked on the various components of the vehicle (see Table 15.1.).

Table 15.1. What to Look for in a Vehicle Inspection

Tire Problems

- not enough (or too much) air pressure
- tires with too much/bad wear
    - Tread depth should be greater than or equal to $\frac{4}{32}$ in. on all major grooves on the front tires.
    - All other tires should have $\frac{2}{32}$ in. tread.
    - Fabric should never show through tread or the sidewall.
- any damage, such as cuts
- separation of tread
- dual tires coming in contact with parts of the vehicle or each other
- tire sizes that are mismatched
- different types of tires used together (radial and bias-ply)
- valve stems that are cracked or cut
- on buses: prohibited regrooved, recapped, or retreaded front wheels

Table 15.1. What to Look for in a Vehicle Inspection

Wheel and Rim Problems

- rims that are damaged
- lock rings that are mismatched, bent, or cracked
- wheel rings with welding repairs (not safe)
- rust around wheel nuts
    - This could signal they are loose.
    - This indicates that the tightness needs to be checked.
    - Always recheck nut tightness shortly after changing a tire.
- Danger is imminent if any of the following are missing:
    - clamps
    - spacers
    - studs
    - lugs

Bad Brake Drums or Shoes

- drums that are cracked
- shoes or pads that have oil, grease, and/or brake fluid on them
- dangerously thin brake shoes
- brake shoes that are missing or broken

Defects to the Steering System

- nuts, bolts, and cotter keys that are missing
- any other missing parts
- parts that are bent, loose, or broken (e.g., steering column, steering gear box, tie rods)
- hoses, pumps, and fluid levels (if equipped with power steering); check for leaks
- a steering wheel play greater than 10°
    - This equates to approximately 2 in. of movement at the rim of a steering wheel that is 20 in.
    - Excessive steering wheel play can make steering difficult.

Defects to the Suspension System

- spring hangers that allow the axle to move from its proper position
- spring hangers that are cracked or broken
- leaves that are missing or broken in any leaf spring

Table 15.1. What to Look for in a Vehicle Inspection

- - o If more than one-fourth of these are missing, the vehicle may be placed out of service.
  - o Any defect to these can be dangerous.
- leaves that are broken in a multi-leaf spring
- leaves that have shifted and are in danger of hitting a tire or other vehicle part
- **shock absorbers that leak**
- axle positioning parts that are damaged, cracked, or missing, including the following:
  - o torque rod or arm
  - o U-bolts
  - o spring hangers
- damaged and/or leaking air suspension systems
- frame members that are broken, cracked, or loose

Exhaust System Defects

Checking the following can prevent poison fumes from entering the cab and/or sleeper berth:
- any of the following that are broken, loose, or missing:
  - o exhaust pipes
  - o mufflers
  - o tailpipes
  - o vertical stacks
  - o mounting brackets
  - o clamps
  - o bolts
  - o nuts
- parts of the exhaust system that rub against the fuel system, tires, or other moving parts
- leaking parts of the exhaust system

Emergency Equipment

- fire extinguishers
- extra electrical fuses (unless the vehicle has circuit breakers)
- warning devices for when the vehicle is parked:
  - o 3 reflective triangles, or
  - o 6 or more fusees, or
  - o 3 liquid-burning flares

15. Vehicle Safety Inspection

Table 15.1. What to Look for in a Vehicle Inspection

Cargo (Trucks)

The following must be checked BEFORE beginning a trip:

- whether the vehicle is overloaded
- whether cargo is balanced and secure
- whether you have the proper papers and placarding (if carrying hazardous materials)

Quick Review Question

2. What should you be on the lookout for when inspecting shock absorbers?

The 7-Step Inspection Method

- Thoroughly inspecting a vehicle involves 7 steps.
- Using a consistent process when conducting vehicle inspections helps ensure you will not forget any of the required steps.
- Before beginning the first step in the inspection process, you must do a visual inspection of the vehicle:
    - Observe its general condition.
    - Check for visible damage.
    - Look to see if the vehicle is leaning.
    - Check under the vehicle for signs of fresh oil, coolant, fuel leaks, or grease.
    - Look for hazards around the vehicle (e.g., people, other vehicles, low wires).

Step 1: Vehicle Overview

- Drivers often must make daily written vehicle inspection reports.
    - Any items listed in these reports must be repaired if they affect safety.
    - Motor carriers must certify that the repairs were either made or unnecessary.
- You must sign the reports ONLY if the defects are certified as having been addressed by the motor carrier.

Step 2: Check the Engine Compartment

- Be sure that parking brakes are on and/or that the wheels are chocked.
- If needed, lift the hood, tilt the cab (secure all loose items), or open the engine compartment door to inspect the following:
    - the level of the engine oil
    - the level of coolant in the radiator
    - the condition of the hoses in the radiator
    - the level of the power steering fluid
    - power steering hoses (if the vehicle is equipped with them)
    - the level of windshield washer fluid
    - the level of battery fluid
    - the battery connections and tie-downs
    - the level of automatic transmission fluid (checking this may require a running engine)
    - the tightness of the belts—alternator, water pump, and air compressor

15. Vehicle Safety Inspection

- - o   excessive wear on belts (recognize beforehand how much "give" these should have)
    - o   engine compartment leaks (fuel, coolant, oil, power steering, hydraulic, and battery)
    - o   worn or cracked electrical wiring insulation
  - When done, lower and secure the hood, cab, or engine compartment door.

Step 3: Inspect the Interior of the Cab

- Get in the cab.
- Make sure that the parking brake is on.
- Shift to neutral (or park if the vehicle has an automatic transmission).
- Start the engine.
- Listen for noises that are unusual.
- Check the antilock braking system (ABS) indicator lights if the vehicle has them.
  - o   The dashboard light should turn on and then turn off.
  - o   If the light stays on, it signals that the ABS is malfunctioning.
  - o   On trailers: a yellow light on the left rear that stays lit signals a malfunctioning ABS.
- Observe the various gauges (see Table 15.2.).

Table 15.2. Checking Gauges During Step Three of the Inspection Process

Gauge Type	What to Check For
Oil pressure	The gauge needle position should be normal within a few seconds of starting the engine.
Air pressure	<ul><li>**Check that pressure builds from 50 to 90 psi within 3 minutes.**</li><li>Know the cutout requirements for your vehicle.</li><li>Build pressure to the governor cutout (typically 120 – 140 psi).</li></ul>
Ammeter and/or voltmeter	Make sure these are within the normal ranges.
Coolant temperature	Make sure that there is a gradual rise to the normal operating range.
Engine oil temperature	Make sure that there is a gradual rise to the normal operating range.
Warning lights and buzzers	Be sure that the oil, coolant, charging circuit warning, and ABS lights go out right away.

- The conditions of the controls should also be checked for looseness, sticking, damage, and improper settings:
  - o   steering wheel
  - o   clutch
  - o   gas pedal (accelerator)
  - o   brake controls
  - o   foot brake
  - o   trailer brake (if equipped with one)

- 15. Vehicle Safety Inspection

    - o parking brake
    - o retarder controls (if equipped with them)
    - o transmission controls
    - o interaxle differential lock (if equipped with one)
    - o horn(s)
    - o windshield wipers
    - o windshield fluid
    - o lights
    - o headlights
    - o dimmer switch
    - o turn signal
    - o hazard lights/4-way flashers
    - o parking switch(es)
    - o clearance switch(es)
    - o identification switch(es)
    - o marker switch(es)
- Check the windshield and mirrors; fix, clean, or adjust the following as needed to ensure a clear view:
    - o cracks
    - o dirt
    - o illegal stickers
    - o any other obstructions that could prevent you from seeing clearly
- Inspect the safety equipment; be sure the vehicle is equipped as needed and items work properly:
    - o spare electrical fuses (exception = if vehicle has circuit breakers)
    - o 3 red reflective triangles, 6 fusees, or 3 liquid-burning flares
    - o a fire extinguisher that is rated and properly charged
- Optional emergency safety items must also be inspected:
    - o chains (for winter use on tires)
    - o equipment to change tires
    - o emergency phone number list (which should be up to date)
    - o accident reporting packet
- Inspect the safety belt and make sure it
    - o is securely mounted,
    - o latches and adjusts as it should, and
    - o is neither frayed nor ripped.

Step 4: Check the Lights

- Ensure that the parking brake is set.
- Shut off the engine.
- Take the keys with you.
- Put the low beams on.
- Put on the hazard lights/4-way flashers.
- Exit the vehicle.

Step 5: Conduct a Walk-Around Inspection

- Walk to the front of the vehicle.
- Make sure the high beams work.
- Check that all of the hazards/4-way flashers are functioning properly.
- Push the dimmer switch; check that the high beams are in working order.

15. Vehicle Safety Inspection

- Turn the headlights and hazards/4-way flashers off.
- Turn on the following lights:
    - parking
    - clearance
    - side-marker
    - identification
- Put the right turn signal on.
- Begin the walk-around inspection (see Table 15.3.).

Table 15.3. Walk-Around Inspection Steps

General

- Walk around the vehicle and do a visual inspection.
- As you walk around, clean off all glass, lights, and reflectors.

Left Front Side

- Make sure the driver's side door glass is clean.
- Check that locks and door latches work properly.
- Look at the left front wheel:
    - Check the condition of the wheel and rim for signs of anything missing, damaged, bent or broken
    - Be sure to check the studs, clamps, and lugs; be on the lookout for indications of misalignment.
    - Check the tire condition: ensure that the tire is properly inflated; the valve stem and cap are in working order; and there are no cuts, bulges, or tread wear that could compromise safety.
- Test rust-streaked lug nuts for looseness by using a wrench.
- Check that the hub oil level is adequate and that there are no leaks.
- Inspect the left front suspension and the condition of
    - the spring,
    - the spring hangers,
    - the shackles,
    - the U-bolts, and
    - the shock absorbers.
- Inspect the left front brake and the condition of
    - the brake drum (or disc), and
    - the hoses.

Front

- Check the condition of the steering system and the front axle:

15. Vehicle Safety Inspection

Table 15.3. Walk-Around Inspection Steps

- - o Make sure there are no parts that are loose, bent, worn, or damaged.
  - o Grab the steering mechanism to make sure it is not loose.
- Check the condition of the windshield:
  - o Make sure there is no damage.
  - o Clean the windshield (inside and out) if it is dirty.
  - o Make sure the wiper arms have the proper spring tension.
  - o Wiper blades should be secure, undamaged, and not have "stiff" rubber.
- Check the lights and reflectors:
  - o Clearance, parking, and ID lights should be clean, in working condition, and amber colored (at front).
  - o Reflectors should be clean and amber colored (at front).
  - o The right front turn signal should be clean, in working order, and colored either amber or white (facing forwarD).

Right Side

- Check all items at the right front as you did for the left front.
- If the vehicle is a cab-over-engine design, make sure the primary and secondary safety cab locks are engaged.
- Make sure the right fuel tank
  - o is securely mounted,
  - o is not damaged or leaking,
  - o has a secure fuel crossover line,
  - o has enough fuel, and
  - o has the cap on securely.
- Check the condition of visible parts.
- Make sure that the rear of the engine is not leaking.
- Check that there are no leaks in the transmission.
- Make sure the exhaust system
  - o is secure,
  - o has no leaks, and
  - o is not touching wires, fuel, or air lines.
- Make sure there are no bends or cracks in the frame and cross members.
- Make sure that the air lines and electrical wiring are secure and will not rub, snag, or wear.

15. Vehicle Safety Inspection

Table 15.3. Walk-Around Inspection Steps

- If the vehicle has one, make sure the spare tire carrier/rack is undamaged.
- Be sure that the spare tire/wheel is mounted securely in the rack.
- Be sure that the spare tire and wheel are the correct size and inflated properly.
- On trucks, check the cargo securement:
    - Cargo should be properly braced, blocked, tied, chained, etc.
    - If needed, the header board (i.e., headboarD) should fit your needs and be secure.
    - Sideboards and stakes (if equippeD) should have enough strength, no damage, and be properly set in place.
    - Any canvas/tarps must be secured to avoid billowing, tearing, or blocking the view from mirrors.
- For oversized vehicles,
    - any required signs must be mounted safely and correctly, and
    - you must have all required permits in your possession.
- The curbside compartment doors must
    - be in good condition,
    - be closed securely,
    - be locked or latched, and
    - have the required security seals in place.

Right Rear

- The following should be neither missing, bent, nor broken on wheels and rims:
    - spacers
    - studs
    - clamps
    - lugs
- The tires should
    - be properly inflated,
    - have valve stems and caps that are in adequate condition,
    - have no bulges, cuts, or wear to the tread that could be dangerous,
    - not rub against each other,
    - have nothing stuck between them,
    - be the same type (not a mix of radial and bias tires),
    - be the same sizes, and

15. Vehicle Safety Inspection

Table 15.3. Walk-Around Inspection Steps

- o have wheel bearings and seals that do not leak.
- Check the suspension:
  - o Inspect the condition of the spring(s), spring hangers, U-bolts, and shackles.
  - o Make sure that the axle is secure.
  - o Check that the powered axle(s) have no leaking gear oil.
  - o Inspect the condition of the bushings and torque rod arms.
  - o Inspect the condition of the shock absorbers.
  - o If there is a retractable axle, make sure the lift mechanism is in good condition.
  - o Check for leaks in air-powered retractable axles.
  - o Check that the air ride components are in safe, working condition.
- Inspect the brakes:
  - o Check the brake adjustment.
  - o Make sure that the brake drums or discs are in safe, working condition.
  - o Make sure that rubbing has not caused any wear on the air hoses.
- Inspect the lights and reflectors:
  - o The side-marker lights should be clean, operable, and colored red in the rear (with the other ones amber).
  - o The side-marker reflectors should be clean and the correct color: red at the rear (with the others amber).

Rear

- Inspect the lights and reflectors:
  - o The rear clearance and identification lights should be clean, in working order, and colored red at the rear.
  - o Reflectors should be clean and colored red at the rear.
  - o Taillights should be clean, in working order, and red at the rear.
  - o The right rear turn signal should be in operating order and colored either red, yellow, or amber at the rear.
- License plate(s) must be on the vehicle, be clean, and be adequately secure.
- The end gates should be undamaged and properly secured and in stake sockets.
- Any canvas/tarps must be secured to avoid billowing, tearing, or blocking the view from mirrors.
- For oversized/overlength vehicles,
  - o any required signs must be mounted safely and correctly, and

15. Vehicle Safety Inspection

Table 15.3. Walk-Around Inspection Steps

- o you must have all required permits in your possession.
- Make sure that the rear doors are closed securely and locked or latched.

Left Side

- Inspect all items on the left side as you did for the right side.
- If batteries are not mounted in the engine compartment, make sure
  - o the boxes are mounted securely to the vehicle,
  - o the boxes have a secure cover,
  - o the batteries are secure and prevented from moving,
  - o the batteries are neither broken nor leaking,
  - o the battery fluid is at the correct level (unless it is a maintenance-free battery),
  - o cell caps are there and tightened securely (unless it is a maintenance-free battery), and
  - o the vents in the cell caps have no foreign materials (unless it is a maintenance-free battery).

Step 6: Check the Signal Lights

- Enter the vehicle and turn off all of the lights.
  - o Turn the stop lights on by using the trailer hand brake OR ask a helper to put the brake pedal on.
- Put the left turn signal lights on.
- Exit the vehicle and check the lights.
  - o Make sure the turn signal on the left front is clean, functioning, and colored amber or white.
  - o Make sure the turn signal light at the left rear is clean, functioning, and colored either red, yellow, or amber.
  - o Make sure BOTH stop lights are clean, functioning, and colored either red, yellow, or amber.
- Enter the vehicle again:
  - o Turn off any lights that are not needed for driving.
  - o Make sure you have the required paperwork, permits, trip manifests, etc.
  - o Ensure any loose items in the cab are secured to prevent interference while driving and protect you from being struck by them in the event of a crash.

Step 7: Check the Brake System

- If the vehicle is equipped with hydraulic brakes, make sure there are no hydraulic leaks:
  - o Pump the brake pedal 3 times.
  - o Firmly apply pressure to the pedal; hold for 5 seconds.
  - o **If the pedal moves, it indicates a leak or other issue.**
  - o If the pedal moves, the issue must be repaired before driving.

- - - If the vehicle is equipped with air brakes, inspect them using the steps described in Chapter 7, which are part of the 7-step inspection method described here.
  - Test the parking brake:
    - Put on your seatbelt.
    - Set the parking brake on the power unit only.
    - If a trailer parking brake is set, release it.
    - Put the vehicle in a low gear.
    - Pull forward gently against the parking brake to be sure it holds.
    - Repeat these steps for the trailer by setting the trailer parking brakes and releasing the power unit parking brakes.
    - If the trailer parking brakes do not hold, repair them before driving.
  - Test the stopping action of the service brake:
    - Drive at a speed of about 5 mph.
    - Firmly depress the brake pedal.
    - If the vehicle pulls to one side, there may be brake issues.
    - Recognize if there are any strange "feels" to the brake pedal or if stopping is delayed; these indicate possible issues.
- If something is found to be unsafe at any point during the inspections, be sure it gets fixed.
- Operating unsafe vehicles is prohibited by federal and state laws.

Quick Review Questions

3. In step 3 of the 7-step inspection method, how much air pressure should build within 3 minutes?

4. When checking hydraulic brakes, what is the indication that there is a leak or other issue?

During-Trip Inspections and the After-Trip Inspection Report

- For safety, inspections should be conducted throughout your trip:
  - Keep an eye on all of the gauges; make sure there are no indications of trouble.
  - Use your senses to identify issues: smell, feel, look, and listen.
- **Whenever you stop, check the following items:**
  - tires, wheels, and rims
  - brakes
  - reflectors and lights
  - trailer brake and electrical connections
  - trailer coupling devices
  - cargo securement devices
- Monitor the vehicle operation regularly by checking the following:
  - instruments
  - air pressure gauge (if equipped with air brakes)
  - temperature gauges
  - pressure gauges
  - ammeter/voltmeter
  - mirrors
  - tires
  - cargo and cargo covers

15. Vehicle Safety Inspection

- o lights, reflectors, and signals
- Always use your senses during a trip: inspect anything unusual that you see, hear, feel, or smell.
- When transporting cargo, remember to inspect the cargo's securement as follows:
    - o within or just after the first 50 mi. of the trip
    - o every 150 mi. (or 3 hours) thereafter—whichever comes first
- You may need to create a written report each day concerning the condition of the vehicle driven.
    - o Always include anything that could affect the safe operation of the vehicle.
    - o Always include anything that could result in a mechanical breakdown of the vehicle.

Quick Review Question

5. What should you check on the vehicle each time you stop?

The Vehicle Inspection Test

- Before beginning the skills test, the examiner will inspect the safety of the vehicle.
- **Test takers with vehicles that do not pass the examiner's safety inspection must reschedule their skills tests.**
- The examiner will look at the following before starting the skills test:
    - o liability insurance (which must be current)
    - o registration (which must be current)
    - o inspection certificate
    - o headlamps (which must have bright and dim functions)
    - o 2 tail lamps (on models made after 1959)
    - o 2 stop lamps (for models made after 1959)
    - o turn signals (for models made after 1959)
    - o horn
    - o exhaust system
    - o license plate (which must be current; the vehicle must have 2 of them)
    - o windshield wipers
    - o rearview mirrors
    - o safety belts
    - o approved glass coating material (if needeD)
    - o clearance lamps
    - o side marker lamps
    - o side reflectors
    - o turn signals
    - o hazard warning lights
    - o fire extinguisher(s) (if requireD)
    - o flashing lights (school buses must have 2 red alternating flashing lights to the front and back)
    - o reflective triangles (if requireD)
    - o full-service brakes
    - o hydraulic brakes
    - o parking brake
- The vehicle inspection test evaluates your knowledge of whether your vehicle is safe to drive.
- The examiner will ask you to inspect the vehicle:
    - o You will be expected to point to or touch items being inspected.

15. Vehicle Safety Inspection

- o You must explain WHAT you are inspecting.
- o You must explain WHY you are inspecting each item.
- The vehicle inspection test you will take depends on the class of CDL you are applying for.
- Applicants for **Class A CDLs** will be asked to do 1 of 4 possible versions of the inspection test:
    - o All 4 tests are equal.
    - o You will learn which of the 4 inspection tests you will take at the time of the test.
    - o You are expected to use the vehicle you brought with you.
- Each of the 4 tests requires
    - o an engine start,
    - o an in-cab inspection, and
    - o a coupling system inspection.
- After completing the components that are the same for each of the 4 tests, you may be asked to complete additional inspections:
    - o You may be asked to perform an inspection of the entire vehicle.
    - o You may be asked to perform an inspection of only a portion of the vehicle.
    - o The examiner will explain what is expected of you.
- Candidates applying for a Class B or Class C CDL will be asked to do 1 of 3 versions of the inspection test:
    - o You must use the vehicle you brought with you.
    - o All 3 tests are equivalent to each other.
    - o You will learn which of the 3 tests you will take moments before the test begins.
- You may be asked to complete additional inspections:
    - o You may be asked to perform an inspection of the entire vehicle.
    - o You may be asked to perform an inspection of only a portion of the vehicle.
    - o You may be asked to inspect special vehicle features, such as those found on a school or transit bus.
    - o The examiner will explain what is expected of you.
- You must understand the type of vehicle you will use on the skills test.
    - o You must be familiar with the parts that are on the vehicle.
    - o You must be able to identify the vehicle parts to the examiner.
    - o You must be able to explain what you are on the lookout for during the inspection.
- **Some vehicles require additional inspections** that are specific to the type of vehicle:
    - o school buses
    - o trailers
    - o transit buses and coaches
- Information concerning the inspection test for these vehicles is described below.

Quick Review Questions

6. What is the point of the vehicle inspection test?

7. Which vehicles require additional inspections that are specific to the type of vehicle being driven?

Engine Compartment

All vehicles require the following engine compartment inspections with the engine off.

Leaks and Hoses

- Make sure there are no puddles on the ground beneath the vehicle.
- Engine underside and transmission: make sure there are no dripping fluids.
- Check the hoses; there should be no leaks and they should be in sound condition.

Oil level

- This should be checked when the engine is off.
- You must indicate the location of the dipstick.
- Ensure that the level is within safe operating range (i.e., above the refill mark).

Coolant level

- The sight glass is on the radiator or coolant reservoir.
- Make sure an adequate level of fluid appears in the sight glass.
- If there is no sight glass, remove the radiator cap and explain what you would look for.

Power steering fluid

- Look at the dipstick to gauge the fluid level (or use the sight glass).
- Be sure that the level is above the refill mark.

Engine compartment belts (power steering, water pump, alternator, and air compressor)

- Ensure these belts are snug (i.e., $\frac{1}{2} - \frac{3}{4}$ in. of play at the center of the belt).
- Make sure the belts do not have cracks, loose fibers, frays, or signs of wear.
- Tell the examiner which, if any, parts are not belt-driven.
- For anything NOT belt-driven, make sure it is in proper working order, undamaged, mounted securely, and has no leaks.

Hydraulic Brakes Master Cylinder and Brake Fluid

- Make sure that the master cylinder has no leaks and is securely attached.
- Check that the brake fluid level in the reservoir is between the "add" and "full" marks.

Safe Start

- For manual transmissions, put the gearshift in neutral.
- For automatic transmissions, put the gearshift in park.
- BEFORE starting the vehicle, depress the clutch.
- Start the vehicle; keep the clutch depressed.
- Release the clutch slowly once the engine hits idling speed.

Quick Review Question

8. What should be inspected if your vehicle is NOT belt-driven?

Cab Check and Engine Start

All vehicles require the following cab check inspections during which you will start the engine.

Oil gauge

- Be sure that the oil pressure gauge is functioning properly.

15. Vehicle Safety Inspection

- Make sure that the warning light turns off or that the gauge indicates increasing or normal oil pressure.
- If the vehicle is equipped with an oil temperature gauge, it should gradually rise to a normal operating range.

Temperature gauge

- Be sure that the temperature gauge is functioning properly.
- Make sure that the temperature starts to rise to normal operating range or that the temperature light turns off.

Air gauge

- Make sure that the air gauge is functioning properly.
- Be aware of manufacturer specifications for governor cutout.
- Make sure that air pressure builds to the governor cutout ($\approx$ 120 – 140 psi or manufacturer specifications).

Ammeter and Voltmeter

- Make sure that the gauges show that the alternator and/or generator is charging.
- Make sure that the alternator and/or generator warning light is off.

Mirrors and Windshield

- Make sure mirrors are clean.
- Make sure mirrors are properly adjusted; adjust them from the inside.
- Be sure that the windshield is clean with no damage to the glass.
- The windshield should have no illegal stickers or obstructions.

Emergency Equipment

- Make sure there are spare electrical fuses.
- Make sure there are 3 red reflective triangles and 6 fusees (or 3 liquid-burning flares).
- Inform the examiner if the vehicle does not have electrical fuses.
- Be sure fire extinguishers are charged and mounted securely.

Wipers and Washers

- Check that the arms and blades are secure.
- Check that the wipers are undamaged.
- Check to make sure that the wipers operate smoothly.
- If the vehicle is equipped with washers, they must function correctly.

Lights, Reflectors, and Reflector Tape Condition

- This step applies to both the sides and rear of the vehicle.
- Make sure the dash indicators work when the lights they correspond with are turned on: **left turn signal, right turn signal, 4-way flashers, high beams,** and **ABS indicator**.
- Check all external lights and reflective equipment for cleanliness and functionality.
- There should be no missing or broken external lights and/or reflective equipment.
- Verify the correct color of lights and reflectors (see Table 15.4.).
- Brake, turn signal, and 4-way flasher inspections are done separately.

Table 15.4. Color Verification for Lights and Reflectors

Item	Correct Color
Clearance lights	- red at rear

15. Vehicle Safety Inspection

Table 15.4. Color Verification for Lights and Reflectors

Item	Correct Color
	• amber elsewhere
Headlights (high and low beams)	white
Taillights	red at rear
Backing/reverse lights	white
Turn signals	red, yellow, or amber at rear
Hazard lights (4-way flashers)	amber (4-way)
Brake Lights	red at rear
Reflectors	• red at rear • amber elsewhere

Horn

- Check that the horn functions.
- This check applies to both air and electric horns.

Heater and Defroster

- Turn on the heater; make sure it works.
- Turn on the defroster; make sure it works.

Parking Brake Check

- Engage the parking brake (release trailer brakes on combination vehicles).
- Build the air pressure to the governor cutout threshold.
- With the parking brake on, pull forward gently; ensure the vehicle is held in place.

Parking Brake Check (Combination Vehicles)

- Build the air pressure to governor cutout.
- Engage the parking brake.
- Pull forward with the trailer parking brake on.
- Be sure the vehicle is held in place while the trailer parking brake is on.

Hydraulic Brakes

- Note: **you must perform BOTH steps of the hydraulic brake check**.
- If you do not perform both steps, you will fail the inspection test automatically.
- **Step 1:** pump the brake pedal 3 times; hold it down for 5 seconds.
- During the 5 seconds in which it is held, the brake pedal should not depress further.
- **Step 2** (if your rig has a backup system [hydraulic brake reserve]): take the key out.
- Depress the brake pedal.
- Listen: you should hear the sound of the reserve system electric motor.
- Make sure that the warning buzzer (or light) is off.

Air Brake Check (for vehicles so equippeD)

- There are 3 parts of the air brake check.

- You will automatically fail the inspection test if you do not perform the 3 parts of the air brake check correctly.
- This check aims to ensure that ANY air brake safety device functions as it should during a decrease in air pressure.
- If there is an incline, you must use wheel chocks during the air brake check.
- **Step 1:** build up the air pressure to the governor cutoff (≈ 120 – 140 psi).
- Shut off the engine; leave the key in the "on" or "battery charge" position.
- Chock the wheels if needed.
- Release the parking brake.
- If using a combination vehicle, release the tractor protection valve.
- Apply the foot brake fully and hold for 1 minute.
- Look at the air gauge: air pressure should drop more than 3 lb. in 1 minute (for a single vehicle) and more than 4 lb. in 1 minute (for a combination vehicle).
- **Step 2:** apply and release the foot brake rapidly to fan off the air pressure.
- Make sure that any warning devices (e.g., a light, flag, or buzzer) for low air activate BEFORE air pressure falls below 55 psi (or as specified by manufacturer).
- **Step 3:** keep fanning off the air pressure.
- On tractor trailers, make sure the tractor protection valve and parking brake valve close/pop out when air pressure hits 20 – 45 psi (or as specified by manufacturer).
- On single vehicles and other types of combination vehicles, the parking brake valve should close/pop out.

Service Brake Check

- This check aims to ensure that the brakes work correctly and do not pull to either side.
- At a speed of 5 mph, pull forward.
- Apply the service brake; stop.
- Make sure the vehicle does not pull to one side or the other.
- Make sure that the vehicle stops when the brake is applied.

Safety Belt

- Make sure the safety belt is mounted securely.
- Be sure that the safety belt latches as it should.
- Make sure the safety belt is neither ripped nor frayed.

Quick Review Question

9. When checking hydraulic brakes during the vehicle inspection test, how many steps must you perform and what do they entail?

External Inspection

The external inspection applies to all vehicles.

Steering Box/Hoses

- Make sure the steering box is mounted securely and has no leaks.
- Be sure there are no missing bolts and/or nuts.
- Check that there are no power steering fluid leaks and/or damage to the power steering hoses.

Steering Linkage

15. Vehicle Safety Inspection

- Check for cracks and/or signs of wear on the connecting links, arms, and rods from the steering box to the wheel.
- Make sure sockets and joints are neither worn nor loose.
- Be sure that there are no missing cotter keys, nuts, or bolts.

Suspension Springs/Air/Torque

- Check that none of the leaf springs are missing, shifted, or cracked.
- Be sure that none of the coil springs are broken or distorted.
- If the vehicle has suspension components such as torsion bars or torque arms, be sure they are securely mounted and undamaged.
- Check air ride suspension for leaks and/or damage.

Suspension Mounts

- Check that no spring hangers are cracked or broken.
- Be sure that there are no damaged or missing bushings.
- Make sure that no bolts, U-bolts, or other axle mounting parts are broken, loose, or missing.
- Be sure to check the mounts at each point where they are secured to the vehicle axle(s) and frame.

Suspension Shock Absorbers

- Make sure shock absorbers are secure and have no leaks.
- You will be expected to perform the above suspension component inspections on every axle.
- If your vehicle has a power unit and trailer, you will need to inspect those suspension components as well.

Brake Slack Adjustors and Pushrods

- Look for parts that are broken, loose, or missing on **slack adjustors** and **pushrods**.
- When the brake is released and manual slack adjustors are pulled by hand, they should move less than or equal to 1 in.

Brake Chambers

- Make sure **brake chambers** have no leaks, cracks, or dents.
- Check that brake chambers are securely mounted.
- Brake chamber clamps should be neither loose nor missing.

Brake Hoses and Lines

- Make sure hoses are neither cracked, worn, nor leaking.
- Make sure lines are neither cracked, worn, nor leaking.
- Make sure couplings are neither cracked, worn, nor leaking.

Drum Brake

- Check that there are no cracks, holes, or dents.
- Be sure that bolts are neither loose nor missing.
- Look for contaminates (e.g., debris, oil, grease).
- If brake linings are visible, make sure they are not worn dangerously thin.

Brake Linings

- If the drum has openings that allow linings to be seen from the outside, make sure that a visible amount of lining is indeed showing.
- Plan to perform this same inspection on each axle.
- If equipped with a trailer and power unit, the inspection described must also take place.

15. Vehicle Safety Inspection

Wheel Rims

- Rims should not be damaged or bent.
- There cannot be any welding repairs on rims.
- Look for rust trails: these could indicate that the rim is loose on the wheel.

Tires (inspect the following items on EACH tire)

- Ensure the minimum tread depth: 4/32 in. (steering axle tires) or $\frac{2}{32}$ in. (all other tires).
- Make sure the tread is worn evenly.
- Be on the lookout for damage, such as cuts, to the tread or sidewalls.
- Check that the valve caps and steps are neither broken, missing, nor damaged.
- Use a tire gauge to make sure tires have proper inflation.
- You will NOT get credit if you kick the tires or use a mallet to check inflation.

Axle Seals and Hub Oil Seals

- The axle and hub oil seals should not be leaking.
- If the wheel has a sight glass, check that there is an adequate level of oil.

Lug Nuts

- Make sure that all lug nuts are present.
- Ensure lug nuts have no cracks and/or distortions.
- Lug nuts should not have rust trails or shiny threads, which can indicate looseness.
- Be sure that all bolt holes are neither cracked nor distorted.

Spacers/Budd Spacing

- If your vehicle has them, ensure that spacers are neither bent, damaged, nor rusted through.
- Spacers should be centered with dual wheels with tires evenly separated.
- Ensure there are no foreign objects or debris between the spacers.
- Plan to perform this same inspection on each axle.
- If equipped with a trailer and power unit, the inspection described must also take place.

Doors and Mirrors

- Doors must not be damaged.
- Doors must properly open and close from the outside.
- Check that the hinges are secure and that their seals are intact.
- Make sure that mirrors and mirror brackets are securely mounted.
- Ensure the mirrors and mirror brackets do not have loose fittings.

Fuel Tank(s)

- Make sure that the tanks are secure.
- Check that the caps are tight.
- Ensure there are no leaks from the tanks or the lines.

Drive Shaft

- Check that the drive shaft is neither bent nor cracked.
- Ensure that couplings are secure and do not have foreign objects in them.

Exhaust System

- Be on the lookout for damage.
- Make sure there is no rust, carbon soot, or other indications of leaks.
- Be sure the system has no holes, cracks, or severe dents.
- Ensure the system is connected tightly and securely mounted.

Exhaust Systems with Emissions After-Treatment Equipment

- Check the diesel exhaust fluid (DEF) tank; be sure it has enough diesel exhaust fluid (more than one-eighth of a tank)
- Ensure that the dashboard's DEF indicator functions as it should.

Frame

- There should be no cracks, holes, broken welds, or damage to any part of the frame.
- Be sure to inspect the longitudinal frame members, cross members, box, and floor.

Splash Guards/Mud Flaps

- These must be securely mounted.
- Ensure that each of these is undamaged.

Doors, Ties, and Lifts

- Doors and hinges should not be damaged.
- Doors and hinges should open, close, and latch properly (if so equippeD).
- Ensure that ties, straps, chains, and binders are secure.
- If the vehicle has a cargo lift, ensure it has no leaks, damage, and/or missing parts.
- Plan to provide an explanation of how to check that cargo lifts are operating correctly.
- The lift will need to be fully retracted and securely latched.

The following inspection steps concern the tractor/coupling:

Air/Electric Lines

- Make sure you do not hear the sound of leaking air.
- Air hoses and electrical lines should be neither cut, chafed, spliced, nor worn.
- If the steel braid on hoses and electrical lines shows, it is worn.
- Air and electrical lines should not be tangled, pinched, and/or dragging against the tractor parts.

Catwalk/Steps

- The catwalk must be solid/sturdy and bolted securely to the tractor frame.
- There should be no objects on the catwalk.
- The steps that lead to the cab entry and the catwalk must also be solid/sturdy and bolted securely to the tractor frame.

Mounting Bolts

- Ensure there are no loose or missing **mounting brackets, clamps, nuts, or bolts**.
- Ensure that the fifth wheel and slide mounting are solidly attached.
- Make sure there are no missing or loose mounting bolts.
- Check that there are no broken or compromised welds for the pintle hook (or other hitch mount).
- Check that there are no broken or compromised welds on the tongue/drawbar assembly.
- There should be no missing and/or broken parts on the coupling components or mounting brackets on other coupling system types.

Hitch Release Lever

- Check that the hitch release lever is in place.
- Ensure that the hitch release lever is secure.

Locking Jaws

- Look inside the fifth wheel gap.
- Make sure the locking jaws are closed fully around the kingpin.

- Ball hitch, pintle hook, and other coupling systems: ensure the locking mechanism has no broken or missing parts and is securely locked.
- Safety cables or chains must be secure.
- Safety cables and chains should have neither kinks nor excessive slack.

Fifth Wheel Skid Plate

- Ensure that this is lubricated properly.
- Make sure that the fifth wheel skid plate is mounted to the platform securely.
- Bolts and pins must be secure.
- There should be no missing bolts or pins.

Platform (Fifth Wheel)

- There should be no cracks or breaks in the platform structure.
- The platform structure must be able to support the fifth wheel skid plate.

Release Arm (Fifth Wheel)

- If so equipped, ensure that the release arm is in the "engaged" position.
- Check that the safety latch is in place.

Kingpin/Apron/Gap

- Explain to the examiner that the kingpin is held in place by the locking jaws.
- Ensure that the kingpin is neither bent nor damaged; explain this to the examiner.
- Check that the visible part of the apron is neither bent, cracked, nor broken.
- Make sure there is no gap: the trailer should be lying flat on the fifth wheel skid plate.
- Make sure there is a kingpin lock.

Locking Pins

- Ensure there are no loose or missing pins in the sliding fifth wheel's slide mechanism.
- Check for leaks if the fifth wheel is air powered.
- Ensure that the locking pins are all fully engaged.
- Be sure that the fifth wheel is positioned to allow the tractor frame to clear the landing gear when turning.

Sliding Pintle

- Ensure there is no excessive wear in the sliding pintle hook.
- Check that it is secure—it should have no loose or missing nuts or bolts.
- Make sure the cotter pin is in place.

Drawbar or Tongue

- This should be neither bent nor twisted.
- Make sure there are no broken welds or stress cracks.
- Make sure that the tongue/drawbar eye does not have excessive wear.

Tongue Storage Area

- Make sure the storage area is secured to the tongue.
- Ensure that the storage area is solid.
- Make sure any cargo in the storage area (e.g., chains, binders) is secure.

Quick Review Questions

10. Which types of vehicles require an external inspection?

11. When inspecting the tractor/coupling, you should hear the sound of leaking air. Is this true or false?

School Buses

Ensure that the school bus has the following emergency equipment:
- spare electrical fuses (if so equippeD)
- 3 red reflective triangles
- 6 fusees OR 3 liquid-burning flares
- a fire extinguisher that is properly charged and rated
- an emergency kit (with contents intact)
- a cleanup kit for bodily fluids

- The following external lights/reflective devices must be secure, operational, correctly positioned, and undamaged:
    - alternately flashing red lights (on the front and back of the bus)
    - alternately flashing amber lights
    - outside left and right side flat mirrors
    - outside left and right side convex mirrors
    - outside left and right side crossover mirrors
    - strobe light (if equippeD)
    - stop arm light (if equippeD)
- Internal and external mirrors used to observe students must be adjusted properly.
- **All mirrors** (external and internal) and **their brackets** must be **undamaged**, have **no loose fittings**, and be **securely mounted**.
- **Mirrors must be clean** and should not impede visibility.
- The **stop arm** (if equippeD) should be securely mounted to the vehicle's frame.
    - It should have no damage or loose fittings.
    - The stop arm should extend fully when in use.
- During the **passenger entry/lift** inspection
    - the entry door must be undamaged and able to close securely from the inside;
    - the entry door should operate smoothly;
    - handrails must be secure;
    - step lights (if so equippeD) must be in working order;
    - entry steps must be clear of obstructions;
    - entry step treads should be neither loose nor excessively worn;
    - handicap lifts must have no leaks, be undamaged, and have no missing parts;
    - plan to explain how to check a handicap lift for correct operation; and
    - the handicap lift should be retracted fully and latched securely.
- During the inspection of the **emergency exit**
    - be prepared to show that at least 1 emergency exit is undamaged, operates smoothly, and can securely close from the inside;
    - ensure the release handle can be properly operated from inside AND outside the vehicle;
    - point out all other emergency exits and be prepared to explain how they operate; and
    - be sure that all emergency exit warning devices function as they should.
- During the inspection of the bus's **seating**
    - no seat frames should be broken,
    - seat frames must be firmly attached to the floor, and

15. Vehicle Safety Inspection

- seat cushions must be securely attached to seat frames.

Quick Review Question

12. What emergency equipment should be on the bus?

Trailers

The following apply to the front of the trailer:

Air and Electrical Connections

- Trailer air connectors should be sealed and in good condition.
- Gladhands must be locked in place.
- Gladhands must be undamaged.
- Gladhands should not have any air leaks.
- The trailer electrical plug must be firmly seated and locked in place.

Header Board/Headboard (if equippeD)

- The header board must be secure and sturdy enough to withstand cargo.
- The header board should be undamaged.
- Canvas or tarp carriers must be securely mounted and fastened.
- Check the front area for damage (e.g., cracks, bulges) on **enclosed trailers**.

*The following apply to the **sides of the trailer**:*

Landing Gear

- Landing gear must be raised fully and have no missing parts.
- The crank handle must be secure.
- Ensure that the support frame and landing pads are undamaged.
- Check for hydraulic or air leaks if landing gear is power operated.

Doors/Ties/Lifts

- Doors should be undamaged.
- Doors must open, close, and latch correctly from the outside.
- Ensure that ties, straps, binders, and chains are secure.
- Cargo lifts (if equippeD) must have no leaks.
- Cargo lifts should be undamaged with no missing parts.
- Plan to explain how to check a cargo lift for correct operation.
- The cargo lift should be retracted fully and latched securely.

Frame

- Ensure there are no cracks, broken welds, holes, or damage to the frame.
- Ensure there are no cracks, broken welds, holes, or damage to the cross members.
- Ensure there are no cracks, broken welds, holes, or damage to the box.
- Ensure there are no cracks, broken welds, holes, or damage to the floor.

Tandem Release Arm/Locking Pins

- Locking pins (if so equippeD) should be locked in place.
- The release arm should be secured.
- For **the rest of the trailer**, complete the inspections of the following components as described in the "Cab Check and Engine Start" and "External Inspection" sections above:
  - wheels

15. Vehicle Safety Inspection

- suspension system
- brakes
- doors, ties, and lifts
- splash guards

Quick Review Question

13. If the trailer's landing gear is power operated, what should you look for during the inspection?

Transit Buses and Coaches

The following apply to the internal inspection of the coach/transit bus:

Passenger Entry/Lift

- Entry doors must operate smoothly and close securely from the inside of the vehicle.
- Ensure handrails are secure.
- If equipped with step lights, be sure they are working.
- Be sure that entry steps are clear.
- Ensure that the tread on entry steps is neither loose nor overly worn.
- Handicap lifts must have no leaks.
- Handicap lifts should be undamaged with no missing parts.
- Plan to explain how to check a handicap lift for correct operation.
- The handicap lift should be retracted fully and latched securely.

Emergency Exits

- All emergency exits must be undamaged.
- Ensure that all emergency exits operate smoothly.
- Make sure that all emergency exits close securely from the inside.
- Ensure that all emergency exit warning devices are functional.

Passenger Seating

- No seat frames should be broken.
- Seat frames must be firmly attached to the floor.
- Seat cushions must be securely attached to seat frames.

Doors and Mirrors

- Entry and exit doors must be undamaged.
- Entry and exit doors should operate smoothly from the outside.
- Ensure that hinges are secure.
- Ensure that hinge seals are intact.
- Ensure that all **passenger exit mirrors** are undamaged, securely mounted, and have no loose fittings.
- Ensure that all **external mirrors** are undamaged, securely mounted, and have no loose fittings.
- Ensure that all **mirror brackets** are undamaged, securely mounted, and have no loose fittings.

The following apply to the external inspection of the coach/transit bus:

Level/Air Leaks

- Make sure that the vehicle is sitting level at both the front and the rear.

15. Vehicle Safety Inspection

- If air equipped, make sure you cannot hear any air leaks from the suspension system.

Fuel Tanks

- Fuel tanks must be secure.
- There should be no leaks from the tank(s) or the lines.

Baggage Compartments

- All exterior baggage and compartment doors must be undamaged and latch securely.
- All exterior baggage and compartment doors must function properly.

Battery/Box

- Make sure the battery (or batteries) is secure, regardless of its location.
- Ensure that connections are tight.
- Check to see that cell caps are present.
- There should be no signs of excessive corrosion.
- The battery box and cover/door should be secure and undamaged.
- For the remainder of the coach/transit bus, complete the inspections described in the "Cab Check and Engine Start" and "External Inspection" sections above.

Quick Review Questions

14. When inspecting the passenger entry/lift area of a transit bus or coach, what should you look for on the tread?

15. Should the front and rear ends of a transit bus or coach be level, or should the front be lifted slightly higher than the rear?

Answer Key

1. The primary reason for vehicle inspections is to help ensure the safety of you and others.

2. Shock absorbers should be inspected for leaks.

3. During step 3 of the 7-step inspection method, air pressure should build from 50 to 90 psi within 3 minutes.

4. After pumping the brake pedal 3 times and firmly applying pressure to the pedal for 5 seconds, the pedal should not move. If the pedal moves, it is an indication that the hydraulic brakes have a leak or other issue.

5. Whenever you stop, you should check the following items: tires, wheels, and rims; brakes; reflectors and lights; the trailer brake and electrical connections; trailer coupling devices; and cargo securement devices.

6. The vehicle inspection test evaluates your knowledge of whether your vehicle is safe to drive.

7. The following vehicles require additional inspections that are specific to the vehicle type: school buses, trailers, and transit buses/coaches.

8. If your vehicle does not have engine compartment belts (i.e., is not belt-driven), check the engine to be sure it is in proper working order, undamaged, mounted securely, and has no leaks.

9. When checking hydraulic brakes during the vehicle inspection test, there are 2 steps that you must perform: Step 1 involves pumping the brake pedal 3 times and holding it down for 5 seconds, during which time the brake pedal should not depress further. Step 2 applies to rigs that have a backup system/hydraulic brake reserve and involves taking the key out, depressing the brake pedal, and listening to the sound of the reserve system electric motor. Be sure that the warning buzzer (or light) is off.

10. All vehicle types require an external inspection.

11. This is false. You should NOT hear the sound of leaking air when inspecting the tractor/coupling.

12. During the inspection—and whenever a bus is being driven—it should contain the following emergency equipment: spare electrical fuses (if so equippeD), 3 red reflective triangles, 6 fusees OR 3 liquid-burning flares, a fire extinguisher that is properly charged and rated, an emergency kit (with contents intact), and a cleanup kit for bodily fluids.

13. If the trailer's landing gear is power operated, you should check for hydraulic or air leaks during the inspection.

14. When inspecting the passenger entry/lift area of a transit bus or coach, you should ensure that the tread on the entry steps is neither loose nor overly worn.

15. Transit buses and coaches should sit level at both the front and the rear

16 Basic Vehicle Control Skills Test

- The basic vehicle control skills test evaluates how skillfully you can control a vehicle as well as your knowledge of **3 of the following maneuvers:**
    - straight line backing
    - offset back/right
    - offset back/left
    - parallel park (driver's side)
    - parallel park (conventional)
    - alley dock
- You can only take the basic vehicle control skills test if you pass the vehicle inspection test.
- You cannot move on to the on-road test if you do not pass the basic vehicle control skills test.
- You will be asked to do the following:
    - move the vehicle forward
    - move the vehicle backward
    - turn the vehicle within a defined area (e.g., marked by lanes, cones, barriers)
- The examiner will explain how each control test should be performed.

Quick Review Question

1. Name 3 driving maneuvers that will be tested during the basic vehicle control skills test.

Scoring

The basic vehicle control skills test is scored based on the following:

Encroachments

- You will be scored on the number of times you cross over or touch (i.e., encroach) a boundary.
- No portion of your vehicle should touch or cross over a boundary.
- Each time you encroach, it will be counted as an error.

Pull-ups

- A pull-up is when a driver stops and pulls forward to get a better position or clear an encroachment.
- A pull-up does not include stopping without changing direction.
- Initial pull-ups will not cause you to be penalized.
- Excessive instances of pull-ups count as errors against your score.

Outside vehicle observations

- These are also known as "looks."

- You may be allowed to stop safely and exit the vehicle in order to check the vehicle's external position.
  - If you exit the vehicle, you must put the vehicle in neutral and set the parking brake(s).
  - If exiting the vehicle, face the vehicle and keep 3 points of contact with it at all times.
  - If you are exiting a bus, keep a firm grasp on the handrail the whole time.
  - **Not safely securing the vehicle can result in an automatic failure of this skills test.**
  - **Not safely exiting the vehicle can also result in automatic failure of this skills test.**
- You have 2 allowable times to do a look EXCEPT for the straight line backing portion, for which you are allowed only 1 look.
- These are all scored as looks: opening the door, moving from a seated position (when in control of the vehicle), and/or walking to the rear of a bus to check the view.

Inside Parallel/Final Position

- You must complete each exercise EXACTLY as instructed by the examiner.
- The examiner will describe the maneuver for the final position.
- Not maneuvering the vehicle into its final position as described will result in a penalty, which could result in failure.

Quick Review Question

2. If you must exit the vehicle during the skills test, what steps must you take?

Exercises

- You may be asked to perform numerous exercises as described in Table 16.1.

Table 16.1. Exercises on the Basic Vehicle Control Skills Test

Exercise	Procedure
Straight line backing	- There will be 2 rows of cones. - Back the vehicle in a straight line. - Do not touch or cross the cones/exercise boundaries.
Offset back/right	- You must back into a space to the right rear of your vehicle. - Pull straight forward to the outer cone or boundary. - From the outer boundary, back the vehicle in the **opposite** lane. - Keep backing in the opposite lane until the front of the vehicle passes the first set of cones without striking any boundaries.
Offset back/left	- You must back into a space that is to the left rear of the vehicle.

16. Basic Vehicle Control Skills Test

Table 16.1. Exercises on the Basic Vehicle Control Skills Test	
Exercise	**Procedure**
	• Pull straight forward to the outer cone or boundary. • From the outer boundary, back into the opposite lane until the vehicle's front passes the first set of cones without striking any boundaries.
Driver's side parallel park	• This entails parallel parking to a space **on your left**. • Drive past the entrance to the parallel parking space; keep the vehicle parallel to the parking area. • Back into the space; do not cross the front, side, or rear boundaries. • The vehicle must fit in the space completely.
Conventional parallel park	• This entails parallel parking to a space **on your right**. • Drive past the entrance to the parallel parking space; keep the vehicle parallel to the parking area. • Back into the space; do not cross the front, side, or rear boundaries. • The vehicle must fit in the space completely.
Alley dock	• This involves sight-side backing into an alley. • Drive past the alley. • Position the vehicle parallel to the outer boundary. • From the outer boundary, back into the alley. • The rear of the vehicle should be within 3 ft. of the rear of the alley; be sure the vehicle is straight and you do not touch or cross any boundaries.

16. Basic Vehicle Control Skills Test

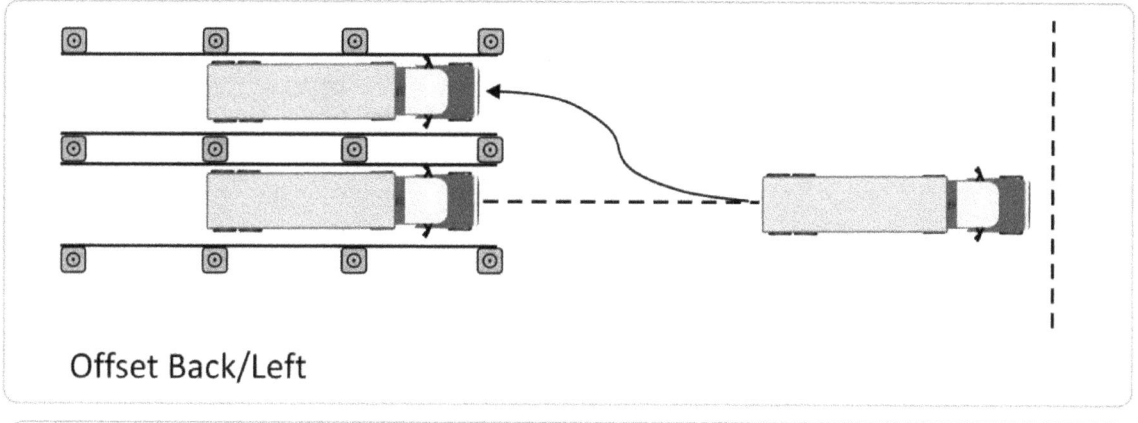

Offset Back/Left

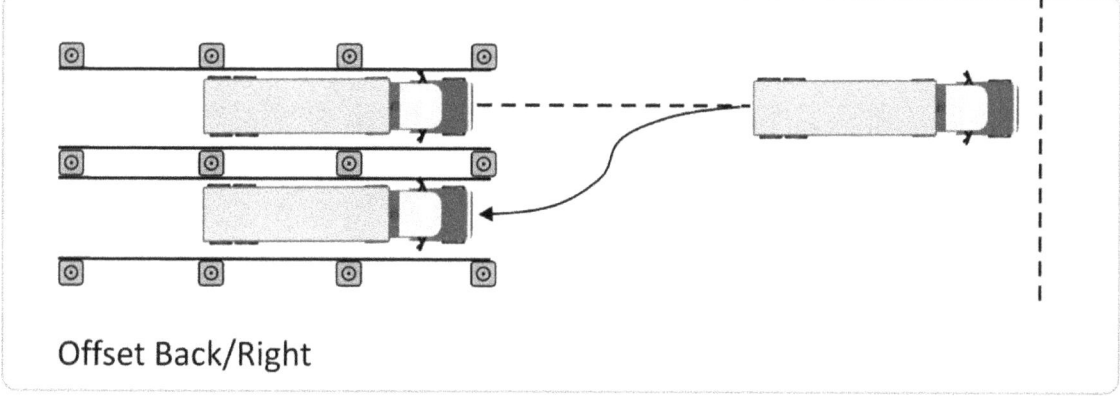

Offset Back/Right

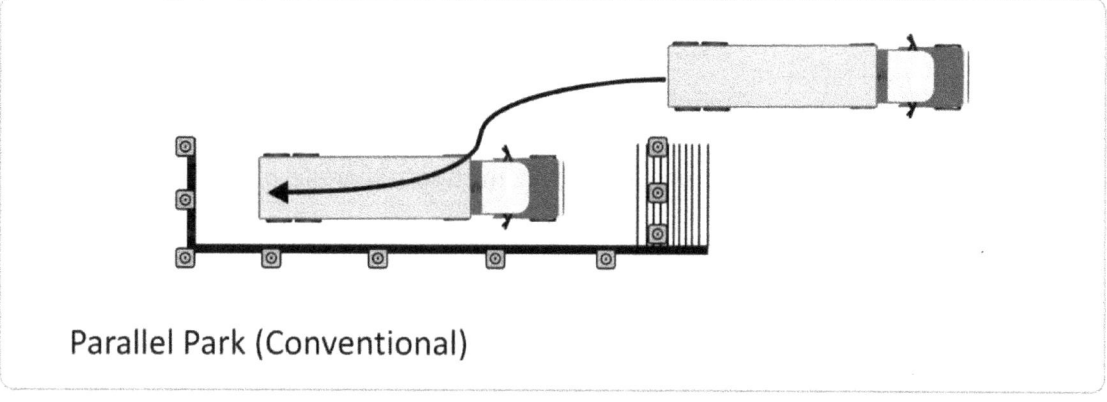

Parallel Park (Conventional)

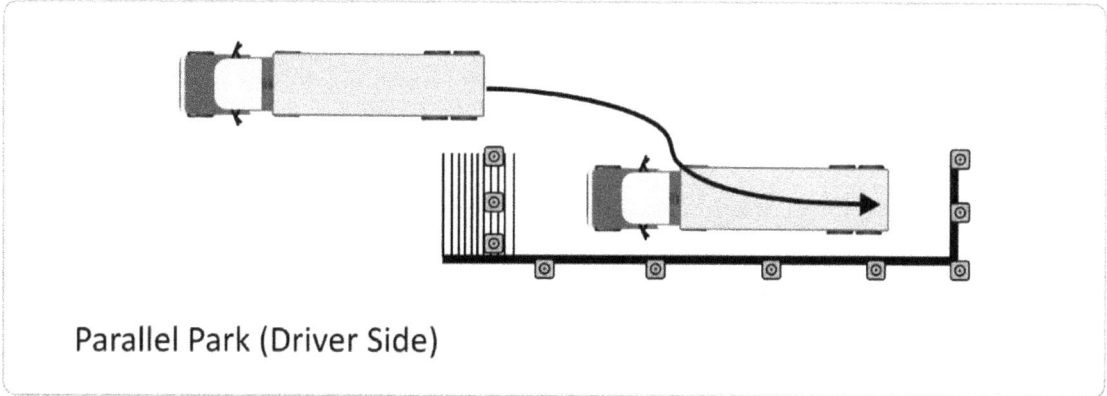

Parallel Park (Driver Side)

16. Basic Vehicle Control Skills Test

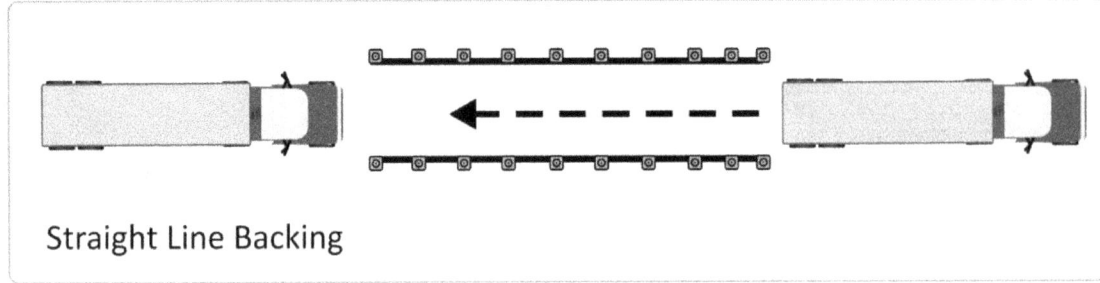

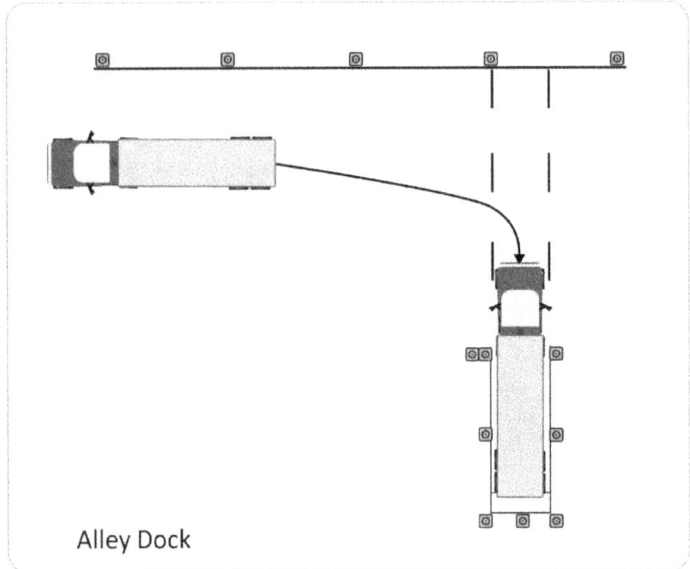

Figure 16.1. Vehicle Control Skills: Maneuvers

Quick Review Question

3. On what side do you park when performing a conventional parallel parking maneuver?

Answer Key

1. Any 3 of the following maneuvers will be tested during the basic vehicle control skills test: straight line backing, offset back/right, offset back/left, parallel park (driver's side), parallel park (conventional), and alley dock.

2. If you must exit the vehicle during the skills test, you must first put the vehicle in neutral and set the parking brake. Upon exiting, be sure to face the vehicle and keep 3 points of contact with it at all times. When exiting a bus, you must keep a firm grasp on the handrail the whole time. If you do not safely exit and/or secure the vehicle, you may receive an automatic failure of the skills test.

3. Conventional parallel parking entails parallel parking to a space on your right.

17 Road Test

The on-road driving portion of the skills tests evaluates your **commercial driving ability**.
- You can only take the on-road skills test if you have passed the basic vehicle control skills test.
- The road test must be taken in the vehicle you plan to drive professionally (or a vehicle in the same class).

Your skills on the following maneuvers will be evaluated on the road test:
- starting
- making a quick, smooth stop
- upshifting
- downshifting
- making a lane change
- merging
- use of lanes
- posture
- right-of-way
- approaching a corner
- traffic signals
- traffic signs
- left turns
- right turns
- intersections
- railroad crossings
- curves
- roadside stop/start

- You will be guided through the road test by the official conducting the exam.
- If you pass, you will be issued a CDL.
- If you do not pass, you must take the road test on a different day.
- **The following will result in failure of your road test:**
    - having more than 30 deductions
    - having an accident
    - causing an accident
    - driving unsafely/dangerously
    - being uncooperative
    - violating laws

17. Road Test

- You will be evaluated on how safely you can drive your vehicle in various traffic conditions:
    - left and right turns
    - intersections
    - railroad crossings
    - up- and downgrades
    - curves
    - single-lane roads
    - multilane roads
    - streets
    - highways

> **Helpful Hint:**
> Experienced and licensed CDL drivers often advise candidates to verbalize their actions during the on-road test. For example, "Checking all mirrors; car behind is speeding, poses a hazard, and is

Quick Review Questions

1. Which skills test must be passed before you are eligible to take the on-road skills test?

2. Name 3 events or behaviors that could cause you to fail the on-road skills test.

How You Will Be Tested

- Your test route will offer a variety of traffic situations.
- Regardless of the specific traffic situation, you must ALWAYS
    - drive safely and responsibly;
    - wear your safety belt; and
    - obey all traffic signs, signals, and laws.
- You will be scored on specific driving maneuvers as well as general driving behavior.
- You must follow the examiner's directions.
    - The examiner will not ask you to drive unsafely.
    - You will have time to ask questions after being given directions.
- The test route may not include certain traffic situations.
    - If this is the case, you may be asked to simulate specific situations.
    - If simulating, explain to the examiner what you would do in the particular situation.

Quick Review Question

3. What are you expected to do if the examiner asks you to simulate a certain traffic condition?

General Driving Behaviors

Your performance of the following general driving behaviors will count toward your score:

Using the Clutch (manual transmissions)

- You must always use the clutch to shift.
- Double-clutch if you will be shifting an unsynchronized manual transmission.
- Never rev or lug the engine.

- **Never do the following:**
    - ride the clutch in order to control speed
    - coast while keeping the clutch depressed
    - pop the clutch

Using Gears (Manual Transmissions)

- Never clash or grind gears.
- Choose a gear that will not rev or lug the engine.
- Never shift during turning.
- Never shift while going through an intersection.

Using Brakes

- Never ride the brake.
- Never pump the brake.
- Never brake harshly; always use steady pressure and brake smoothly.

Using Lanes

- The vehicle should not go over curbs, sidewalks, and/or lane markings.
- Always stop BEHIND stop lines, stop signs, and crosswalks.
- On multiple-lane roads, always complete turns in the proper lane.
    - A left turn should be finished in the lane directly right of the center line.
    - A right turn should be finished in the curb, or rightmost, lane.
- Unless a lane is blocked, move to (or remain in) the rightmost lane.

Steering

- You should neither under- nor oversteer the vehicle.
- Unless shifting, both hands must be on the steering wheel at all times.
- Return your hands to the steering wheel as soon as you finish shifting.

Regular Traffic Checks

- Be sure to check the traffic and mirrors regularly
    - before an intersection,
    - while in the intersection, and
    - after the intersection.
- Scan and check for traffic in high-volume areas and where pedestrians are anticipated.

Using Turn Signals

- Turn signals should always be used properly and activated when required.
- Remember to cancel turn signals once turns and lane changes are completed.

Quick Review Questions

4. Name 3 things you should never do on the on-road skills test if you are using a clutch.

5. Is there ever an excuse to not have both hands on the wheel while steering?

Urban Driving

Check traffic regularly.

- Keep a safe following distance.
- Make sure your vehicle is centered and in the proper (i.e., rightmost) lane.

17. Road Test

- Keep up with the traffic flow, but do not exceed posted speed limits.

Quick Review Question

6. Is it OK to slightly exceed the speed limit in order to keep up with the flow of traffic?

Turns

When you are asked to make a turn
- o always check for traffic in ALL directions;
- o if a lane change is needed to make the turn, remember to use the turn signal; and
- o change lanes safely before turning (if requireD).
- As you are approaching the turn
  - o warn others by using the correct turn signal;
  - o be sure to slow down smoothly;
  - o if needed, change gears to maintain power; and
  - o do not coast unsafely (i.e., being out of gear or in neutral for a distance greater than the length of your vehicle).
- If a stop is required before making the turn
  - o stop smoothly—do not skid or roll;
  - o stop completely behind the crosswalk, stop sign, or stop line;
  - o ensure a safe gap if a vehicle is ahead of you (i.e., be sure you can see the rear tires of that vehicle);
  - o be sure that the front wheels of your vehicle are aimed straight ahead.
- When you are ready to turn
  - o be sure to check traffic in ALL directions,
  - o ensure both hands are kept on the steering wheel during the turn,
  - o check your mirrors regularly to ensure you will not hit anything on the inside of the turn,
  - o remember that your vehicle should NOT move into oncoming traffic, and
  - o ensure the vehicle is in the correct lane when the turn is finished.
- When the turn is finished
  - o be sure that the turn signal is off;
  - o increase your speed so that it matches that of the traffic;
  - o if you are not already in the rightmost lane, put the turn signal on and move to that lane; and
  - o continue to check mirrors and traffic.

Quick Review Question

7. How can you be sure that there is a safe gap between your vehicle and the one in front?

Intersections

When approaching an intersection

- o thoroughly check for traffic in ALL directions;
- o slow down gently and brake smoothly;
- o change gears if needed;
- o come to a complete stop if needed (e.g., at a stop sign)—do not coast;
- o ensure a safe gap if a vehicle is ahead of you (i.e., be sure you can see the rear tires of that vehicle); and
- o make sure your vehicle does not roll forward or backward.
- As you are driving through an intersection
  - o make sure to thoroughly check traffic in all directions,
  - o slow down,
  - o yield to traffic and pedestrians,
  - o never change lanes, and
  - o always keep your hands on the wheel.
- Once you are through an intersection
  - o continue using your mirrors to monitor traffic,
  - o speed up smoothly, and
  - o change gears as needed.

Quick Review Question

8. When driving through an intersection, you have the right-of-way and pedestrians and other traffic must wait for you. Is this true or false?

Lane Changes and Expressway or Limited Access/Rural Highway

Portions of the test will take place in multiple lanes; the examiner will ask you to change lanes to the left and then return to the right lane.

- Before you enter an expressway
  - o always check for traffic;
  - o remember to use turn signals properly; and
  - o merge smoothly, making sure you are in the proper lane.
- When you are on the expressway
  - o ensure proper positioning in your lane,
  - o maintain proper vehicle spacing,
  - o maintain proper vehicle speed, and
  - o check traffic in all directions thoroughly and continuously.
- When exiting an expressway
  - o check for traffic,
  - o make sure to use the proper turn signals,
  - o slow down smoothly in the exit lane,
  - o continue to slow down upon reaching the exit ramp,
  - o stay within lane markings on the exit ramp, and
  - o ensure adequate spacing between your vehicle and others.

17. Road Test

Quick Review Question

9. When you are driving on an expressway, what are the 4 rules you need to follow?

Stopping and Starting

You will be asked to pull your vehicle over to the side of the road and stop (as if to check something).

- Check all traffic in all directions thoroughly.
- When safe to do so, prepare to move to the rightmost lane (or shoulder).
    - Continue to check traffic.
    - Turn on your vehicle's right turn signal.
    - Slow down smoothly and brake evenly.
    - If needed, change gears.
    - Stop the vehicle fully—do not coast.
- Once you are stopped
    - ensure the vehicle is parallel to the curb (or shoulder),
    - ensure the vehicle is safely away from the flow of traffic,
    - check that your vehicle is not blocking driveways or fire hydrants,
    - cancel the turn signal if it is still on,
    - turn on your hazard lights/4-way flashers,
    - put the parking brake on,
    - shift into neutral or park, and
    - take your foot off of the brake and clutch pedals.
- When the examiner asks you to resume driving
    - thoroughly check your mirrors and the traffic in all directions;
    - turn your hazard lights/4-way flashers off;
    - put your vehicle's left turn signal on;
    - release the parking brake when traffic permits;
    - pull straight ahead;
    - **never turn the wheels before the vehicle moves;**
    - check the traffic in all directions—pay close attention to traffic to your left;
    - when safe to do so, accelerate and steer smoothly into the proper lane; and
    - cancel the turn signal once your vehicle returns to the flow of traffic.

Quick Review Question

10. During the stopping and starting portion of the exam, when should you turn the wheels after the examiner gives you the go-ahead to resume driving?

Curves

As you approach a curve

- thoroughly check the traffic in ALL directions,
- reduce speed BEFORE the curve to avoid braking or shifting while in the curve,
- ensure your vehicle stays in its lane, and
- continuously monitor the traffic in all directions.

Quick Review Question

11. Why should speed be reduced before taking a curve?

Railroad Crossings

Before reaching a railroad crossing
- slow down;
- brake smoothly;
- shift gears as needed; and
- use your eyes and ears: look AND listen for trains in either direction.
- When any part of your vehicle is in a crossing or going across the tracks
  - NEVER stop,
  - NEVER change gears, and
  - NEVER change lanes.
- If driving **a coach/transit bus, school bus, or placarded vehicle**
  - put the hazard lights/4-way flashers on;
  - stop within 50 ft. of the nearest rail;
  - ensure you are no fewer than 15 ft. from the nearest rail;
  - look and listen along the track in BOTH directions for approaching trains;
  - look for signals that indicate a train is approaching;
  - prepare to open the window and door (if requireD) BEFORE crossing if driving a bus;
  - ensure both hands remain on the steering wheel as you cross the tracks;
  - never stop, switch gears, or change lanes if ANY part of the vehicle is crossing the tracks;
  - remember to shut off hazard lights/4-way flashers AFTER crossing the tracks; and
  - continuously monitor traffic and check your mirrors.
- If your test route does not have a railroad crossing, prepare to
  - explain how you would perform the railroad crossing, and
  - demonstrate the proper procedures at a simulated location.

Quick Review Question

12. Within what distance of the nearest rail should you stop?

Bridges and Overpasses

Pay close attention if you will need to drive under an overpass or over a bridge:
- **The examiner may ask what the posted height was after you drive under an overpass.**
- **You may be asked what the posted weight limit was after going over a bridge.**
- If the route does not have bridges or overpasses, the examiner may ask you the details of other posted signs.

17. Road Test

Quick Review Question

13. During the exam, why is it especially important to pay attention to overpasses, bridges, and other posted signs?

Discharging (Loading and Unloading) Students on a School Bus

Candidates applying for a school bus endorsement must demonstrate how to do a student discharge.

- Review Chapter 13 for specific guidance on this procedure.
- Be mindful of differences between unloading on a route, unloading at school, and special dangers related to discharging students.
- When approaching a stop to pick up students
    - approach the pickup location at a slow rate of speed;
    - continuously check traffic;
    - put on the right turn signal;
    - put on the amber warning lights;
    - on the traveled part of the road, move as far to the right as possible; and
    - check traffic again.
- When stopping to pick up students, you must
    - stop the bus completely,
    - stop at least 10 ft. from the students,
    - put the transmission in neutral or park,
    - set the parking brake, and
    - turn on the stop arm and red warning lights.
- When unloading students
    - be sure to communicate with them clearly,
    - check traffic regularly,
    - open the door for students, and
    - check for students.
- While students are crossing
    - check traffic continuously,
    - communicate with the students, and
    - check for students.
- When student pickup or drop-off is complete
    - check all mirrors thoroughly,
    - turn off the warning lights,
    - turn off the stop arm,
    - close the door,
    - check thoroughly for traffic, and
    - depress the accelerator to drive away from the stop area.

Quick Review Question

14. When stopping to pick up students, at what distance from the students should you stop?

Answer Key

1. You must pass the basic vehicle control skills test before you are eligible to take the on-road skills test. Remember: you must also pass the vehicle inspection test before you can take the basic vehicle control skills test; the on-road skills test is the last of the 3 skills tests you need to pass in order to earn your CDL.

2. Any 1 of the following can result in failure of your on-road skills test: having more than 30 deductions, having an accident, causing an accident, driving unsafely/dangerously, being uncooperative, or violating laws.

3. If you are asked to simulate a certain traffic condition, you should explain to the examiner what you would do if confronted with the given situation.

4. If using a clutch during your on-road skills test, you should never 1) ride the clutch in order to control speed, 2) coast while keeping the clutch depressed, or 3) pop the clutch.

5. Shifting gears is the only excuse to not have both hands on the wheel while steering.

6. It is never OK to exceed the speed limit—even a little—in order to keep up with the flow of traffic.

7. If you can see the rear tires of the vehicle ahead of you, the gap distance is considered safe.

8. This is false. You must always yield to traffic and pedestrians when driving through an intersection.

9. When you are driving on an expressway, you must 1) ensure proper positioning in your lane, 2) maintain proper vehicle spacing, 3) maintain proper vehicle speed, and 4) check traffic in all directions thoroughly and continuously.

10. During the stopping and starting portion of the exam, you should only turn the wheels once the vehicle starts moving—never turn the wheels before the vehicle moves.

11. Before taking a curve, speed should be reduced in order to avoid having to brake or shift while in the curve.

12. You should stop within 50 ft. of the nearest rail.

13. It is especially important to pay attention to overpasses, bridges, and other posted signs during the exam because the examiner may ask you about the posted height, weight limit, or details of other posted signs.

14. When stopping to pick up students, you must stop at least 10 ft. from the students.

Practice Test #1

General Knowledge

1. What is the most important reason for doing a vehicle inspection?
    A) to make sure the vehicle looks clean
    B) to ensure the vehicle is safe to drive
    C) to check the vehicle's oil level
    D) to ensure registration is current

2. What should gradually rise to the normal operating range after the engine is started?
    A) engine oil pressure
    B) voltmeter
    C) engine oil temperature
    D) ammeter

3. When transporting cargo, how often must drivers inspect its securement throughout the day?
    A) every hour or 50 mi.
    B) every 2 hours or 100 mi.
    C) every 3 hours or 150 mi.
    D) every 4 hours or 200 mi.

4. What should drivers do as they approach a vehicle for inspection?
    A) initial the inspection report
    B) notice the vehicle's general condition
    C) check that the parking brake is on
    D) review the last inspection report

5. According to the vehicle inspection guide, what is the first step of the vehicle overview?
    A) Test the parking brake.
    B) Check the tires and fill them with air.
    C) Check the electrical fuses.
    D) Review the last vehicle inspection report.

6. How can the driver determine when to shift up?
    A) judge according to the speed of passing vehicles
    B) listen for a grinding engine sound
    C) watch the engine tachometer
    D) look at the number of gears

Practice Test #1

7. What are the 4 basic types of retarders?
    A) electric, motor, filter, shaft
    B) exhaust, engine, hydraulic, electric
    C) hydraulic, flywheel, drivetrain, motor
    D) drivetrain, shaft, exhaust, generator

8. What type of mirror is often used on large vehicles to increase a driver's field of vision?
    A) convex mirror
    B) arched mirror
    C) concave mirror
    D) plane mirror

9. What should be done after turning if a vehicle does not have self-canceling signals?
    A) flash the brake lights
    B) turn off the turn signal
    C) tap the brake pedal
    D) use the hazard lights

10. How long does a driver have to put out emergency warning devices after stopping on the shoulder of any road?
    A) 30 seconds
    B) 1 minute
    C) 5 minutes
    D) 10 minutes

11. While conducting a walk-around inspection, what should the driver do after inspecting the left side, the front, the right side, and the rear?
    A) test the parking brakes
    B) start the engine and check it
    C) do a general overall check
    D) check the signal lights

12. How should a driver back out a truck safely?
    A) by reversing straight back without turning
    B) by steering with the vehicle moving toward the driver's side
    C) by turning the wheel toward the passenger's side
    D) by turning back first to the right and then to the left

13. How do drivers know if a car is in their "blind spot"?
    A) by accelerating quickly to see if a car was in the blind spot
    B) by looking in the mirrors that have been aligned to show the blind spots
    C) by looking out the window to see if there is a car in the lane
    D) by checking the mirrors frequently to see the other vehicles in the other lanes

14. If a 70-ft. truck is driving 40 mph down the road, at least how much following distance should the driver allow?
    A) 7 seconds
    B) 6 seconds
    C) 5 seconds
    D) 4 seconds

Practice Test #1

15. Which action should a driver take if an aggressive driver gets into a crash within a visible distance of the driver?
    A) check and see if the crash victims are injured
    B) call and wait for the police
    C) block the aggressive driver's car
    D) confront the aggressive driver

16. Which of the following problems of nighttime driving is one of the leading causes of traffic collisions?
    A) drunk drivers
    B) lack of headlight usage
    C) glare
    D) fatigue

17. How far away should an oncoming car be for the driver to dim the vehicle's lights at night in order to prevent blinding others?
    A) up to 1,000 ft.
    B) within 500 ft.
    C) at least 50 ft.
    D) one-half mile away

18. For what reason should a driver begin in low gear prior to starting to drive up a mountain?
    A) The driver will be able to effectively use the braking effect of the engine.
    B) The driver will be able to accelerate gradually up the mountain.
    C) The driver will not be able to downshift after accelerating.
    D) A higher gear may damage the transmission.

19. What is the difference between newer and older ABSs with regard to the malfunction lamp staying on at start-up?
    A) The lamp on the newer system flashes 3 times.
    B) The lamp on the older system remains on longer.
    C) The older system's lamp will turn off after 5 minutes.
    D) A lamp will remain on until reaching speeds of 5 mph on the newer models.

20. What is usually involved in fires on or around trucks?
    A) air
    B) tires
    C) fuel
    D) cargo

21. When driving under 40 mph, what is the amount of space—in seconds—that should be maintained for every 10 ft. of vehicle length?
    A) 1 second
    B) 3 seconds
    C) 10 seconds
    D) 30 seconds

22. What should be done when traveling near other vehicles in heavy traffic?
    A) drop back so as to be visible to other drivers
    B) flash the lights
    C) stay close to the other vehicles
    D) increase the vehicle's speed

Practice Test #1

23. To drive a truck safely in heavy traffic, what is the most appropriate action?
    A) drive 10 mph faster than the other vehicles
    B) drive 10 mph slower than the other vehicles
    C) drive the speed of the other vehicles
    D) use flashing hazard lights

24. What is the number one cause of injury and death in roadway work zones?
    A) texting while driving
    B) using a handheld mobile communication device
    C) speeding
    D) poor road conditions

25. Which of the following activities is considered a distraction for drivers?
    A) smoking
    B) checking mirrors
    C) scanning the road
    D) checking gauges

26. Which of the following is the best way for a driver to stay safe when encountering fog?
    A) pull over to the side of the road until the fog has passed
    B) maintain normal speed
    C) use high-beam headlights
    D) turn off headlights and turn on 4-way flashers

27. How long does it take a typical tractor trailer combination unit to clear a double track?
    A) 5 seconds
    B) 15 seconds
    C) 30 seconds
    D) 45 seconds

28. If it is necessary to leave the roadway during an emergency, a driver should
    A) accelerate off the pavement.
    B) slow the vehicle as much as possible before leaving the roadway.
    C) keep 1 set of wheels on the pavement.
    D) turn sharply onto the shoulder.

29. ABSs prevent
    A) tire burnouts.
    B) slow braking.
    C) wheel lockup.
    D) overheated brakes.

30. A 12-ounce glass of 5% beer has the same amount of alcohol as
    A) A 6-ounce glass of 12% wine
    B) A 1 ½ ounce shot of 80 proof liquor
    C) An ounce shot of 80 proof liquor
    D) 1 ¼ ounce shot of 90 proof liquor and a 5-ounce glass of 12% wine

Practice Test #1

31. When does a vehicle inspection report need to be signed by the driver?
    A) as soon as it is written
    B) if defects were noted and certified to be repaired
    C) when no defects are noted on the vehicle inspection report
    D) after all repairs are completed

32. Before applying firm pressure to the brake pedal, how many times should the pedal be pumped in order to test for hydraulic leaks?
    A) 1
    B) 2
    C) 3
    D) 4

33. What is the main function of the pitman arm in the steering system?
    A) to convert rotary motion from the steering gear into linear motion
    B) to absorb the energy of vibration to prevent overheating of the engine
    C) to provide power assistance to the steering
    D) to absorb vibrations from the road surface

34. What needs to be done to the windshield wipers during the walk-around inspection?
    A) rotation of the wiper blades
    B) a check of the spring tension in the wiper arms
    C) testing of the windshield wiper controls
    D) removal of the wiper blades

35. What should be applied when leaving the vehicle?
    A) low-beam lights
    B) parking brake
    C) seat belt
    D) clutch

36. What is the initial method for shifting down a manual transmission?
    A) release the accelerator, push in the clutch, and simultaneously shift to neutral
    B) push in the clutch, press the accelerator, and shift to a lower gear
    C) press the accelerator, shift to neutral, and simultaneously push the clutch
    D) press the accelerator, push in the clutch, and shift to a lower gear

37. What usually controls the auxiliary transmission in a vehicle?
    A) pedals
    B) selector knob
    C) brake lever
    D) steering wheel

38. Objects appear smaller and farther away than they actually are in which type of mirror?
    A) concave
    B) plane
    C) arched
    D) convex

Practice Test #1

39. When it is difficult for drivers to see one other at dawn or dusk, which lights should be used?
    A) high-beam headlights
    B) low-beam headlights
    C) identification lights
    D) clearance lights

40. What is the perception distance for an alert driver?
    A) $\frac{1}{2}$ second
    B) $\frac{3}{4}$ second
    C) $1\frac{3}{4}$ seconds
    D) $2\frac{1}{2}$ seconds

41. What additional inspection criteria must be met if cargo contains hazardous materials?
    A) correct load balance
    B) proper papers and placarding
    C) presence of a fire extinguisher
    D) decreased cargo weight

42. What amount of "give" in the steering wheel could make it more difficult to steer?
    A) more than 1 in. of movement
    B) more than 2 in. of movement
    C) more than 5 in. of movement
    D) more than 10 in. of movement

43. How fast should a driver be going to test service brake stopping action?
    A) 5 mph
    B) 10 mph
    C) 20 mph
    D) 35 mph

44. Which of the following is a proper operating psi for oil pressure?
    A) 12
    B) 22
    C) 42
    D) 82

45. When using mirrors, what should the driver check and adjust each mirror to show?
    A) the cabin interior
    B) the center lane
    C) the shoulder of the road
    D) some part of the vehicle

46. How many warning devices must be placed if stopped on a one-way or divided highway?
    A) 2
    B) 3
    C) 4
    D) 5

47. When driving on a wet road, what speed should be used to maintain comparable dry road stopping time?
   A) $\frac{1}{3}$ of dry road speed
   B) twice the dry road speed
   C) less than 20 mph
   D) the same as the dry road speed

48. Which system is responsible for keeping the axles in place?
   A) steering system
   B) fuel system
   C) suspension system
   D) braking system

49. What should drivers do when operating wide commercial vehicles?
   A) keep their vehicle centered in the lane
   B) stay to the right side of the lane
   C) stay to the left side of the lane
   D) drive alongside other vehicles

50. If the driver of one car (car A) cuts in front of another car (car B), what is the safest action the driver of car B can take?
   A) accelerate quickly
   B) maintain speed and ignore the driver
   C) swerve around the vehicle
   D) slow down

Combination Vehicles

1. What is a difference between driving a combination vehicle and driving a single vehicle?
   A) A combination vehicle has more gears.
   B) A combination vehicle takes longer to start.
   C) Driving a combination vehicle requires more ability and skill.
   D) A combination vehicle is more likely to skid.

2. Where should cargo be placed in a rig in order to better prevent a rollover?
   A) stacked high
   B) along the perimeter of the truck
   C) low to the ground
   D) with heavier cargo in the front

3. In a "crack-the-whip" effect, what action primarily causes the trailer part of the truck to overturn?
   A) increasing speed
   B) changing lanes
   C) traveling uphill
   D) stopping abruptly

Practice Test #1

4. How will a driver most likely detect that the truck has skidded?
    A) by looking in the mirrors
    B) by feeling the truck shudder
    C) by hearing a screeching sound
    D) by smelling smoke from the skid

5. What is the purpose of the relay valves on a truck?
    A) to supply trailer brakes faster
    B) to carry air to other areas
    C) to control the emergency brakes
    D) to prevent a loss of pressure

6. What is the most likely cause of spring brakes not releasing when the driver pushes the trailer air supply control?
    A) Air was leaking from the air lines.
    B) Emergency lines were mixed up with service lines.
    C) Air lines were crossed.
    D) Older trailers did not have the spring brakes.

7. How often should the driver drain the air tank?
    A) once a week
    B) each day
    C) monthly
    D) at normal inspections

8. In what gear should the transmission be placed while securing the vehicle?
    A) park
    B) reverse
    C) drive
    D) neutral

9. While uncoupling tractor semitrailers, why should a driver check the surface of the parking area?
    A) to ensure it can support the trailer's weight
    B) to ensure there is no rough terrain
    C) to make sure the surface is dry
    D) to make sure there is a large enough area for the truck to maneuver safely

10. If the driver is not sure whether a trailer has spring brakes or not, what should be done?
    A) lower the landing gear
    B) chock the trailer wheels
    C) shut off the trailer air supply
    D) lock the trailer brakes

11. Which part must be secure when inspecting the pintle hook?
    A) the latch
    B) the lock handle
    C) the mount
    D) the tethered wire

12. What should be rotated to transfer the weight of the trailer tongue?
    A) the brake switch
    B) the jack handle
    C) the mount
    D) the pintle hook

13. What is the next step if, while coupling a drawbar, the safety cover bar will not fit completely into the seating?
    A) Document the issue to be fixed at the next inspection.
    B) Apply enough force so the safety cover bar is in the correct place.
    C) Do not drive until the issue is resolved.
    D) Use a fixture to hold the safety cover bar in place.

14. Where should the jaws be locked when inspecting the coupling system area?
    A) around the head of the kingpin
    B) in between the upper and lower fifth wheel
    C) around the shank
    D) in conjunction with the base

15. While checking the air flow to all trailers, what should the driver do if air is not heard escaping from both the emergency and service lines?
    A) open the service line valve
    B) check the shut-off valve at the rear
    C) test the tractor protection valve
    D) push the trailer air supply knob again

16. Which valve should be used to test the trailer service brakes when applying the trailer brakes with the hand control?
    A) trailer
    B) trolley
    C) emergency
    D) air brake

17. How should a driver begin to couple a gooseneck hitch?
    A) lower the gooseneck trailer into position and latch the clamp
    B) position the trailer's coupler directly over the ball
    C) lubricate the gooseneck ball
    D) open the clamp latch on the gooseneck coupler

18. What increases the probability of a rollover in combination vehicles?
    A) incorrectly loaded cargo
    B) faulty brakes
    C) insufficient tire pressure
    D) slow lane changes

19. What is the primary feature of a bobtail tractor?
    A) It does not have wheels.
    B) It does not have a trailer.
    C) Its trailer is partially loaded.
    D) Its trailer has no cargo.

20. What is the main reason for off tracking when turning with a combination vehicle?
    A) the length of the vehicle
    B) the weight of the vehicle
    C) the speed at which the turn is taken
    D) the type of road surface

21. When should the trailer hand valve be used?
    A) when the vehicle is skidding
    B) when driving, to control the trailer brakes
    C) when parking the vehicle
    D) to test the trailer brakes

22. What color is the air service line running between vehicles?
    A) red
    B) blue
    C) green
    D) yellow

23. What should a driver do if ABS malfunctions?
    A) stop driving and call for a tow
    B) drive normally but get the system serviced soon
    C) disable the regular brakes
    D) apply the handbrake

24. How should a driver position the tractor when coupling a trailer?
    A) at an angle
    B) directly in front of the trailer
    C) anywhere as long as the fifth wheel touches the trailer
    D) at the back of the trailer

25. When checking air flows, how does a driver supply air to the emergency lines?
    A) by pushing in the red tractor air supply knob
    B) by pushing in the red trailer air supply knob
    C) by using the tractor handbrake
    D) by using the trailer parking brake

Double and Triple Trailers

1. When compared to other commercial vehicles, what is an area of concern when pulling 2 or 3 trailers?
    A) fuel efficiency
    B) vehicle stability
    C) slow traffic conditions
    D) passing a vehicle inspection

2. For a vehicle with triple trailers, which part of the combination is most likely to turn over?
    A) the tractor
    B) the first trailer
    C) the middle trailer
    D) the last trailer

3. Which factor is directly related to managing driving space for double trailers?
    A) the type of cargo being transported
    B) the driver's personal preferences
    C) ensuring large enough gaps when crossing traffic
    D) the age of the vehicle or trailers

4. When coupling a second trailer that does not have spring brakes, what should be done before charging the air tank?
    A) connect the emergency line
    B) raise the landing gear
    C) release the dolly brakes
    D) chock the wheels

5. When coupling a second trailer, the dolly can be positioned by hand to align with what component?
    A) the truck axle
    B) the landing gear
    C) the suspension system
    D) the kingpin

6. After locking the pintle hook, the dolly support is secured in which position?
    A) lowered
    B) angled
    C) raised
    D) inverted

7. How should a rig be parked to uncouple a rear trailer?
    A) the rig on level ground, with trailers angled away from the tractor
    B) the rig on level ground, with trailers in a straight line
    C) the rig on a slight incline, with the rear trailer lower
    D) the rig on a slight incline, with the trailers angled toward the tractor

8. Which of the following is required for a successful walk-around inspection of the release arm and safety latch?
    A) The release arm moves freely, and the safety latch is engaged.
    B) The release arm moves freely, and the safety latch is disengaged.
    C) The release arm is seated, and the safety latch is engaged.
    D) The release arm is seated, and the safety latch is disengaged.

9. What color is the trailer air supply knob?
    A) red
    B) blue
    C) yellow
    D) green

10. To properly check for service pressure through all the trailers, what does the test assume?
    A) the engine is off
    B) the service brake pedal is on
    C) the emergency lights are on
    D) the wheels are aligned

11. To test the tractor protection valve, how does the driver reduce air pressure in the tanks?
    A) by turning the engine on
    B) by disconnecting the air hose
    C) by stepping on and off the brake pedal
    D) by using the trailer handbrake

12. What is the first step when testing trailer service brakes?
    A) Move the vehicle forward slowly.
    B) Release the parking brake.
    C) Check for normal air pressure.
    D) Apply the trailer brakes with the hand control.

13. Overall, why is it safer to pull single trailers than double and triple trailers?
    A) It is easier to turn a single trailer out of a skid.
    B) Single trailers can be managed better in inclement weather.
    C) Single trailers are less likely to cause an accident.
    D) Single trailers remain more stable.

14. Why should a truck driver allow for more pre-trip preparation for a triple trailer before beginning a run?
    A) An inspection takes longer to check all critical parts.
    B) More problems are likely to occur.
    C) It takes more time to hook up the trailers.
    D) More paperwork is required for additional trailers.

15. On doubles and triples, which part causes the truck to be more prone to skidding?
    A) the prop shaft
    B) dead axles
    C) drive shafts
    D) the rear suspension

16. How would a driver realize that the converter dollies are "current"?
    A) the date label on the dolly
    B) a converter dolly credential
    C) a yellow lamp on the left side
    D) a red indicator light

17. What should be the final step in securing the second (rear) trailer while coupling after charging the trailer air tank?
    A) Check the antilock brakes.
    B) Disconnect the emergency line.
    C) Connect the emergency line.
    D) Check the rear suspension.

18. How should the driver wheel the dolly into position in front of the second (rear) trailer if the dolly and the trailer are close to each other?
    A) by hand
    B) by tugging the dolly with a rope
    C) by moving the trailer closer
    D) by slowly driving closer

19. While using the tractor and first semitrailer to pick up the converter dolly, where should the dolly first be moved to?
    A) the rear of the second semitrailer
    B) the front of the first semitrailer
    C) the rear of the first semitrailer
    D) the rear of the third semitrailer

20. Where should the semitrailer be positioned when connecting the converter dolly to the front trailer?
    A) in front of the dolly tongue
    B) behind the kingpin
    C) to the side of the ring hitch
    D) to the left of the dolly brakes

21. What is considered to be the correct trailer height?
    A) at the level of the air and electrical connections
    B) slightly lower than the center of the fifth wheel
    C) above the ring hitch
    D) under the air hoses

22. When performing a visual check of the coupling, how close should the upper and lower fifth wheel be?
    A) touching together
    B) 1 in. apart
    C) 1 ft. apart
    D) 5 in. apart

23. What would be an effective way to release weight from the dolly when uncoupling twin trailers?
    A) setting the dolly brake
    B) lowering the landing gear of the second semitrailer
    C) slightly raising the landing gear of the second semitrailer
    D) disconnecting the semitrailer

24. What should be pulled out when uncoupling the third trailer rig?
    A) the dolly
    B) the tow bar
    C) the pintle hook
    D) the kingpin

25. When coupling system areas and inspecting the lower fifth wheel, how much space should be between the upper and lower fifth wheel?
    A) 1 in.
    B) no visible space
    C) ¼ in.
    D) enough to allow the kingpin to be above the fifth wheel jaws

Passengers

1. What must be considered while driving a bus with an emergency roof hatch open?
    A) the bus's higher clearance
    B) the need for a fire extinguisher nearby
    C) the need for emergency lights
    D) the presence of an additional blind spot

Practice Test #1

2. What is the safe "design speed" when driving a bus on a banked curve in good weather?
    A) 20 mph
    B) 15 mph
    C) 10 mph
    D) the safe design speed varies depending on the terrain

3. Which of these may remain open while driving a bus?
    A) emergency roof hatches
    B) emergency windows
    C) emergency doors
    D) access panels

4. Bus drivers must have a CDL if their vehicle is designed to seat how many people, including themselves?
    A) at least 10
    B) 12 or more
    C) 16 or more
    D) more than 20

5. On a bus, the brake and accelerator interlock system apply the brakes and hold the throttle in idle position when which of the following is open?
    A) the front door
    B) the rear door
    C) the roof hatch
    D) an emergency window

6. When doing a vehicle inspection on a bus, the driver should ensure the bus has
    A) emergency reflectors.
    B) seat belts.
    C) regrooved tires.
    D) a full tank of fuel.

7. Which of the following cannot be carried on a bus?
    A) small-arms ammunition labeled "ORM-D"
    B) emergency hospital supplies
    C) more than 100 lb. of solid Class 6 poisons
    D) children under the age of 3

8. When a bus arrives at an intermediate stop, the driver should announce all of the following EXCEPT
    A) the reason for stopping.
    B) the next stop.
    C) the bus number.
    D) the next departure time.

9. A bus should NOT be refueled when
    A) it has not been properly inspected.
    B) the engine is hot.
    C) the tank is not completely empty.
    D) passengers are on board.

Practice Test #1

10. When should a bus driver sign off on a previous driver's safety report?
    A) if the previous driver did not sign the report
    B) never; the bus driver can only sign his own report
    C) if the defects have been certified as repaired
    D) with permission from a bus mechanic

11. What may be used in place of emergency reflectors on a bus?
    A) a flashing light
    B) 3 liquid-burning flares
    C) orange cones
    D) a red electric lantern

12. If a bus rider has carry-on luggage, where should it be stored?
    A) near the door
    B) next to the aisle
    C) away from a doorway or aisle
    D) under the seat

13. How would someone know that cargo on a bus has been approved and contains hazardous materials?
    A) by the presence of a red hazard warning sign
    B) by the presence of a diamond-shaped hazard label
    C) by the word *hazardous* stamped on the cargo
    D) by the bright-yellow hazard box containing the cargo

14. Which of the following is permitted to be carried on a bus?
    A) lighter fluid
    B) asbestos
    C) pharmaceutical medicine
    D) battery acid

15. Where must a bus rider stand if the bus is moving?
    A) in the very back of the bus
    B) next to the bus driver
    C) behind the bus driver's seat
    D) away from the other riders

16. When should rules be mentioned to charter and intercity bus riders?
    A) when the trip begins
    B) if the riders ask about a rule
    C) when a rule is first disobeyed
    D) when riders are seated

17. How should a bus driver deal with a disruptive rider?
    A) confront the rider in front of the rest of the passengers
    B) unload the unruly passenger at a well-lit area
    C) tell the disruptive rider to move to the back of the bus
    D) pull over and wait for the authorities to handle it

Practice Test #1

18. What should a bus driver consider when accelerating to merge into traffic?
    A) clearing poles and tree limbs
    B) a signal or stop sign nearby
    C) scraping mirrors on passing vehicles
    D) how much room is needed for the bus

19. How should a bus driver interpret the design speeds posted on a curve?
    A) Bus drivers should drive more slowly because the posted design speed is intended for cars in good weather conditions.
    B) Posted design speeds refer to the speed to drive in bad weather for both bus drivers and drivers of cars.
    C) The posted design speed would be slower on a curve for cars in poor weather conditions.
    D) Good traction is needed for the posted design speed, which buses do not have.

20. What should a bus driver do after a train goes through a railroad crossing?
    A) wait for the crossing arm to raise
    B) slowly approach the crossing with caution
    C) look for another train approaching
    D) cross the train tracks normally

21. How should a bus approach a railroad crossing?
    A) with a complete stop
    B) by stopping far back and then rolling slowly
    C) by slowing way down but not stopping
    D) at normal speed

22. Which type of bus company requires an inspection report at the end of a shift?
    A) charter bus
    B) private enterprise
    C) intercity
    D) interstate carrier

23. How should bus drivers act professionally when interacting with other riders?
    A) briefly speak to riders to be friendly
    B) remain quiet and keep to themselves
    C) identify the riders' destinations
    D) observe each rider for drunkenness

24. If a bus breaks down in the middle of the interstate during rush hour, what should the bus driver do with the riders?
    A) tell the riders to get off the bus and move to the shoulder
    B) have the riders push the disabled bus
    C) have the riders stand next to the bus
    D) have the riders remain on the bus

25. What should happen if a rider carries a can of gasoline onto a bus?
    A) The driver should not allow the rider onto the bus.
    B) The rider should place the can at the back of the bus.
    C) The driver should keep the gas can near the driver's seat.
    D) The rider should empty the can and then enter.

Tank Vehicles

1. An unbaffled tank is required for which tanker?
   A) oil
   B) liquid chemical
   C) gas
   D) sanitation

2. What do baffles prevent?
   A) rollovers
   B) side-to-side surge
   C) liquid flow
   D) forward-and-back surge

3. What is the main disadvantage of unbaffled tanker trucks?
   A) They are more expensive.
   B) They are less fuel efficient.
   C) They are less stable when driving.
   D) They are less durable.

4. A tank vehicle with a high center of gravity is at increased risk of what?
   A) stalling
   B) brake failure
   C) rolling over
   D) forward-and-back surge

5. For a vehicle with a Class B CDL, a tank endorsement is needed to haul liquids in tanks having an aggregate rated capacity of how many gallons?
   A) 10
   B) 100
   C) 1,000
   D) 10,000

6. What factor necessitates that drivers have special skills to haul liquids in tanks?
   A) fluid movement
   B) low visibility
   C) poor fuel economy
   D) a low center of gravity

7. Where are bulkheads located on a tank?
   A) on top of the tank
   B) inside the tank
   C) under the tank
   D) at the rear of the tank

8. What action can a driver take to help control surge when braking?
   A) delay braking as long as possible
   B) keep steady pressure on the brakes
   C) steer quickly while braking
   D) over brake

Practice Test #1

9. What is the proper configuration for valves and manhole covers while driving a tank vehicle?
    A) valves and manhole covers closed
    B) valves open and manhole covers closed
    C) valves closed and manhole covers open
    D) valves and manhole covers open

10. What is the primary challenge of hauling liquids in a tanker truck?
    A) complex driving patterns
    B) low fuel efficiency
    C) poor road conditions
    D) fluid movement in the tank

11. Based on weight, which of the following would require transport by a tank vehicle?
    A) tobacco products
    B) solid radioactive materials
    C) hazardous materials
    D) water

12. Which requirement differentiates having a Class C endorsement from having a Class A or Class B CDL endorsement?
    A) heavy capacity cargo
    B) hazardous materials
    C) liquid materials
    D) long-distance transportation of materials

13. What would definitely take place if a driver were pulled over by law enforcement for a leaking tank vehicle?
    A) a deduction from the driver's company paycheck
    B) suspension of the driver's commercial driver's license
    C) a jail term
    D) a citation

14. While checking the valves, what should a tank vehicle driver make certain about them?
    A) their length in service
    B) their appearance
    C) their position
    D) their type

15. What should be ensured with regard to the vents during the inspection of a tank vehicle?
    A) that they are covered
    B) that they are undamaged
    C) that they are clean
    D) that they are clear

16. What makes a transport of liquid different than a gas transport?
    A) the light weight of gas
    B) movement
    C) evaporation
    D) location

17. Which type of tanker would be best for an amateur driver since it would be easier to drive?
    A) liquid
    B) gas
    C) hazardous materials
    D) heavy-weighted

18. On which part of the highway would a tank driver need to slow way down?
    A) on highway curves
    B) on ramps
    C) beneath underpasses
    D) on the straight part of the road

19. What happens to the liquid in a tank when there is a liquid surge?
    A) It moves side to side.
    B) It moves back and forth.
    C) It gets warmer.
    D) It begins to evaporate.

20. How could a driver of tanks that transport liquids improve her skills?
    A) by riding along with an expert tank driver
    B) by gaining education through information about transporting liquids
    C) through practice and experience with transporting liquids

D.) through practice driving at a slow pace

21. Why do bulkheads have holes in baffled liquid tanks?
    A) to control the temperature of the liquid
    B) to stop skids and jackknifing
    C) to allow for an increase in tank speed
    D) to lessen forward-and-back surge

22. Which type of tank requires the driver to drive extremely carefully when starting and stopping?
    A) smooth bore tanks
    B) baffled tanks
    C) gas tanks
    D) smaller tanks

23. Before driving, what must a driver know about the liquid being transported when considering the outage requirements?
    A) the amount the liquid could expand
    B) the initial weight of the liquid
    C) whether the liquid is a hazardous material
    D) the makeup of the liquid

24. How should a tank driver operate the vehicle when transporting a liquid?
    A) with quick but confident maneuvers
    B) with a tandem driver
    C) with smooth maneuvers
    D) as slowly as legally allowed

25. When is stab braking needed with a tank truck?
    A) while putting slight pressure on the brakes
    B) when stopping quickly
    C) in a controlled situation
    D) at an intersection

Hazardous Materials

1. If a driver recently acquired a CDL with a hazardous materials endorsement, what minimum action was required to secure it?
    A) completing a course in hazardous materials and security risks followed by a written test
    B) taking a written test and a road test with hazardous materials
    C) taking a written test and training about hazardous materials
    D) completing employer-led training and a 90-day probationary period

2. If a driver has left the vehicle, where should the hazardous materials shipping papers be properly placed in the driver's absence?
    A) in the glovebox
    B) in a pouch on the driver's door
    C) secured to the dashboard
    D) on the driver's seat

3. Which term, if it appears on a shipping paper or package, must be placed on a placard?
    A) Corrosives
    B) Combustible Liquids
    C) Poison Gas
    D) Oxidizers

4. What must the driver carry when transporting hazardous wastes?
    A) a Forbidden Waste Document
    B) International Civil Aviation Organization Instructions
    C) an EPA Registration Form
    D) a Uniform Hazardous Waste Manifest

5. Where should liquid corrosive materials in Class 8 be loaded into the truck?
    A) separated from other containers
    B) in the middle of a stack
    C) on the bottom of a stack
    D) on a smooth surface

6. What would a driver be transporting if required to have an approved gas mask in the truck?
    A) gasoline
    B) propane
    C) radioactive materials
    D) chlorine

7. In which class would propane, oxygen, and helium be placed based on the Hazard Class Definitions Table B?
   A) Flammable
   B) Oxidizers
   C) Gases
   D) ORM-D (Other Regulated Material-Domestic)

8. What is the driver's responsibility in a hazardous materials accident?
   A) to continue transporting the shipment to its destination
   B) to contact a hazardous waste disposal company immediately
   C) to report the accident or incident only to the shipper
   D) to report the accident or incident to the appropriate government agency

9. What is the function of shipping papers in hazardous materials transportation?
   A) to provide instructions on how to transport hazardous materials
   B) to describe the hazardous materials being transported
   C) to provide an inventory of all items being transported
   D) to provide the recipient's contact information

10. What telephone number must shippers include on shipping documents?
    A) the shipper's phone number
    B) the recipient's phone number
    C) the driver's phone number
    D) an emergency response phone number

11. Who is responsible for accurately describing hazardous materials on shipping documents?
    A) the carrier
    B) the driver
    C) the recipient
    D) the shipper

12. When transporting a hazardous substance in a reportable quantity or greater in a single package, the shipper must display which letters on the shipping papers and package?
    A) QR
    B) RQ
    C) PQ
    D) RP

13. How can hazardous materials be distinguished from nonhazardous products on shipping papers?
    A) by emphasizing them with a contrasting color
    B) by putting them at the end of the list
    C) by adding the letter *H* before their description
    D) by including their technical name

14. What must a shipper of hazardous wastes put on the shipping papers before the proper shipping name of the material?
    A) a warning label
    B) an identification number
    C) a waste code
    D) the word *waste*

15. What should be done if the driver doesn't recognize the hazardous material being transported?
    A) accept the shipment anyway
    B) contact the driver's office for assistance
    C) refuse the shipment
    D) request that the shipment be delivered to another carrier

16. What is the name of the document that must be carried and signed by hand when transporting hazardous wastes?
    A) Uniform Hazardous Waste Manifest
    B) shipping paper
    C) bill of lading
    D) commercial bill

17. Why shouldn't hooks be used when loading hazardous materials?
    A) They may cause damage to the containers.
    B) They could start a fire.
    C) They have the potential to agitate the contents.
    D) They may violate regulations.

18. Why are hazardous materials containers required to be braced during transportation?
    A) to keep the packages from moving
    B) to keep packages from catching fire
    C) to avoid leaking
    D) to deter theft

19. Which hazardous materials require a closed cargo space?
    A) Classes 1 and 3
    B) Classes 4 and 5
    C) Classes 1 and 2
    D) Classes 3 and 5

20. Which of the following may be loaded with corrosive liquids?
    A) Division 1.4 materials
    B) Division 4.2 materials
    C) Division 1.6 materials
    D) Class 5 materials

21. What must the cargo space floor be like if a vehicle lacks racks to hold compressed gas cylinders?
    A) tiered
    B) sloping
    C) flat
    D) curved

22. What is the maximum total transport index for all packages in a single vehicle transporting Class 7 materials?
    A) 100
    B) 75
    C) 50
    D) 25

23. What is the most common cargo tank for liquids?
    A) MC331
    B) MC306
    C) MC307
    D) MC308

24. What should a driver do if a Division 6.2 package becomes damaged in transit?
    A) accept the package and report the damage later
    B) contact the driver's supervisor right away
    C) ignore the damage and continue with the package handling
    D) open the package to inspect the contents

25. What is the purpose of the Emergency Response Guidebook (ERG)?
    A) to advise drivers on how to transport hazardous materials safely
    B) to advise emergency personnel on protecting themselves and others from hazardous materials
    C) to advise shippers on how to package hazardous materials for transport properly
    D) to advise manufacturers on how to manufacture hazardous materials safely

School Bus

1. Where is the danger zone located around a school bus?
    A) in front of the bus
    B) behind the bus
    C) on the left side of the bus
    D) on all sides of the bus

2. How far can the blind spot extend behind a school bus?
    A) 50 – 100 ft.
    B) 150 – 200 ft.
    C) up to 300 ft.
    D) up to 400 ft.

3. What is the function of the overhead inside rearview mirror on a school bus?
    A) to keep an eye on traffic approaching from the bus's rear
    B) to allow a clear view of the area directly behind the driver's seat
    C) to monitor passenger activity on the bus
    D) to provide a view of the side of the bus

4. What should a driver do when stopping at a school bus stop?
    A) stop next to the students to prevent them from walking
    B) put the transmission in neutral and release the parking brake
    C) turn on alternating red lights when traffic is passing by
    D) stop the bus with the front bumper at least 10 ft. from the students

5. What should the driver do first when preparing to leave a designated unloading area?
    A) close the door
    B) check all mirrors
    C) turn off the alternating flashing red lights
    D) engage the transmission

Practice Test #1

6. Under which condition must the driver evacuate the bus?
    A) if a student becomes ill on the bus
    B) if there are downed powerlines
    C) if the bus is stalled on a railroad crossing
    D) if the bus is running low on fuel

7. What is the safest position for students if there is no shelter and the bus is directly in the path of a sighted tornado?
    A) remaining upright in seats on the bus
    B) lying face down on the bus floor
    C) evacuating and lying face down next to the bus
    D) evacuating to a nearby ditch and lying face down

8. What traffic control devices are found at an active crossing?
    A) stop signs
    B) yield signs
    C) flashing red lights with bells and gates
    D) yellow advance warning signs

9. Where should a driver stop the bus when approaching a railroad crossing for the safest and best view of the tracks?
    A) as close to the nearest rail as possible
    B) no closer than 5 ft. from the nearest rail
    C) no closer than 15 ft. from the nearest rail
    D) no closer than 200 ft. from the nearest rail

10. What is the purpose of the roof-mounted white strobe lights on a school bus?
    A) to indicate that the bus has passengers
    B) to indicate that the bus is empty
    C) to improve the visibility of the bus
    D) to indicate that the bus is running late

11. What is the potential danger of strong winds for a school bus?
    A) Strong winds can increase the speed of the bus.
    B) Strong winds can cause the bus to stall.
    C) Strong winds can push the bus sideways.
    D) Strong winds can reduce the fuel efficiency of the bus.

12. How large is a tail swing on a school bus?
    A) 1 ft.
    B) 2 ft.
    C) 3 ft.
    D) 4 ft.

13. What should a driver do if leaving the driver's compartment when loading a bus at a school campus?
    A) release the parking brake
    B) turn off the flashing lights
    C) remove the key
    D) engage the transmission

14. What do pavement markings at a highway-rail crossing consist of?
    A) a straight line with the letters *RR*
    B) a circle with the letters *RR*
    C) an X with the letters *RR*
    D) a diamond shape with the letters *RR*

15. Which of the following is a bus's most important safety feature?
    A) a safe driver
    B) ABS
    C) emergency exits
    D) flashing lights

16. What does a sign below the crossbuck at a highway-rail crossing indicate?
    A) the speed limit at the crossing
    B) the distance to the nearest train station
    C) the number of tracks at the crossing
    D) the number of trains that pass per day

17. Where should bus drivers learn about operating their own buses?
    A) state and local regulations
    B) the information on the National Transportation Safety Board's website
    C) the federal guidelines for driving a school bus
    D) the Department of Motor Vehicles' school bus manual

18. How should all the mirrors on a bus be aligned and adjusted?
    A) to see what is directly behind the bus
    B) pointed toward a single area of the bus depending on the mirror's purpose
    C) so children can be seen in each mirror while leaving the bus
    D) pointed toward the front or rear of the bus

19. A child tells the driver that she would like to be dropped off 2 blocks past her normal bus stop, which is not an official bus stop. What should the driver do?
    A) drop her off there and then get written approval afterwards
    B) require her to get off at her normal bus stop
    C) allow her this one time to be dropped off where she wants
    D) tell her to get off at the bus stop closest to the location she wants

20. After all students have been accounted for while unloading a group at a bus stop, which step should the driver take next?
    A) engage the transmission
    B) release the parking brake
    C) turn off the alternating flashing lights
    D) close the door

21. If a bus driver is not on the bus at the school's unloading place at the beginning of the school day, where would the driver's keys most likely be found?
    A) with the driver
    B) in the ignition
    C) on the driver's seat
    D) on the dashboard

Practice Test #1

22. Which of the following scenarios would qualify for a school bus evacuation?
    A) The bus has stalled next to the railroad tracks.
    B) A car crash has occurred on the side of the road.
    C) A hazardous materials spillage has occurred down the street.
    D) The police have pulled over the school bus.

23. What would a bystander see on the side of a bus that would indicate the bus had been evacuated due to an emergency?
    A) a printed "emergency" sign attached to the side of the bus
    B) triangular reflectors showing an emergency
    C) the bus driver's radio hanging outside the window
    D) all the lights off on the side of the bus

24. If there is no white line to indicate where to stop at a railroad crossing, where should a driver stop?
    A) an appropriate distance away as gauged by the driver
    B) 3 car lengths from the railroad tracks
    C) 15 ft. from the railroad tracks
    D) in front of the railroad crossing sign

25. Given that the length of an average bus is 30 ft., if a car is stopped 40 ft. away on the other side of railroad tracks, what should the school bus driver do when crossing the tracks?
    A) roll slowly over the railroad tracks, giving the car enough time to move
    B) wait until the car moves out of distance of the school bus
    C) remain on the bus's side of the railroad tracks until the car moves back another 5 ft.
    D) continue over the railroad tracks so that the bus clear the tracks

Metal Coil

1. What does a direct tie-down through the eye of a coil help prevent?
    A) backwards movement
    B) forward movement
    C) side-to-side movement
    D) falling off the truck

2. What is wrong if a shipment of 5 metal coils is secured with an eyes vertical orientation in a row tie-down at a 50-degree angle?
    A) There should be an even number of metal coils.
    B) The securement should be for an eyes crosswise orientation.
    C) The coils should be secured at no more than a 45-degree angle.
    D) Instead of rows, the placement of the coils should be in a circle.

3. How could the direction of 2 tie-downs best be described in an eyes vertical orientation?
    A) diagonal
    B) parallel
    C) at a 180-degree angle
    D) circular

Practice Test #1

4. What restricts movement of a pallet with a metal coil on top of it while in transit?
    A) a metal box
    B) a friction mat
    C) a wooden crate
    D) metal side barriers

5. Why would there be a problem if the tie-downs through the metal coils were crossed?
    A) This method is not allowed.
    B) It would damage the inner coil.
    C) The coil would produce a loud sound.
    D) The tie-down could break more easily.

6. Which of the following is prohibited from being used for securement in an eyes crosswise orientation?
    A) timbers
    B) chocks
    C) nailed blocking
    D) wedges

7. Which factor influences whether a driver needs an "M" endorsement with metal coil shipments?
    A) the height of the metal coils
    B) the weight of the shipment
    C) the material used in the making of the metal coils
    D) the amount of metal coils being shipped

8. With an eyes lengthwise orientation, how does the driver prevent the coil from rolling?
    A) by using a tie-down above the deck
    B) by placing the tie-downs through the eye
    C) by crossing a tie-down over the top
    D) by placing friction mats underneath the coil

9. Where should a direct tie-down be placed when carrying 3 or more coils in the front and rear rows?
    A) over the coils and attached to the next closest row of coils
    B) on each side of the end coils and attached to the middle coil
    C) weaving in and out of all of the coils
    D) outside a channel that will be able to bear against all coils in the front and back rows

10. How would a driver determine the securement requirements for metal coils?
    A) by the placement of the metal coils on the truck
    B) by the positioning of the coils' eyes on the vehicle
    C) by the type of vehicle transporting the metal coils
    D) by the length of the trip

11. How is an indirect tie-down different from a direct tie-down?
    A) Indirect tie-downs run through the eyes of the coils.
    B) An indirect tie-down is attached to the vehicle and passes over the cargo.
    C) Indirect tie-downs are attached to the tops of the coils.
    D) Direct tie-downs are more secure than indirect ones.

Practice Test #1

12. What is the purpose of blocking?
    A) to prevent other drivers from seeing around the vehicle
    B) to help cargo be more evenly distributed
    C) to stabilize cargo and prevent it from moving horizontally
    D) to ensure other vehicles cannot pass while dangerous cargo is being transported

13. While transporting metal coils secured in the eyes crosswise orientation, what might slide if friction mats are not used?
    A) the chocks
    B) the cradle
    C) the pallet
    D) the wood block

14. With 6 metal coils in shipment in an eyes vertical orientation, what is the smallest number of tie-downs needed to meet the requirements?
    A) 4
    B) 6
    C) 8
    D) 12

15. Which category of securement rules would a load be in if there were 4 metal coils that weighed 3,500 lb.?
    A) securement of rows rules
    B) metal-coil-specific securement rules
    C) general cargo securement rules
    D) main metal cargo securement rules

16. What is the potential difference in movement with a coil in the eyes crosswise orientation as compared to the eyes vertical orientation?
    A) tipping over
    B) shifting
    C) rocking
    D) shaking

17. What constitutes a row of metal coils?
    A) There are at least 3 coils in a line.
    B) The metal coils are secured in the eyes vertical orientation.
    C) Metal coils are placed in a row.
    D) Ropes and chocks are used to secure the shipment.

18. Which type of vehicle has securement requirements for metal coils?
    A) van-type vehicles
    B) slope-nosed trucks
    C) reefer semi-trucks
    D) raised-roof sleepers

19. How is the orientation of the metal coil's securement different for the eyes vertical and eyes crosswise?
    A) An eyes crosswise metal coil has a smaller diameter, whereas the eyes vertical has a larger diameter.
    B) An eyes vertical position means that the metal coil has 4 constraints, but the crosswise only needs 2 constraints.
    C) The crosswise way is lying in a container, whereas the vertical is lying on the truck without anything underneath it.
    D) Vertical is standing straight up, whereas crosswise is lying down.

20. If an intermodal container lacks an anchor point, what should be used in its place to tie down the metal coils?
    A) the side of the truck
    B) the coil
    C) an indirect tie-down
    D) a nailed wood cradle

21. How are the securements of metal coils measured so that they meet the requirements?
    A) by the type of securement and the amount of the load
    B) by measuring tie-down tightness and the strength of the ropes
    C) by using a height and movement percentage
    D) by weight and working load limits

22. What is an anchor point regarding the shipment of metal coils?
    A) a looped fastener used to secure cables or ropes
    B) a part of the structure on a piece of cargo to which tie-downs are attached
    C) a bar that provides support for an object
    D) a mechanism that presses 2 separate parts to keep together

23. How many options does a driver have to safely secure individual coils loaded with eyes lengthwise?
    A) 1
    B) 2
    C) 3
    D) 4

24. For what reason would a driver secure a single metal coil using a pallet and the eyes vertical orientation?
    A) to further secure the metal coil from movement during transit
    B) so the metal coil will be protected and not damaged
    C) because a pallet must be used when using the eyes vertical orientation
    D) because the ropes or cables tying the metal coil down must pass through the pallet to secure it

25. Which characteristic must a pallet possess in order to be used for securement requirements?
    A) sufficient length
    B) sufficient strength
    C) wooden materials
    D) sufficient height

Practice Test #1 Answer Key

General Knowledge

1. B: A vehicle inspection is essential for safety and legal reasons, as it ensures that the vehicle is safe to drive and meets all state regulations.

2. C: The engine oil will start to warm up after the engine is started. As it warms up, the engine oil should gradually reach its operating range temperature.

3. C: Cargo should be inspected every 3 hours or 150 mi.—whichever comes first.

4. B: When approaching a vehicle for inspection, the driver should notice the vehicle's general condition and check around the vehicle for hazards.

5. D: The first step of the vehicle overview is to review the last vehicle inspection report.

6. C: A driver can know when to shift by learning the operating rpm range for the vehicle and monitoring the tachometer.

7. B: The 4 basic types of retarders that help slow a vehicle are exhaust, engine, hydraulic, and electric.

8. A: A curved or convex mirror shows a larger area than a flat mirror and increases the driver's field of vision.

9. B: Drivers without self-canceling signals should not forget to turn off their turn signal after turning.

10. D: A driver must put out emergency warning devices within 10 minutes after stopping on the shoulder of any road.

11. D: After inspecting the left and right sides, the front, and the rear of the vehicle during a walk-around inspection, the driver should check the signal lights before entering the truck.

12. B: The driver should back the truck out turning to the driver's side so that the driver can see better.

13. D: Drivers should frequently check the mirrors to know what cars are around but also to see if a car enters their blind spot.

14. A: The heavy vehicle formula states that there should be 1 second for every 10 ft. of vehicle length when a truck is driving at 40 mph.

15. B: The driver should call and wait for the police, and then inform them of what she witnessed; however, the driver should remain a safe distance away from the crash.

16. D: Over 100,000 crashes occur annually due to drowsy driving according to the National Highway Traffic Safety Administration.

17. B: The driver should dim the vehicle's lights when driving within 500 ft. of a vehicle that is oncoming or following the driver's vehicle.

Practice Test #1 Answer Key

18. C: The driver will not be able to shift into a lower gear after the speed has been built up.

19. B: The older systems will keep the malfunction lamp of the antilock braking system (ABS) on until driving at least 5 mph.

20. C: There are two main causes of fires that involve fuel: 1) improper fueling and 2) spilled fuel after an accident.

21. A: Safe following distance, or traveling space, is often expressed in terms of time. When driving under 40 mph, a following distance of 1 second for every 10 ft. of vehicle length is required.

22. A: If it is necessary to travel near other vehicles in heavy traffic, a driver should drop back or pull forward in order to be visible to other drivers.

23. C: Vehicles going at the same speed in the same direction are less likely to crash into one another, making this the safest option for driving a truck in heavy traffic.

24. C: Speeding traffic is the number one cause of work zone-related injuries and death.

25. A: Smoking takes the driver's attention off the road.

26. A: The best way to stay safe when encountering fog is to pull to the side of the road and not drive through it.

27. B: It takes 15 seconds for a typical tractor trailer combination unit to clear a double track.

28. C: Keep 1 set of wheels on the pavement to help maintain control if it is necessary to leave the roadway during an emergency.

29. C: Antilock braking systems (ABSs) prevent wheel lockup, helping the driver maintain control during braking.

30. B: A 12-ounce glass of 5% beer has the same amount of alcohol as a 1 ½ ounce shot of 80 proof liquor and a 5-ounce glass of 12% wine.

31. B: The driver must only sign the vehicle inspection report if defects were noted and certified to be repaired or deemed unnecessary.

32. C: Before applying firm pressure to the brake pedal, pump the pedal 3 times when performing a test for hydraulic leaks.

33. A: The pitman arm is a linkage that connects the steering gear to the steering arm of the system. It converts rotary motion of the steering gear into the linear motion required to turn the wheels.

34. B: During the walk-around inspection, the windshield wiper arms should be checked for proper spring tension.

35. B: The parking brake should be applied when the driver leaves the vehicle.

36. A: The initial procedure for shifting down a manual transmission is to release the accelerator, push in the clutch, and simultaneously shift to neutral.

37. B: Auxiliary transmissions provide extra gears, usually controlled by a selector knob or switch on the gearshift lever.

38. D: Objects appear smaller and farther away in a curved or convex mirror when compared to looking at the same thing directly.

39. B: Drivers should turn on their low-beam headlights to be more visible during low-light conditions.

40. **C:** The average perception distance for an alert driver is 1 ¾ seconds.

41. **B:** The driver must inspect for proper papers and placarding if the cargo contains hazardous materials.

42. **B:** More than 2 in. of movement at the rim of a 20-in. steering wheel, or 10 degrees, can make it difficult to steer.

43. **A:** To test the service brake stopping action, the driver should go about 5 mph before pushing the pedal firmly.

44. **C:** An ideal operating psi for oil pressure is 42; oil pressure ranges are between 35 and 75 psi.

45. **D:** To have a reference point for judging other images, the driver should adjust each mirror to show some part of the vehicle.

46. **B:** Warning devices should be placed 10 ft., 100 ft., and 200 ft. toward the approaching traffic if stopped on a one-way or divided highway.

47. **A:** On a wet road, speed should be reduced to 1/3 to stop at the same distance as on a dry road.

48. **C:** The suspension system holds up a vehicle and its load and keeps the axles in place.

49. **A:** Wide vehicles should manage their space by staying centered in their lane and avoiding driving alongside other vehicles.

50. **D:** When a driver cuts in front of another car, the safest action the driver who was cut off can take is to slow down and give the other driver room to change lanes safely.

Combination Vehicles

1. **C:** It takes more ability and skill to drive a combination vehicle because there is more to learn about driving a combination vehicle.

2. **C:** The lower to the ground and the more evenly distributed the cargo is, the more likely it is that a rollover will be prevented.

3. **B:** An overturned truck usually occurs when the truck changes lanes too fast.

4. **A:** A driver can determine a skid by looking in the mirrors for a moving trailer.

5. **A:** The relay valves make it so that the driver can apply the brakes to the trailer more quickly.

6. **C:** If the spring brakes do not release, it is likely that the air lines were accidentally crossed.

7. **B:** The air tank should be drained every day.

8. **D:** The driver should put the gear in neutral when securing the vehicle.

9. **A:** The trailer's weight is important; a trailer therefore cannot be placed on just any surface.

10. **B:** The trailer wheels should be chocked if there are no spring brakes on the truck or if the driver is unsure whether the truck has spring brakes.

11. **C:** The mount must be secure when inspecting the pintle hook; an unsecured pintle hook could separate from the vehicle, resulting in injury or death if it strikes someone.

12. **B:** The jack handle should be rotated to move the weight to another part of the truck.

13. **C:** It is imperative for the safety cover bar to fit completely into the seating.

14. **C:** It is important for the jaws to be locked around the shank and not the kingpin.

Practice Test #1 Answer Key

15. B: Drivers who do not hear air escaping from the emergency and service lines should make sure that the trailer and dolly shut-off valves are in the open position.

16. B: To test the trailer service brakes, use the trolley valves.

17. D: To couple a gooseneck hitch, the driver should open the clamp latch on the gooseneck coupler.

18. A: Rollover risks increase when cargo is not loaded correctly, which can cause an imbalance of weight and increase the risk of the vehicle tipping over.

19. B: A bobtail tractor is a tractor without a semitrailer.

20. A: When a vehicle goes around a corner, the rear wheels take a different path than the front wheels. This is referred to as off tracking and occurs more with longer vehicles.

21. D: The trailer hand valve should be used only to test the trailer brakes—not while driving—because it increases the risk of skidding or jackknifing.

22. B: Colors are used to mark air lines to help avoid mistakes: blue is used for service lines; red is used for emergency or supply lines.

23. B: If the antilock braking system (ABS) malfunctions, the driver can still use the regular brakes to stop the vehicle, but it is important to get the system serviced as soon as possible.

24. B: The tractor should be positioned directly in front of the trailer to avoid pushing the trailer sideways and breaking the landing gear.

25. B: Pushing in the red "trailer air supply" knob will supply air to the emergency (supply) lines.

Double and Triple Trailers

1. B: Pulling more trailers means that more can go wrong; doubles and triples are also less stable than other commercial vehicles.

2. D: The last trailer in a combination is most likely to turn over in a vehicle with triple trailers.

3. C: Doubles and triples take up more space than other commercial vehicles. The driver should ensure large enough gaps before entering or crossing traffic.

4. A: If the second trailer does not have spring brakes, the emergency line should be connected before charging the trailer air tank.

5. D: If the distance is not considerable, the dolly can be positioned by hand to line up with the kingpin.

6. C: Secure the dolly support in the raised position after locking the pintle hook.

7. B: When uncoupling a rear trailer, the rig is parked on firm, level ground with the trailers in a straight line.

8. C: In a satisfactory walk-around inspection, the release arm is seated, and the safety latch is engaged, preventing the trailer from becoming disconnected.

9. A: The red trailer air supply knob supplies air to the emergency lines.

10. B: Checking for service pressure throughout all trailers assumes that the service brake pedal is on.

11. C: Stepping on and off the brake pedal several times reduces the air pressure in the tanks.

Practice Test #1 Answer Key

12. C: The first step in testing the trailer service brakes is to check for normal air pressure.

13. D: Double and triple trailers are less stable and secure than single trailers.

14. A: All critical parts must be checked on all trailers during the inspection, which will take more time since there are more trailers.

15. B: More dead axles are needed to pull the drive axles on a double or triple, and having more dead axles to pull can increase the likelihood of skidding.

16. C: A converter dolly built after March 1, 1998, would have a yellow lamp on the left side of it.

17. B: After charging the trailer air tank, disconnecting the emergency line should be the final step when securing the second (rear) trailer.

18. A: If the distance between the dolly and its position in front of the second (rear) trailer is not too great, then it is best to position the dolly by hand.

19. C: The dolly should be moved to the rear of the first semitrailer if the driver is using the tractor and first semitrailer to pick up the converter dolly.

20. A: The first semitrailer should be backed into position in front of the dolly tongue.

21. B: The trailer height should be correct when connecting the converter dolly to the rear trailer, and that height is a little lower than the fifth wheel's center.

22. A: There should be no space between the upper and lower fifth wheel.

23. B: Lowering the landing gear of the second semitrailer will take some of the weight off the dolly.

24. A: The dolly should be pulled out so that it can be unhitched.

25. B: There should be no visible space between the upper and lower fifth wheel.

Passengers

1. A: When driving a bus with an emergency roof hatch open, the driver should consider the bus's higher clearance when navigating overhead objects.

2. D: On banked curves, the posted safe "design speed" is safe for cars in good weather; however, it may be too high for buses depending on the terrain.

3. A: To allow fresh air to circulate when driving a bus, emergency roof hatches may be locked in a partly open position.

4. C: A commercial driver's license is needed if the bus being driven is designed to seat 16 or more people, including the driver.

5. B: The brake and accelerator interlock system apply the brakes and hold the throttle idle when the rear door is open on a transit bus.

6. A: A bus must carry 3 reflective triangles or at least 6 fusees or 3 liquid-burning flares.

7. C: Buses must never carry more than 100 lb. of solid Class 6 poisons.

8. B: The driver should announce the location, the reason for stopping, the next departure time, and the bus number when arriving at an intermediate stop or destination.

9. D: Buses should not be refueled when passengers are on board.

Practice Test #1 Answer Key

10. C: A bus driver may only sign off and begin driving the bus if the issues have been repaired.

11. B: Three liquid-burning flares are alternatives to using emergency reflectors on a bus.

12. C: To avoid injuries while riding (or driving) a bus, luggage should not be placed in the doorway, aisle, or in a place from which luggage items could fall into the doorway or aisle.

13. B: A diamond-shaped hazard label on a bus denotes that a hazardous material is being transported.

14. C: There are a few exceptions as to the hazardous materials and other items that may be brought on board a bus; these include pharmaceutical medicines, which are considered legal drugs.

15. C: A standee line exists right behind the bus driver's seat and indicates where riders may stand.

16. A: Rules should be stated at the start of a trip on a charter or intercity bus so that all passengers are aware of the rules.

17. B: Bus drivers are responsible for passenger safety—even if the passenger is disruptive. Disruptive and/or intoxicated passengers should be let off at stops that are well lit and populous. Carriers have specific guidance on dealing with intoxicated or otherwise disruptive passengers, so drivers should be sure to understand their carrier's rules.

18. D: When merging into traffic, the bus driver should be aware of the length of the bus.

19. A: Even though a posted design speed means that a vehicle should not exceed the design speed, other factors usually require bus drivers to drive below the design speed.

20. C: After a train passes, the bus driver should look both ways for another train.

21. A: When approaching a railroad crossing, all bus drivers must come to a complete stop.

22. D: A bus driver for an interstate carrier must fill out an inspection report at the end of the shift.

23. B: Even though bus drivers need to be friendly, they should keep to themselves in order to focus.

24. D: For safety reasons, riders should remain on the bus during high-traffic hours.

25. A: Gasoline is a hazardous material that is banned and should not be brought onto a bus.

Tank Vehicles

1. D: Unbaffled tanks, or smooth bore tanks, do not have partitions on the inside to slow the flow of liquid and are therefore easier to clean. Sanitation tanks must be unbaffled to allow for easier cleaning.

2. D: Baffles help to control the forward-and-back surge of liquids.

3. C: Unbaffled tanker trucks lack internal partitions, causing the liquid inside to slosh around during transport and creating instability.

4. C: A high center of gravity makes a vehicle top-heavy and easy to roll over.

5. C: A tank endorsement is required for a vehicle with a Class B CDL to haul liquids in tanks with an aggregate rated capacity of 1,000 or more gal.

6. A: Hauling liquids in tanks requires particular skill due to fluid movement and a high center of gravity.

7. B: Bulkheads are dividers that are located on the inside of a tank. They are used to separate the tank into smaller compartments.

8. B: To help control surge, the driver should keep a steady pressure on the brakes when stopping.

Practice Test #1 Answer Key

9. A: A tank vehicle should only be driven when valves and manhole covers are closed.

10. D: Vehicle instability due to fluid movement, or surge, is a primary challenge of hauling liquids.

11. D: Tank vehicles transport gases or liquids, including water.

12. B: A Class C tank endorsement is required in order to transport hazardous materials that are in liquid or gas form based on their weights.

13. D: At the very least, the driver would be cited for driving a leaking tank vehicle because that is illegal. The driver might also be responsible for cleaning up the spill.

14. C: The valves should be in the correct position during the inspection, and tanks should never be driven with open valves.

15. D: The vents should be kept clear so they will work correctly.

16. B: Movement of liquid will occur while a tank vehicle is in transport.

17. B: Since liquid tanks roll over more easily, it would be best for an amateur driver to drive a gas tanker.

18. B: Trucks should drive well below the posted speed limit on ramps.

19. B: The liquid moves back and forth during a surge.

20. C: The driver needs to become familiar with driving a tank that transports liquids, which will allow for better handling of the vehicle.

21. D: The holes in the bulkheads lessen the likelihood that the liquid will move back and forth.

22. A: Smooth bore tanks require drivers to be extremely cautious by slowing down their speed when starting and stopping.

23. A: Since the liquid could expand at certain temperatures, the driver must know the outage requirements; this will allow the driver to know how much of the liquid can be hauled.

24. C: Safe driving practices require the driver to maneuver slowly when operating vehicles transporting liquids. The driver must consider a smooth ride for a liquid, which would cause it to be safe.

25. B: Sometimes a tank may need to stop suddenly, and the driver may have to resort to stab braking.

Hazardous Materials

1. C: Before a truck driver may transport hazardous materials, the driver must pass a written test and participate in employer training for hazardous materials transport; other requirements must also be met according to certain states and materials.

2. D: When the driver leaves a vehicle containing hazardous materials, the shipping papers should be placed on the driver's seat.

3. C: If the shipping papers contain the words *Inhalation Hazard*, *Poison Inhalation Hazard*, or *Poison Gas*, those words must be on the placard.

4. D: A Uniform Hazardous Waste Manifest must be carried and signed by hand by the driver when transporting hazardous wastes.

5. D: Liquid corrosive materials should be placed on an even floor surface.

6. D: An approved gas mask must be in the vehicle when a cargo tank is transporting chlorine.

Practice Test #1 Answer Key

7. C: The Hazard Class Definitions Table B provides the examples of propane, oxygen, and helium as gases in Class 2.

8. D: While in physical control of the shipment, the driver is responsible for reporting accidents and incidents involving hazardous materials to the appropriate government agency.

9. B: The hazardous materials being transported are described in shipping papers. The shipping papers aim to inform carriers, drivers, and emergency responders about hazardous materials in the event of an accident, spill, or leak.

10. D: Shippers must include an emergency response phone number on shipping documents for emergency responders in case of an accident, hazardous materials spill, or leak.

11. D: Shippers are responsible for accurately describing hazardous materials on shipping documents, including the correct identification number, shipping name, hazard class, packing group, and emergency response phone number.

12. B: When transporting a hazardous substance in a reportable quantity or greater in one package, the letters *RQ* must be displayed on the shipping papers and package.

13. A: If shipping papers contain hazardous and nonhazardous materials, the hazardous materials are highlighted in contrasting colors. Highlighting aids in quickly determining which products are dangerous.

14. D: Hazardous waste shippers are required by law to include the word *waste* before the proper shipping name of the material on the shipping papers.

15. B: If the driver is unfamiliar with the hazardous material being transported, requesting that the shipper contact the driver's office for assistance is best.

16. A: The Uniform Hazardous Waste Manifest must be carried and signed by hand when transporting hazardous materials.

17. A: Hooks can physically damage containers and packaging, resulting in leaks and spills.

18. A: Bracing is required to prevent containers from shifting or collapsing during transportation, which can result in damage and spills.

19. B: Class 4 (flammable solids) and Class 5 (oxidizers) must be securely covered or loaded into a closed cargo space.

20. C: Corrosive liquids may be loaded with Division 1.6 materials (extremely insensitive explosives).

21. C: The cargo space floor must be flat if a vehicle lacks racks for compressed gas cylinders.

22. C: The total transport index of all packages in a single vehicle must not exceed 50 for Class 7 (radioactive) materials.

23. B: MC306 is the most common cargo tank for liquids. MC331 is the most common cargo tank for gases.

24. B: If a Division 6.2 package is damaged during transportation, the driver's supervisor must be notified immediately so that appropriate action can be taken.

25. B: The Emergency Response Guidebook (ERG) is designed to instruct firefighters, police officers, and industry workers on protecting themselves and the public from hazardous materials.

Practice Test #1 Answer Key

School Bus

1. D: The area around a school bus where kids are most likely to be hit by another vehicle or their own bus is called the "danger zone." This area is on all sides of the bus.

2. D: The blind spot behind a school bus can extend up to 400 ft., depending on the length and width of the bus.

3. C: The overhead inside rearview mirror on a school bus is mounted directly above the windshield on the driver's side and is used to monitor passenger activity inside the bus.

4. D: When stopping at a school bus stop, bring the school bus to a complete stop with the front bumper at least 10 ft. away from the students at the designated stop.

5. A: When all students are accounted for and the driver is preparing to leave, the door should be closed first.

6. C: A bus that stalls on or adjacent to a highway-rail crossing requires a mandatory evacuation.

7. D: If the bus is in the path of a sighted tornado and evacuation is ordered, students should be directed to lay face down in a nearby ditch or culvert with their hands covering their heads.

8. C: Active crossings employ traffic control devices at the crossing to regulate traffic. Flashing red lights with bells and gates are an example.

9. C: For the best—and safest—view of the train tracks, drivers should stop no closer than 15 ft. from the nearest rail and no farther than 50 ft. from the nearest rail.

10. C: The purpose of the roof-mounted white strobe lights on a school bus is to improve the visibility of the bus in situations of limited visibility, such as during heavy rain, fog, or snow.

11. C: Strong winds can push a school bus sideways, move it off the road, or even tip it over.

12. C: A school bus can have up to a 3-ft. tail swing.

13. C: When students are loading at the school campus, the driver should remove the key if leaving the driver's compartment to supervise.

14. C: Pavement markings mean the same as the advance warning sign and consist of an X with the letters *RR* and a no-passing marking on 2-lane roads.

15. A: A safe driver is the most important bus safety feature.

16. C: The number of tracks is indicated by the sign beneath the crossbuck sign.

17. A: Since different states have different laws and regulations, the bus driver should consult the applicable state and local regulations.

18. C: Each mirror should be placed so that children can be seen in the mirror as they walk to the street.

19. B: Bus drivers must stop only at official school bus stops, and they can only add bus stops to their route with prior written approval from the school district.

20. D: The first step for the school bus driver after the students get off the bus is to close the door before doing anything else.

21. A: The driver should always remove and take the keys upon leaving the driver's compartment.

22. A: The bus must evacuate if the bus stalls on or near railroad tracks.

Practice Test #1 Answer Key

23. C: The bus driver should dangle the radio or telephone outside the window in case it needs to be used later.

24. D: The crossbuck sign is the place where a bus should stop if there is no painted white line on the road near the tracks.

25. C: To cross the railroad tracks, there should be an extra 15 ft. in addition to the length of the bus.

Metal Coil

1. B: When a tie-down goes directly through the eye, it is keeping the coil from moving forwards.

2. C: The degree of the tie-down could be 45 degrees or less, but not more.

3. A: In an eyes vertical orientation, 2 of the ropes are crossed over one another in a diagonal fashion.

4. B: The friction mat as well as the tie-downs restrict movement of the metal coil on the truck.

5. A: This method of the tie-downs forming an X-pattern is prohibited.

6. C: Timbers, chocks, and wedges can be used for securement in an eyes crosswise orientation, but nailed blocking to secure them cannot.

7. B: Metal coil shipments that weigh in excess of 5,000 lb. may only be shipped with a driver who has an "M" endorsement.

8. A: The tie-down is placed above the deck to prevent rolling.

9. D: When transporting more than 2 metal coils in the front and rear rows, it is required to have a direct tie-down run outside a channel that bears against all of the coils in the front and back rows.

10. B: Since there are 3 ways to position coils, the positioning of the coils' eyes will determine the securement requirements.

11. B: Indirect tie-downs are attached to the vehicle only, but direct tie-downs are attached to both the vehicle and cargo.

12. C: Blocking is a device or type of structure that is placed around or against cargo in order to stabilize it and prevent it from moving horizontally.

13. B: By placing friction mats under the timbers and coil bunks, the sliding of the cradle may be limited.

14. C: 8 tie-downs would be needed: 1 over each coil, a tie-down across the front, and another across the back.

15. C: The general cargo securement rules apply to metal coil shipments that weigh less than 5,000 lb.

16. C: When the metal coils are in an eyes crosswise orientation, there is a chance they could rock back and forth.

17. A: When there are 3 or more coils in a load, it is called a row.

18. A: There are 3 types of vehicles that have securement requirements for metal coils: 1) flatbed vehicles, 2) van-type vehicles, and 3) intermodal containers that have anchor points.

19. D: An eyes vertical metal coil stands straight up, but the eyes crosswise is lying down.

20. B: If an anchor point is not available, then the coil itself should be used to tie down the metal coils and keep them in place.

21. D: The sum of the working load limits must be greater than or equal to 50% of the coils' weight.

22. B: Anchor points are part of the fitting, structure, or attachment on a vehicle or an item of cargo and are the points from which tie-downs are attached.

23. C: When using the eyes lengthwise orientation, there are 3 options for effectively securing the metal coils in place.

24. A: To better support the metal coil during movement, a strong pallet may be placed underneath it.

25. B: The pallet must be strong enough to meet the movement and securement requirements.

Online Resources

Trivium includes online resources with the purchase of this study guide to help you fully prepare for the exam.

Practice Tests

In addition to the practice tests included in this book, we also offer an online exam. Since many exams today are computer based, practicing your test-taking skills on the computer is a great way to prepare.

From Stress to Success

Watch "From Stress to Success," a brief but insightful YouTube video that offers the tips, tricks, and secrets experts use to score higher on the exam.

Reviews

Leave a review, send us helpful feedback, or sign up for Cirrus promotions—including free books!

Access these materials at: www.triviumtestprep.com/cdl-online-resources

www.ingramcontent.com/pod-product-compliance
Lightning Source LLC
Chambersburg PA
CBHW080332170426
43194CB00014B/2537